Common Sense

In *Common Sense*, Noah Lemos presents a strong defense of the common sense tradition, the view that we may take as data for philosophical inquiry many of the things we ordinarily think we know. Lemos discusses the main features of that tradition as expounded by Thomas Reid, G. E. Moore, and Roderick Chisholm.

For a long time, common sense philosophers have been subject to two main objections: that they fail to give any non-circular argument for the reliability of memory and perception, and that they pick out instances of knowledge without knowing a criterion for knowledge. Lemos defends the appeal to what we ordinarily think we know in both epistemology and ethics, and thus rejects the charge that common sense is dogmatic, unphilosophical, or viciously question-begging.

Written in a clear and engaging style, *Common Sense* will appeal to students and philosophers in epistemology and ethics.

Noah Lemos is Professor of Philosophy at DePauw University.

RECENT TITLES

Common Sense

A Contemporary Defense

NOAH LEMOS

DePauw University

CAMBRIDGE
UNIVERSITY PRESS

PUBLISHED BY THE PRESS SYNDICATE OF THE UNIVERSITY OF CAMBRIDGE
The Pitt Building, Trumpington Street, Cambridge, United Kingdom

CAMBRIDGE UNIVERSITY PRESS
The Edinburgh Building, Cambridge CB2 2RU, UK
40 West 20th Street, New York, NY 10011-4211, USA
477 Williamstown Road, Port Melbourne, VIC 3207, Australia
Ruiz de Alarcón 13, 28014 Madrid, Spain
Dock House, The Waterfront, Cape Town 8001, South Africa

http://www.cambridge.org

First published 2004

Printed in the United States of America

Typeface Bembo 10.5/13 pt.   *System* LATEX 2$_\varepsilon$ [TB]

A catalog record for this book is available from the British Library.

Library of Congress Cataloging in Publication Data

Lemos, Noah Marcelino, 1956–
Common sense : a contemporary defense / Noah Lemos.
p.   cm. – (Cambridge studies in philosophy)
Includes bibliographical references and index.
ISBN 0-521-83784-7
1. Common sense.   I. Title.   II. Series.
B105.C457L46   2004
149–dc22   2003069664

ISBN 0 521 83784 7 hardback

Contents

Acknowledgments

I am deeply grateful to several people who have been kind enough to read all or large parts of the manuscript. These include Michael Bergmann, Fred Feldman, Dan Parks, Matthias Steup, and Erik Wielenberg.

I have also benefited over the years from discussions with my colleagues at DePauw University concerning the issues taken up in this book, most especially Marthe Chandler, Marcia McKelligan, and Roger Gustavsson.

I would like to thank DePauw University and John and Janice Fisher for their support through Faculty and Fisher Fellowships. Though it has been more than twenty years since I sat in their classrooms, I remain deeply grateful to my teachers, Roderick Chisholm, who introduced me to the works of Thomas Reid; James Van Cleve, who gave me a deeper understanding of Reid; and, most especially, Ernest Sosa, whose influence is evident throughout this book.

To my father, Ramon Lemos, who has read all that I've sent him, I owe a debt that I can never repay.

Finally, I wish to thank my wife Lisa, to whom this book is dedicated.

charges are made quickly within the first few pages of philosophical works, and very little more is said in support of them. It is as though the author assumes that the reader can readily see for himself the philosophical inadequacy of the approach of the common sense tradition. In other cases, however, these charges are often based on well-considered philosophical views about the nature of knowledge and justification. So, for these critics, the popular jibe "What's common sense got to do with philosophy?" may be raised as a serious philosophical question, one that calls for the common sense tradition and its assumptions to be examined philosophically and critically.

In this book, I discuss the views of some of the main figures in that tradition – namely, Thomas Reid, G. E. Moore, and Roderick Chisholm. My approach will be philosophical and conceptual, rather than historical. I will discuss some of the views of each thinker, views that I think are characteristic of, or important to understanding, the common sense tradition. I also discuss some recent criticisms of these views. In this way, I hope, we might be better able to appreciate the common sense tradition from a contemporary perspective, one that takes into account contemporary views about relevant philosophical matters, such as recent views on the nature of knowledge and justification. I will, for the most part, defend the views of Reid, Moore, and Chisholm. I will be satisfied if the reader at least comes away with the view that the common sense tradition is not unphilosophical, dogmatic, intemperate, or viciously question-begging.

In Chapter 1, I present some of the main features of the common sense tradition. I lay out some views characteristic of the tradition and some views to which it is not committed. One view common to members of the tradition is, roughly, that we may take as data for philosophical inquiry many of the things we ordinarily think we know. This is no doubt part of what Reid means in claiming that philosophy is rooted in common sense. Among the things we ordinarily think we know are various "common sense" propositions such as that there are other people, that they think and feel and have bodies. But why should we take these propositions as data? Members of the common sense tradition have given different sorts of answers, and some of them do not seem very compelling. Some members of the tradition, Reid for example, hold that we may take such propositions as data because we simply cannot give them up. On this view, we may take certain claims as data for philosophical inquiry because we cannot give them up, because we find them doxastically compelling. An alternative answer, and one more central to the common sense tradition, is that these are things that we do know or that we are justified in believing. In other words, we may take these things as data because they enjoy some positive epistemic status. But this sort of answer leaves the common sense philosopher open to a variety of objections. Two of the most important are the following. First, we cannot pick out instances of knowledge or justified belief without first knowing a criterion of knowledge. Since the common sense philosophers do not offer us one, their claims to know the epistemic propositions they take as data are false. Second, the beliefs that the common sense philosopher takes as data are instances of knowledge only if those beliefs are reliably formed. But the only satisfactory way to know that those beliefs are reliably formed is on the basis of some "non-circular" argument. Yet philosophers in the common sense tradition simply haven't provided the necessary argument. So they have no reason to think that the beliefs they take as data are reliably formed. Much of this book explores what the common sense tradition has said or should say in response to these objections. In Chapters 2 and 3, I will focus primarily on the second objection. In Chapter 6, I will focus on the first.

In Chapter 2, I take up the second objection. I consider some reasons in favor of the view that perceptual and mnemonic knowledge require that one know or be justified in believing that one's perception and memory are reliable. I argue that we should reject such a requirement, in part because it would preclude children and brute animals from having perceptual and mnemonic knowledge. But even if we reject the requirement, I argue that we cannot simply ignore the question of the reliability of our ways of forming beliefs. Does knowledge of the reliability of our ways of forming beliefs really require the sort of non-circular argument that the critic demands? I examine how William Alston and Ernest Sosa answer this question. I will also look at "track record" and "Neo-Moorean" arguments for the reliability of our doxastic sources. Following Sosa, I will hold that knowledge of the reliability of one's way of forming beliefs simply doesn't require the sort of non-circular argument the critic demands.

In Chapter 3, I continue the discussion of the issues raised in Chapter 2, examining some criticisms of the view defended by Sosa. I will explore some objections to this view raised by Richard Fumerton and Jonathan Vogel and argue that they do not show that the only way to know that one's ways of forming reliable beliefs is on the basis of a non-circular argument. I will argue that even if we accept the view that a reflective being knows that p only if he is justified in believing that his belief that p is reliably formed, this does not imply that we must reject track-record arguments or the Neo-Moorean argument for the reliability of perception and memory.

In Chapter 4, I look at the views of Thomas Reid concerning our knowledge of the reliability of our ways of forming beliefs. Reid holds that it is a "first principle" that our natural cognitive faculties are reliable. In addition, he seems to endorse some ways in which the reliability of our faculties can be supported. Reid seems to hold the view that we can know on the basis of our natural faculties that they are in fact reliable. Yet Reid also *seems* to criticize Descartes's attempts to defend the reliability of his faculties as "question-begging," and some of the criticisms that Reid makes of Descartes would seem no less applicable to Reid's own views. I will argue, however, that Reid's criticism of Descartes is mistaken, that it is a wrong turn on his part.

In Chapter 5, I begin by looking at Moore's proof of an external world and his response to skepticism. It is sometimes charged that philosophers in the common sense tradition do not take skepticism seriously. Well, certainly they aren't skeptics, but they do address and consider skeptical arguments, though many critics think their responses unsatisfactory. In the first section, I look at Moore's proof for an external world and defend it against the charge that it is "question-begging." In the second section, I consider a Moorean response to skepticism and defend it against a criticism raised by Barry Stroud. The third section focuses on the "sensitivity requirement" prominent in recent "relevant alternative" and "contextualist" criticisms of Moore's views.

In Chapter 6, I return to the objection that picking out particular instances of knowledge or justified belief depends upon knowing some general criterion of knowledge or justified belief. I begin with Chisholm's discussion of particularism, methodism, and skepticism. Chisholm defends particularism against methodism and skepticism. Methodism holds that in order to pick out instances of knowledge or justified belief, one has to know a criterion of knowledge or justification. Particularism denies this. I believe that Chisholm is right and the methodists are wrong. I look at one attempt to support methodism by appealing to the "supervenient" character of evaluative concepts such as knowledge and justification. I also look at some criticisms of common sense particularism raised by Paul Moser, Laurence BonJour, and Panayot Butchvarov.

Chapter 7 addresses the relationship between *a priori* knowledge and common sense particularism. On "strong" accounts of *a priori* knowledge and justification, such as Chisholm's, basic *a priori* knowledge is certain and indefeasible. What enjoys basic *a priori* justification is thus "insulated" from defeat by conflict with our common sense beliefs. This presents a problem for the common sense particularist who holds *both* that some epistemic principles are justified *a priori* and that our common sense beliefs can defeat various epistemic principles. Moreover, the strong account makes it very unlikely that many, if any, interesting epistemic principles can be known or justified *a priori*. Some philosophers might welcome such a view. William Lycan, for example, defends a Moorean response to skepticism by calling into question the epistemic credentials of alleged *a priori* intuitions. I defend a "modest" view of *a priori* knowledge and justification, one that does not require that basic *a priori* knowledge be certain and indefeasible. Such a view leaves open the possibility of *a priori* justification for epistemic principles, including those in skeptical arguments, while also leaving open the possibility of defeat by other considerations.

In Chapter 8, I look at some recent views on the role that our moral judgments should play in moral philosophy. If the common sense tradition holds that we may take as data much that we ordinarily think we know in formulating criteria of knowledge and evidence, then may we do the same when we attempt to formulate criteria of right action? I think the answer is "yes." Particularists in epistemology hold that we can pick out particular instances of knowledge and justified belief. Particularists in moral philosophy assume that we can pick out particular instances of right and wrong action, that we can know that some particular actions are right and others wrong. Several philosophers have taken the opposing view, and hold that in attempting to formulate criteria of right action, we should not rely upon our moral judgments or "intuitions" about what is right or wrong. In some cases, this opposition is rooted in arguments similar to those raised against particularism and the common sense tradition in epistemology. I argue that these objections fare no better when they are raised in moral philosophy. In other cases, however, the opposition to particularism in moral philosophy does not rest on such grounds. Some philosophers, who endorse a form of act utilitarianism, have suggested that we simply cannot know whether particular actions are right or wrong. They hold that we simply cannot pick out particular instances of right and wrong action. Such a view seems to be held, surprisingly perhaps, by Moore. I look critically at such views.

Finally, let me make two cautionary points. First, much of the discussion in this book concerns epistemology and what we may assume when we try to answer the epistemological questions that concern us. However, I don't give any detailed analysis of the nature of knowledge or criteria for knowledge and justified belief. I leave many substantive epistemological

1

The Common Sense Tradition

In this chapter, I begin by describing some of the main features of the common sense tradition, whose chief representatives include Thomas Reid, G. E. Moore, and Roderick Chisholm. There are certainly important differences among the views of Reid, Moore, and Chisholm, but I think one can give a rough account of some central features of the common sense tradition. In the first section, I describe some of the main views accepted by members of the tradition as well as some views to which they are not committed. In the second section, I consider some views about *why* we should take various common sense propositions as data for assessing philosophical theories. Philosophers in the common sense tradition have offered different sorts of answers to this question. Sometimes they suggest that we simply have no alternative to taking these propositions as data. Sometimes, however, it is suggested that such propositions are "irresistible" – that we cannot give up our belief in them. Reid, for example, appears in places to take this view. In other cases, they point, not to irresistibility, but to the positive epistemic character of our beliefs in such propositions as that which makes them worthy of being taken as data. On this view, it is the fact that we know or are justified in believing certain propositions that makes them worthy of being taken as data. This "epistemic answer" seems to me to be the best. However, appealing to the epistemic character of various common sense beliefs invites a variety of objections and criticisms that we shall consider in various forms throughout this book.

1.1 SOME MAIN FEATURES OF THE COMMON SENSE TRADITION

Roderick Chisholm, along with Thomas Reid and G. E. Moore, is one of the most prominent defenders of the common sense tradition in philosophy. Chisholm once wrote that in investigating the theory of knowledge from a philosophical or "Socratic" point of view,

We presuppose, first, that there *is* something that we know and we adopt the working hypothesis that *what* we know is pretty much that which on reflection we think we know. This may seem like the wrong place to start. But where else *could* we start?[1]

Elsewhere, we find Chisholm saying:

It is characteristic of "commonsensism," as an alternative philosophical tradition, to assume that we do know, pretty much, those things we think we know, and then having identified this knowledge, to trace it back to its sources and formulate criteria that will set it off from those things we do not know.[2]

Chisholm held that we can pick out instances of knowledge and reasonable belief and use them as "data" for formulating and assessing criteria of knowledge and evidence. He held, roughly, that our criteria of knowledge and evidence should fit or cohere with what we take ourselves to know or to be justified in believing. If some proposed criterion of knowledge implies that we do *not* know many of the things we ordinarily take ourselves to know – for example, that there are other people and they have bodies – then so much the worse for that proposed criterion. Our philosophical theory of knowledge, our criteria of knowledge and evidence should be, in his view, adequate to the fact that we *do* know such things.

Chisholm saw himself as belonging to the common sense tradition, a tradition that includes the eighteenth-century Scottish philosopher Thomas Reid and the influential English philosopher, G. E. Moore. Reid was a contemporary and critic of that better known Scottish philosopher, David Hume. It is Hume who gets credit for awakening Immanuel Kant from his "dogmatic slumbers," but it is Reid who gets things more nearly right, or so think Chisholm and the other commonsensists. Hume belonged to the great tradition of British Empiricism that included John

---

1 Roderick M. Chisholm, *Theory of Knowledge*, 2nd edition (Englewood Cliffs, N. J.: Prentice Hall, Inc., 1977), p. 16.
2 Roderick M. Chisholm, *The Foundations of Knowledge* (Minneapolis: The University of Minnesota Press, 1982), p. 113.

Locke and Bishop Berkeley. But it was the intrepid Hume who, to many, including Reid, drew out the implications of British Empiricism. Reid took Hume to have shown that empiricism implies that we have no knowledge of the material world; no knowledge of the future, the past, other minds; nor, indeed, any knowledge of ourselves as continuing subjects of consciousness. Reid took Hume to have shown that the wages of empiricism are a rather thoroughgoing skepticism. Reid writes:

A traveller of good judgment may mistake his way, and be unawares led into a wrong track; and while the road is fair before him, he may go on without suspicion and be followed by others but, when it ends in a coal pit, it requires no great judgments to know he hath gone wrong, nor perhaps to find out what misled him.[3]

According to Reid, since we do know many things of the sort that empiricism would rule out, so much the worse for empiricism. Since the theory implies that we do not know things we *do* know, we should reject the theory. A similar stance was taken by Moore. Concerning skeptical arguments in general, Moore writes:

But it seems to me a sufficient refutation of such views as these, simply to point to cases in which we do know such things. This, after all, you know, really is a finger; there is no doubt about it: I know it, and you all know it. And I think we may safely challenge any philosopher to bring forward any argument in favour either of the proposition that we do not know it, or of the proposition that it is not true, which does not at some point rest upon some premiss which is beyond comparison, less certain, than the proposition which it is designed to attack.[4]

Elsewhere, Moore writes:

There is no reason why we should not, in this respect, make our philosophical opinions agree with what we necessarily believe at other times. There is no reason why I should not confidently assert that I do really *know* some external facts, although I cannot prove the assertion except by simply assuming that I do. I am, in fact, as certain of this as of anything; and as reasonably certain of it.[5]

3 Thomas Reid, *Inquiry and Essays*, ed. Ronald E. Beanblossom and Keith Lehrer (Indianapolis: Hackett, 1983), p. 11.
4 G. E. Moore, "Some Judgments of Perception," *Philosophical Studies* (London: Routledge and Kegan Paul, 1960), p. 228.
5 G. E. Moore, "Hume's Philosophy," *Philosophical Studies*, p. 163.

Like Reid, Moore holds that if some philosophical theory or some philosophical argument implies that we do not know anything about "external" objects, then so much the worse for the theory or the argument. That we do know such things is more evident, more reasonable to believe, than the theory or one of the premises for the opposing view.

As we have seen, Chisholm takes it to be characteristic of the common sense tradition to hold that we do know much of what we ordinarily think we know. Not surprisingly, some of what we think we know might be considered common sense. But what does it mean to say that some proposition is "common sense"? I think the notion of a common sense proposition is rather vague, and that one could take it to mean many things. But suppose we take a common sense proposition to be one that is deeply and widely held. If this is what we mean by a "common sense proposition," then the common sense tradition holds that there are common sense propositions. It holds that there are propositions that are deeply and widely held. Examples of such propositions would be that there are other people, that they have bodies, that they think, that they know various things about the world around them. Clearly, many other examples could be given. In any case, in holding that there are common sense propositions, the tradition implies that there are other people and that they believe things.

Moreover, the common sense tradition holds that *some* common sense propositions are *known* to be true. For example, it holds that we do *know* that there are other people, that they have bodies, that they think, and that they know various things about the world. Indeed, the tradition holds that these and many other common sense propositions are such that almost everyone knows them. In this respect, the tradition holds that *some* common sense propositions are matters of *common knowledge*. Certainly these would be among the things that Chisholm takes to fall within the scope of what we ordinarily take ourselves to know. Furthermore, it is worth noting that among those things that are matters of common knowledge are some *epistemic* propositions – that is, propositions about what is known or what it is reasonable to believe. Thus, the proposition that people *know* various things about the world around them would be for the common sense philosopher an epistemic proposition that is *both* a common sense proposition and a matter of common knowledge.

Though the common sense tradition does hold that *some* common sense propositions are known, it is *not* committed to the view that *everything* that might be called a "common sense" belief or proposition is true or known or even reasonably accepted. In his essay, "A Defence of Common Sense," Moore is quite clear on this point. Moore writes:

The phrases 'Common Sense view of the world' or 'Common Sense beliefs' (as used by philosophers) are, of course, extraordinarily vague; and, for all I know, there may be many propositions which may be properly called features in 'the Common Sense view of the world' or 'Common Sense beliefs', which are not true, and which deserve to be mentioned with the contempt with which some philosophers speak of 'Common Sense beliefs'. But to speak with contempt of those 'Common Sense beliefs' which I have mentioned is quite certainly the height of absurdity. And there are, of course, enormous numbers of other features in 'the Common Sense view of the world' which, if these are true, are quite certainly true too: e.g. that there have lived on the surface of the earth not only human beings, but also many different species of plants and animals, etc.[6]

In spite of the title of his essay, Moore's defense of common sense is clearly limited. Though he clearly thinks that some common sense beliefs are true, he avoids endorsing them all. As Arthur E. Murphy notes, Moore "takes great pains to specify the kinds of statement he is talking about and to add that it is statements of these kinds and not 'the common sense view of the world' in general that he claims to know for certain, in some cases, to be true."[7] The common sense tradition is simply not committed to the view that *all* widely held propositions are true or even reasonable.

In sum, I think we may make the following general points about the common sense tradition. First, it holds that we do know pretty much what we think we know. Second, it holds that there are some propositions that almost everyone knows, that are matters of common knowledge. Third, it holds that we may take these propositions as data for assessing various philosophical theories. It holds that a philosophical theory about the nature and scope of knowledge should be compatible with the fact that people *do* know such things, and it should seek to explain how people know such things. Fourth, it assigns a great deal of weight to these propositions, holding it to be more reasonable to accept them than any philosophical theory or premise that implies that they are false. The preceding points would be accepted, I believe, by Chisholm, Reid, and Moore.

In suggesting that the common sense philosopher takes as data some common sense propositions, I do not imply that these are the *only*

---

6   G. E. Moore, "A Defence of Common Sense," *Philosophical Papers* (London: George Allen and Unwin, 1959), p. 45.

7   Arthur E. Murphy, "Moore's Defence of Common Sense," *The Philosophy of G. E. Moore*, 3rd edition, ed. Paul Schilpp (LaSalle, Illinois: Open Court, 1968), p. 302.

propositions that he takes as data for philosophical inquiry. If we take the Chisholmian view that we know pretty much what we think we know, this would certainly include propositions that are *not* deeply and widely believed. Thus, among the propositions I think I know would be that I had eggs for breakfast and that I live in Indiana. Similarly, Moore may take as data propositions such as those expressed by the sentences "My name is Moore" and "I live in England." These propositions are not common sense propositions in the sense that they are widely or deeply believed, nor are they matters of common knowledge. Yet we may hold that a philosophical theory of knowledge must be adequate to the fact that people do know such things.

Moreover, though the common sense tradition does hold that *some* common sense propositions are epistemically justified for us, it is not committed to the view that they are epistemically justified for us *in virtue of* their being common sense propositions or in virtue of their being deeply and widely held. It is not committed to the view that being widely and deeply believed confers, or is a source of, any positive epistemic status upon a proposition. Similarly, though it holds that some common sense propositions are known, it doesn't claim that they are known *because* they are common sense propositions. Furthermore, the common sense tradition is not committed to, and in fact rejects, the view that we know various common sense propositions on the basis of inferring them from the general principle, (1) Whatever is a common sense proposition is true, and (2) *p* is a common sense proposition. Our knowledge that there are other people does not depend on an inference of that sort. (Reid *seems* to think that *knowing* that a proposition is widely and deeply held by almost everyone now and in the past is *some* reason for believing it. But even for Reid, this is a defeasible reason. And such a view is not to be found in Moore or Chisholm.)

It is important to emphasize that Moore and Chisholm do not take being a common sense proposition in the sense that it is widely and deeply held to imply that the proposition is true or epistemically justified. They are not "methodists" who begin with a criterion such as "Whatever is a common sense proposition is true or epistemically justified." On the contrary, they are particularists who believe that we can pick out instances of knowledge and justified belief without such a criterion. (I say more about methodism and particularism in Chapter 6.) I do not think that we should see them as appealing to common sense in the following way: (1) If something is a proposition of common sense, then it is true or reasonable. (2) Theory T denies a proposition of common sense.

(3) Therefore, Theory T is false or unreasonable. One might well find this form of argument unsatisfactory. "Why," one might ask, "should we reject a metaphysical, epistemological, or scientific theory simply because it conflicts with some proposition of common sense? Indeed, why assume that premise 1 is true?" But I would stress that there is no reason why we must view common sense philosophers such as Moore and Reid as committed to this sort of argument. As we have seen, Moore would reject premise 1, and there is no reason to attribute such a view to Chisholm. (Again, Reid, I think, would not accept premise 1. Reid *seems* to hold the weaker view that our knowing that some proposition is widely and deeply held by almost everyone now and in the past is a defeasible reason for believing it.) What Moore, Chisholm, and Reid *do* maintain is that there are some common sense propositions that we know. We might take them frequently to be arguing: (1′) *P* is a common sense proposition that I and many others know. (2) Theory T implies that *p* is false. (3) Therefore, Theory T is false or unreasonable. I do not see that arguing in this fashion is objectionable. Rejecting a metaphysical, epistemological, or scientific theory because it conflicts with something one knows is not an unreasonable procedure. In arguing this way, the emphasis is on the fact that the theory conflicts with something known, something that also happens to be common sense. We might say, then, that Moore, Reid, and Chisholm reject certain views because they conflict with something that happens to be common sense, but not because it is common sense.

Still, the fact that some common sense propositions are matters of common knowledge is not utterly without significance for the common sense philosopher. If some propositions are matters of common knowledge, then there must be some way of knowing them which is not unique to an elite few. Thus, for example, since it is common knowledge that there are other people, such knowledge cannot rest on philosophical arguments or considerations grasped only by a handful of philosophers and it can't be the fruit of philosophical reasoning followed only by a philosophical elite. Our account of such knowledge must be adequate to the fact that it is, after all, *common* knowledge. Thus, if a philosopher suggests that one's belief that there are other people or that there are external objects is a mere matter of faith until grounded in some philosophical argument that he hopes to develop, then, I think, such a view is antithetical to the common sense tradition. Similarly, one doesn't need to know a philosophical analysis of knowledge or have a sophisticated theory of what makes a belief an instance of knowledge. That people do know things about the world around them is a matter of common knowledge, and ordinary men and women, who know such epistemic facts, do not have a philosophical analysis of knowledge or have a satisfactory epistemic theory. This is not, of course, to deny that having such an analysis or such a theory might yield a deeper, richer, or better sort of knowledge of various epistemic facts. It is simply to claim that such things, desirable as they might be for a variety of reasons, are unnecessary for the sort of ordinary knowledge most people enjoy.

In addition to noting the preceding points, I think it is important to note certain other claims that are not accepted by the common sense tradition. First, the common sense tradition is not committed to the view that there is "a faculty of common sense" or that one's considered judgments are known *via* such a faculty. Such a view is not found in Moore or Chisholm. Reid, of course, does refer to a faculty of common sense. It is not clear, however, that Reid considers it to be a *sui generis* faculty. Indeed, he suggests that "common sense" is "only another name for one branch or degree of reason."[8] In any event, it would be a mistake to assume that the common sense tradition in general holds that there is some special faculty of common sense by which we know various propositions.

Second, though the common sense tradition holds that we can pick out instances of knowledge and justified belief, and use these in assessing criteria of knowledge and justification, it is also important to note that the common sense tradition does not insist that *everything* we take to be known is known. It does not insist that it can never be reasonable to abandon what we might have taken to be instances of knowledge. Indeed, this is part of Chisholm's point in calling himself a "critical commonsensist."[9] Philosophical reflection sometimes reveals that some of what we take ourselves to know conflicts with other things we take ourselves to know. Plato's dialogues artfully illustrate the puzzles that arise through thoughtful examination of one's beliefs. Such self-examination sometimes requires revision of one's commitments, but it does not require that one withhold *ab initio* belief in what one takes oneself to know. Nor does it require

---

8 Thomas Reid, *Essays on the Intellectual Powers of Man* (Cambridge, MA: The M. I. T. Press, 1969), Essay VI, Chapter II, p. 567.

9 Roderick Chisholm, *Theory of Knowledge*, 3rd edition (Englewood Cliffs, N. J.: Prentice-Hall, 1989), p. 64. The point that Chisholm emphasizes is that accepting some proposition *h* does not make it probable that *h* is true. Instead, Chisholm endorses the principle that "If S accepts h and if h is not disconfirmed by S's total evidence, then h is probable for S." Thus, simply accepting that *h* does not make it probable that *h* is true. Whether *h* is probable for S also depends on the fact that S's total evidence does not disconfirm *h*. Whether it is reasonable to believe some proposition, including the epistemic proposition that one knows that *p*, depends on the fact that the proposition is not disconfirmed by one's total evidence.

that one assume initially that one knows nothing or that one cannot pick out instances of knowledge or reasonable belief. In this respect at least, the Socratic tradition of self-examination agrees with the common sense tradition. It is important that we see the quest for coherence and the willingness to revise some of our beliefs as compatible with the common sense tradition.

Perhaps it would be useful to understand better the common sense tradition to consider what John Rawls calls "the method of wide reflective equilibrium." In the method of wide reflective equilibrium, one begins with (1) one's particular considered judgments, (2) one's beliefs in general principles, and (3) general background theories. One then seeks to achieve a coherent balance or "equilibrium" between these various elements. In some cases, this might require abandoning or revising one's particular judgments in favor of, say, a general principle that seems, on reflection, more reasonable. In other cases, one might give up or revise the general principle in favor of the particular judgment. The method of "wide" reflective equilibrium can be contrasted with the method of "narrow" reflective equilibrium. In the latter, we seek coherence only within a particular domain. For example, one might seek merely coherence between one's particular moral judgments and one's general moral principles, ignoring the relevance of considerations outside the domain of the moral. But in wide reflective equilibrium, one does not restrict oneself to beliefs within a given domain. One seeks a wider harmony between one's particular judgments and general principles and whatever other considerations might seem relevant. So, conceptions of the person and the functioning of social institutions as well as principles of economic theory might be brought to bear on particular moral judgments and general principles. What favors the method of wide reflective equilibrium is that nothing that seems relevant is excluded.

I suggest that the common sense tradition is compatible with the method of wide reflective equilibrium. The common sense philosopher begins with various considered judgments, general principles, and background theories and attempts, insofar as he can, to bring them into reflective equilibrium. He wants his philosophical theories and his criteria of knowledge and evidence to fit and cohere with his considered particular judgments, including his considered particular judgments about some common sense propositions.

Still, one can certainly take up the method of wide reflective equilibrium without belonging to the common sense tradition. For example, suppose that a philosopher held that the only things he knows and the only things he may take as data are propositions about his own mental states and some simple logical and metaphysical propositions. Suppose that his considered judgments were restricted in this way. He might then seek to achieve a coherence between his particular judgments and his general principles, but he would not be, I suggest, a common sense philosopher. Similarly, some proponents of the method of wide reflective equilibrium seem to hold that our initial beliefs, our considered judgments, have only a low degree of credibility.[10] The credibility of these judgments may, however, be increased as we weave them into a coherent body of beliefs. However, the view that our considered judgments or initial judgments have only a low degree of credibility conflicts with the common sense tradition. For the common sense philosophers, there are various truisms that they know and that almost everyone knows, and to hold that they are known is incompatible with holding that they have only a low degree of credibility. It is contrary to the common sense tradition to hold that all considered judgments have only a low degree of credibility until anchored in a philosophical web. Thus, simply taking up the method of wide reflective equilibrium is not sufficient for being a "commonsensist." One's considered judgments must have a certain breadth and scope, extending beyond, say, one's own mental states, and one must take at least some of them to be instances of knowledge and to be highly credible.

Again, it seems that one can take up the method of wide reflective equilibrium without being a commonsensist, even if one's considered judgments have broad scope and one takes them to be highly credible. Consider, for example, the follower of Zeno who shares many of the considered judgments of the common sense philosopher, finds them highly credible, and yet abandons them on hearing his master's arguments. Or consider the skeptic who finds at least initially credible most of what the common sense philosopher finds credible and yet comes to believe, on the basis of a philosophical argument, that he in fact knows nothing about

10   See Catherine Elgin, *Considered Judgment* (Princeton: Princeton University Press, 1996), Chapter 4. Elgin holds that in adopting the method of reflective equilibrium, we begin with those sentences we accept without reservation. She says, "Being our best current estimate of how things stand, such sentences have some claim on our allegiance" (p. 101). Such claims are "initially tenable." So my belief that "I have hands" and that "there are other people" are initially tenable. Later, however, she tells us that "Initially tenable claims are woefully uncertain, but are not defective on that account. They are not taken as true or incontrovertible or even probable, but only as reasonable starting points in a reflective self-correcting enterprise" (p. 110). I think philosophers in the common sense tradition would reject the view that the claims that "one has hands" or that "there are other people" are "woefully uncertain." Moreover, they would take these claims to be true.

other people. Such thinkers would not, I suggest, belong to the common sense tradition. Though the follower of Zeno or the philosophical skeptic might reach his position through the method of wide reflective equilibrium, that would not be sufficient for his being a commonsensist.

As noted here, philosophers in the common sense tradition assign a great deal of weight to various of their considered judgments. They assign a great deal of weight, for example, to the judgments that there are other people, that they have bodies, that they think and feel, and that we know such things. Of course, that much might also be said of the follower of Zeno and the philosophical skeptic. What is significant, though, is that the common sense philosopher does not regard such judgments as merely claims that might weigh against some philosophical theory, but that might, all things considered, be reasonably abandoned in favor of the theory. The weight he assigns such propositions is not outweighed by any competing philosophical view or criterion of knowledge. It is in this spirit that Moore says we can safely challenge any philosopher to bring forward an argument against our knowing such propositions that does not rest on a proposition less certain than that it is designed to attack.

In this section, I have stated some of the main features of the common sense tradition and identified some views to which it is not committed. It has not been my aim, however, to provide a set of necessary and sufficient conditions for being a "commonsensist" or to provide some principle of philosophical taxonomy by which we can identify all and only those who belong to the tradition. I do assume, however, that there are some propositions that one cannot reject and still be a member of the common sense tradition. I assume, for example, that one cannot deny that there are other people who know a lot about the world around them and be a member of the common sense tradition. I also assume, for example, that one cannot deny the existence of material objects and be a member of the common sense tradition. Thus, Bishop Berkeley is not a member of the common sense tradition however much he insists that his denial of the existence of material objects is compatible with common sense and thinks it important that his philosophical views be compatible with common sense.

Denying the existence of material objects excludes one from the common sense tradition. You do that and you are out. The same is true of a great many other propositions – for example, that there are other people, they have bodies, they think, the earth has existed for many years. But there are other propositions that are not so clearly essential for belonging to the common sense tradition. Consider the propositions that people have free will, that what they do is sometimes up to them, and that there is such a thing as "agent causation." Could one deny all or some of these propositions and still belong to the common sense tradition? There is perhaps a certain unavoidable "fuzziness" around the fringe of any reasonable philosophical taxonomy even when there are clear cases of who belongs to a tradition and who does not. Perhaps that is the way it is for many interesting and complex views. So, for example, we might think that there are certain core views that one must accept in order to be a Christian. One must accept the divinity of Jesus, for example. But must one also accept that the Holy Spirit proceeds from the Son as well as the Father? Must one believe in transubstantiation as opposed to consubstantiation? Could one accept the tenets of the Mormon faith and be a Christian? Mormons and many Baptists, for example, would certainly disagree over that one. I won't try to settle some thorny issues of taxonomy. Fortunately, the main philosophical objections to the common sense tradition that we will consider in this work don't really turn on those matters.

Finally, I would like to make a few comments about different sorts of philosophical projects. The common sense tradition takes as data various propositions about ourselves and the world around us and various epistemic propositions. It uses such data in assessing various philosophical theories about the nature of knowledge and justification and proposed analyses of philosophically interesting concepts. It seeks to understand and deepen our knowledge about various philosophically important issues. Still, there are some philosophical projects where such appeals are simply out of place. Two examples might illustrate this point. First, suppose that one grants that much of his putative knowledge is knowledge. One might thus grant that he does indeed know there are other people, that they walk and talk, and so on. But one might also believe that there is knowledge and there is "super knowledge" – knowledge that is certain and indubitable. Super knowledge would comprise only a small subset of one's knowledge. Some of the things we ordinarily take ourselves to know, including some things that are common sense propositions and matters of common knowledge, are not certain and indubitable. One might then undertake the philosophical project of discovering criteria of knowledge or evidence while restricting oneself to those bits of data that are thus super known. If one undertakes this sort of philosophical project, appeals to what one ordinarily thinks one knows might be simply out of place. Given the aim of this sort of project, the appeal to many of the things the common sense philosopher takes as data might be unacceptable.

Second, suppose one takes oneself to know various propositions about the past and the external world, but realizes that there are skeptics who deny such things. One might undertake the task of showing to the skeptic that such things are known. One might attempt, for example, to infer from *mutually accepted* premises that someone knows that there is an external world. In developing such an argument, appeals to propositions about the external world are dialectically irrelevant since the skeptic to whom they are addressed simply doesn't accept such claims. Given such projects, appeals to what we ordinarily think we know are out of place. They seem precluded by the nature of these philosophical projects.

I think we must be cautious, therefore, and not conclude that every philosopher who eschews appeal to what we ordinarily think we know is *ipso facto* holding that the views of the common sense tradition are false. Perhaps he is simply engaged in a project where appeals to what we ordinarily think we know are out of place. By the same token, however, one should not assume that the common sense philosopher is engaged in one of *those* projects. One should not assume that he is concerned to confine his data to what is super known, or that he is trying to refute or convince the skeptic by arguing from mutually accepted premises. It would be a mistake to criticize the common sense philosopher for not abiding by the tenets of some task he is not undertaking, just as it would be a mistake to criticize a musician's performance for not sounding like Bach when he is playing Brahms. If there are some philosophical projects where appeals to what we ordinarily think we know are out of place, it hardly follows that they are irrelevant to the questions that concern the common sense philosopher. It hardly follows, for example, that they are irrelevant to discovering criteria of knowledge or evidence.

1.2 EVIDENCE OR IRRESISTIBILITY?

The common sense philosopher takes various sorts of propositions as data for philosophical reflection. These include, but are not limited to, various truisms that almost everyone knows. But if we ask *why* should we take such claims as data, we find within the common sense tradition a variety of different answers.

As we have seen, Chisholm says that in investigating the theory of knowledge from a philosophical point of view, we assume that what we know is pretty much that which, on reflection, we think we know. He goes on to say, "This may seem like the wrong place to start. But where else *could* we start?" As a defense of the common sense tradition, this doesn't seem compelling. Surely, there are alternatives that one *could* adopt. One could, for example, confine one's data to what is certain and indubitable or one could confine one's data to propositions about one's own mental states. I don't think one can defend the common sense tradition on the ground that it is the only approach available.

As we have seen, Chisholm, Moore, and Reid hold that they can pick out instances of knowledge and justified belief and use these in assessing philosophical theories, including theories of knowledge and evidence. If we ask why should our philosophical views be consistent with such claims, one answer is that such claims really are instances of knowledge. On this view, then, we should take such claims as data because they have some positive epistemic status for us, because they are either known or epistemically justified for us. It is the epistemic character of these claims that makes it reasonable for us to take them as data.

Such claims expose the common sense philosopher to a battery of criticism. Critics often object that what the common sense philosopher takes as data lacks the positive epistemic status he takes it to have. These critics charge that the common sense philosopher does not know or is not justified in believing much of what he takes as data, and therefore it is a mistake for the common sense philosopher to use them in assessing epistemic principles or theories. Such critics often hold that the common sense philosopher is missing something important, something necessary, for his beliefs to have the positive epistemic status he attributes to them.

But what is it that the common sense philosopher lacks? There seem to be a variety of different answers. Some critics hold that what is lacking is knowledge of, or justified belief in, a criterion of knowledge or justification. This sort of view is, of course, characteristic of the view that Chisholm calls "methodism." It holds that in the absence of knowing a criterion of knowledge or justification, one cannot know that any particular belief is an instance of knowledge or that it is justified. More generally, it holds that in order to know that a particular belief has some epistemic property, F, one needs to know some criterion that tells us that beliefs of a certain sort have F. Such a view has its analogue in ethics. Mill, for example, in the first chapter of *Utilitarianism* tells us, "A test of right and wrong must be the means, one would think, of ascertaining what is right or wrong, and not a consequence of having already ascertained it."[11] Mill suggests that our knowledge of particular instances of right action is epistemically dependent on our knowing some general criterion

---

11   John Stuart Mill, *Utilitarianism* (Indianapolis: Hackett Publishing, 1979), p. 2.

of right action. In his view, knowledge of the criterion of right action is epistemically prior to knowledge of particular instances. The point of such an objection when raised against the common sense philosopher is that without knowing a criterion of knowledge or justified belief, one cannot know that some particular belief is an instance of knowledge or that it is justified. Knowledge of a criterion of knowledge or justification is epistemically prior to knowledge of particular instances of knowledge or justification.

A second objection focuses not on epistemic criteria but on reliability. There are different forms this doubt about the common sense tradition may take. There are differences about whether lack of knowledge of the reliability of a faculty or a source precludes "object-level knowledge," such as knowing that this is a pencil, or whether it precludes "second-level knowledge," such as knowing that one knows it is a pencil. But in either case, the objection is that the sorts of propositions that the common sense philosopher takes as data depend for their positive epistemic status upon knowledge that one's faculties or sources of belief formation are indeed reliable. Thus, in order to know that this is a pencil or to know that one knows such a thing, one must know that perception is indeed reliable. But knowledge of the reliability of one's faculties cannot be simply assumed, according to the objection. Knowledge of the reliability of one's faculties must be had through some form of philosophical argument that does not presuppose or assume the reliability of those faculties. It is held that such an argument – one free from "epistemic circularity" – is crucial for having the sort of knowledge that the common sense philosopher claims. Yet, the objection concludes, the common sense philosophers have notoriously failed to provide the necessary argument, and their claims to knowledge and justified belief are thus built on sand.

Both sorts of objections are important objections to the common sense tradition. Both imply that the beliefs that the common sense philosopher takes as data do not have the positive epistemic status he takes them to have. According to the first objection, his particular epistemic beliefs are not known or justified in the absence of knowing some general epistemic criterion. According to the second, his beliefs are not known or justified until he has provided the relevant argument, one free from epistemic circularity, for the reliability of the sources that yield those beliefs. In either case, the refusal or reluctance to take common sense beliefs as data is not based, as was suggested in Section 1.1, on the desire to confine one's data to what is certain or indubitable or to premises that are mutually acceptable to the skeptic. The refusal is based rather on the view that the

15

common sense philosopher is missing something crucial for the beliefs he takes as data to be known or justified. In the next two chapters, I will focus on the second sort of objection concerning our knowledge of the reliability of our ways of forming beliefs. In Chapter 6, I will take up the first objection, that knowledge of particular epistemic propositions depends on knowledge of general epistemic criteria.

But there is another sort of answer to the question as to why take our ordinary beliefs as data, one that focuses not on their epistemic character, but rather on their irresistibility. Consider the following striking passage from Reid's *Inquiry*:

To what purpose is it for philosophy to decide against common sense in this or any other matter? The belief of a material world is older, and of more authority, than any of the principles of philosophy. It declines the tribunal of reason, and laughs at all the artillery of the logician. It retains its sovereign authority in spite of all the edicts of philosophy, and reason itself must stoop to its orders. Even those philosophers who have disowned the authority of our notions of an external world, confess that they find themselves under a necessity of submitting to their power.

Methinks, therefore, it were better to make a virtue of necessity; and, since we cannot get rid of the vulgar notion and belief of an external world, to reconcile our reason to it as well as we can; for, if Reason should stomach and fret ever so much at this yoke, she cannot throw it off; if she will not be the servant of Common Sense, she must be her slave.[12]

Reid counsels us to "make a virtue of necessity"; since we can't get rid of certain common sense beliefs, such as a belief in the existence of a material world, we should make our philosophical views fit these deeply held beliefs. Indeed, Reid often points to the difficulty in giving up certain sorts of beliefs and to the futility of skeptical arguments. In explaining why he does not give up or ignore the testimony of his senses in the face of skeptical arguments, Reid says, "because it is not in my power; why then should I make a vain attempt . . . My belief is carried along by perception, as irresistibly as my body by the earth."[13] Here Reid seems to be defending the appeal to various sorts of common sense beliefs on the basis of their power or irresistibility.

The stance that Reid seems to take here resembles that which P. F. Strawson attributes to Reid's contemporary, David Hume. Hume tells us "that we assent to our faculties, and employ our reason only because we

12 Thomas Reid, *Inquiry and Essays*, p. 4.
13 *Ibid.*, p. 85.

cannot help it. Philosophy would render us entirely *Pyrrhonian*, were not nature too strong for it."[14] Strawson takes Hume to hold that "we simply *cannot help* believing in the existence of body, and *cannot help* forming beliefs and expectations in general accordance with the basic canons of induction."[15] Strawson agrees with Hume in this assessment of our basic "framework" beliefs – for example, beliefs in the existence of bodies, other people, and a determinate past. Such framework beliefs are "unavoidable natural convictions, commitments or prejudices, . . . ineradicably implanted in our minds by Nature."[16] From the claim that these framework beliefs are ineradicable, Strawson draws the following moral for dealing with skeptical arguments, one he finds already in Hume:

According to Hume the naturalist, skeptical arguments are not to be met with argument. They are simply to be neglected (except, perhaps, in so far as they supply a harmless amusement, a mild diversion to the intellect). They are to be neglected because they are *idle*; powerless against the forces of nature, of our naturally implanted disposition to belief. . . Our inescapable natural commitment is to a general frame of belief and to a general style (the inductive) of belief-formation. But *within* that frame and style, the requirement of Reason, that our beliefs should form a consistent and coherent system, may be given full play.[17]

For Strawson, skeptical arguments are idle insofar as they cannot lead us to abandon our framework beliefs. The proper response to skeptical arguments is to neglect or ignore them. But, by the same token, Strawson sees attempts to rebut skepticism as equally idle. He argues that "skeptical arguments and rational counter-arguments are equally idle – not senseless, but idle – since what we have are original, natural, inescapable commitments which we neither choose nor could give up."[18]

On Strawson's view, to argue in defense of our framework beliefs is idle because those beliefs are original, natural, inescapable commitments. Our original, natural, and inescapable commitments include the disposition to form beliefs in accordance with the basic canons of induction. Presumably, we may also include our dispositions to form beliefs about

14 David Hume, *A Treatise of Human Nature*, 2nd edition, ed. L. A. Selby-Bigge (Oxford: Clarendon Press, 1978), p. 657. This passage is taken from Hume's abstract to the *Treatise*.
15 P. F. Strawson, "Skepticism, Naturalism, and Transcendental Arguments," *Human Knowledge*, 2nd edition, ed. Paul K. Moser and Arnold vander Nat (Oxford: Oxford University Press, 1995), p. 407.
16 *Ibid.*, p. 410.
17 *Ibid.*, p. 408.
18 *Ibid.*, p. 414.

the external world on the basis of perception and beliefs about the past on the basis of memory. What is more, the proper business of philosophical reflection is not to evaluate critically the reliability of such dispositions, and it certainly isn't to try to provide arguments for the reliability of such dispositions. Such arguments would be idle. What, then, is the proper task of philosophy? Strawson suggests, it is "to establish the connections between the major structural features or elements of our conceptual scheme – to exhibit it, not as a rigidly deductive system, but as a coherent whole whose parts are mutually supportive and mutually dependent, interlocking in an intelligible way – to do this may well seem to our naturalist the proper task of analytical philosophy. As indeed it does to me. (Whence the phrase "descriptive" [as opposed to validatory or revisionary] metaphysics.[19]) The proper task of philosophy is to see how our conceptual scheme holds together and, perhaps, when elements within the framework conflict, to resolve the conflict as seems best within the light of Reason in a way compatible with our inescapable framework convictions.

Perhaps one might see an advantage in the naturalistic appeal to the irresistibility of framework beliefs. The advantage is that it seems to allow us to sidestep questions about their epistemic status or about the credibility of common sense beliefs. The appeal to irresistibility might thus be construed as telling us that whether or not we know or are justified in believing these propositions, it is reasonable for us to take them as data. In this respect, such an appeal is like Chisholm's suggestion that we have no place else to start. In each case, these responses seem to permit the common sense philosopher to appeal to various propositions as data without taking a stand on their epistemic status. Indeed, some of Strawson's remarks suggest that he is not committed to a positive epistemic status for our framework convictions, since he refers to them as "unavoidable natural commitments, convictions, or prejudices."

We should ask, then, whether the "naturalist" perspective Strawson endorses and sees in Hume provides an answer to the question, "Why take our common sense beliefs as data?" As we have seen, Reid holds that we accept various propositions and principles by a necessity of our nature. Could this be why we should take them as data? Can we view the common sense tradition as an expression of Strawsonian or Humean naturalism?

---

19 *Ibid.*, p. 412.

I do not think so for three reasons. First, perhaps many common sense beliefs are irresistible. Perhaps this is true of beliefs such as there are bodies and there are other people. Perhaps it is true, too, of beliefs such as I have a body. But as we have seen, the common sense philosopher takes as data various epistemic propositions in attempting to formulate criteria of knowledge and evidence. Such epistemic propositions might include: I *know* that I have a body, I *know* there are other people, and people know many things about themselves and their environment. Is it really clear that these epistemic propositions cannot be given up? Could one not hold, for example, "Yes, I have a body. I cannot give up that belief. But it isn't something I know. Maybe it's more likely than not, maybe it isn't. But I don't know it." It is far from obvious that *all* the propositions that various common sense philosophers would take as data are irresistible. It is not clear, therefore, that the common sense philosopher would or should point to their irresistibility as what makes it reasonable to take such propositions as data. Such an answer would not explain, for example, why he takes various epistemic propositions as data.

Second, whatever the merits of an appeal to irresistibility, I suggest that it is not the main reason the common sense tradition takes as data the various propositions that it does. The common sense tradition does not sidestep questions about the epistemic status of what it takes as data. It does not regard them as mere "prejudices." On the contrary, it takes a clear stand on the epistemic status of a great many propositions. Consider the proposition that people have bodies. Perhaps this proposition is irresistible for us. Still, common sense philosophers such as Reid, Moore, and Chisholm hold not only that people have bodies, but that they *know* they have bodies, and almost everyone knows that people have bodies. It is a matter of common knowledge. Thus, the common sense philosopher could point, not to the ineradicable nature of such beliefs, but to their positive epistemic status, to their being known, as that which makes it reasonable to take them as data in philosophy. What would make it reasonable to take as a datum the proposition that there are bodies would not be that it is irresistible, but that it is known or evident. Similarly, what makes it reasonable for us to take as a datum the epistemic proposition that most people know their names is the fact that this epistemic proposition is itself known or evident. Indeed, according to the common sense tradition, it is a matter of common knowledge. Almost everyone knows that most people know their own names. What makes it reasonable to take such things as data is that they are known or justified for him, rather than being irresistible. Thus, Chisholm says in defense of his theory of knowledge and his critical commonsensism, "it corresponds with what we do know."[20]

Among Reid, Moore, and Chisholm, the naturalistic stance seems strongest in Reid. But even Reid does not rest his appeal to common sense beliefs merely upon their irresistibility. In Reid's view, various principles of common sense are evident to us. Their being evident to us is a good reason for taking them seriously and giving them weight in philosophical reflection. In the passage just quoted, Reid counsels us to make "a virtue of necessity," but he also points to the *authority* of various common sense beliefs. To say that they have authority is to make a *normative* or *evaluative* claim. This authority consists in their being worthy of acceptance. Reid tells us that various principles of common sense have more authority than competing philosophical claims. I take him to hold that they are more worthy of acceptance than the competing philosophical claims. At least, part of what Reid is telling us is that the belief in a material world is more worthy of acceptance than the philosophical assumptions that would imply that it is false or that we should withhold belief in it.

Finally, we might ask why should irresistibility matter? Why should the irresistibility of some belief or set of beliefs matter for our philosophical inquiries? One possible reply might be that we want a *consistent* set of beliefs. If some philosophical view conflicts with beliefs that we cannot give up, and we can give up the philosophical view, then the latter must go. In other words, given an interest in overall consistency, the only philosophical views we should adopt are those that fit with our irresistible common sense beliefs.

This reply is not entirely satisfactory. First, the common sense tradition does not simply accept various common sense propositions. It takes them as data for philosophical inquiry. It takes various common sense beliefs as *good reasons* or *evidence* for accepting various theories of knowledge and evidence. But how could such beliefs be good reasons for adopting or rejecting a philosophical view if they were not justified, if they did not have some positive epistemic status? The goal of consistency doesn't seem to require that we treat deeply held or irresistible beliefs as good reasons for accepting or rejecting philosophical views. After all, if our interest is simply in being consistent, then why must we adopt any philosophical views at all? Could we not simply eschew philosophy altogether? Could not consistency be had without adopting any philosophical theory about, say, the nature of knowledge and evidence? Suppose, for example, that one

---

20 Roderick Chisholm, *Theory of Knowledge*, 2nd edition, p. 121.

holds various irresistible common sense beliefs p, q, and r, and that these beliefs are mutually consistent. Suppose further that some philosophical proposition T is inconsistent with those beliefs, but another philosophical proposition T' is not. Given that one can't give up the common sense beliefs and that one wants a consistent body or beliefs, then it seems reasonable for one to give up T. But one would not have any good reason for adopting T', since one could have a consistent body of beliefs simply by continuing to hold one's common sense beliefs. The aim of mere consistency would not require that we add or adopt any further philosophical propositions. The fact that some philosophical proposition is consistent with our irresistible beliefs would not constitute a good reason for us to believe it. Second, even if one aspires to a philosophical view of the world, one might hold that inconsistency between our philosophical views and our overpowering common sense beliefs is not such a bad thing. If the only thing to be said in favor of our common sense beliefs is that they are irresistible, why should we not view them the way we view bad habits, such as smoking or overeating, that we continue to engage in even when reason convinces us that they should be given up? Reid suggests that the philosophical rejection of various common sense beliefs is a kind of intermittent "metaphysical lunacy." But could one not take instead the opposite view and be grateful for those brief moments of philosophical lucidity, freed from the insistent promptings of nature? The philosopher in her study, rejecting common sense beliefs, is, on this alternative view, no lunatic, but rather an enchanted princess who enjoys, while the moon is on the lake, a few moments of rational clarity before becoming once more a swan. She might thus value her philosophical views in spite of the fact they are inconsistent with what she finds herself irresistibly believing at other times. Furthermore, suppose that we do find our philosophical views conflicting with our common sense beliefs. Even if we do not take our philosophical views as more likely to be true, or see our common sense beliefs as ineradicable prejudice, could we not simply recognize the inconsistency, continue to hold our philosophical views, and hope that further reflection will remove the impasse?

"But," one might object, "even if we cannot give up various common sense beliefs, could we not accept certain philosophical views because accepting them brings us greater overall coherence? Even if some set of irresistible beliefs form a consistent set of beliefs, we might adopt a philosophical theory T' because of the greater coherence it brings to our views. What we want is not simply a consistent body of beliefs, but one that enjoys coherence." In response to this objection, I would make the following two points. First, why should coherence with our irresistible beliefs matter if the latter have no positive epistemical status? Suppose that one could weave one's wildly false, indeed crazy or paranoid beliefs, into a more coherent body. What would be desirable about this? Would not such coherence simply lead one further away from the truth and knowledge? It is not clear that achieving greater coherence by adopting a philosophical theory that coheres with our irresistible beliefs is epistemically desirable if our irresistible beliefs have no positive epistemic status. Second, even *if* one viewed mere coherence itself as a source of epistemic justification, could not our irresistible common sense beliefs enjoy some degree of coherence without adopting some philosophical view? If coherence is seen as being itself a source of justification, then it is not clear why the naturalist should eschew the claim that our irresistible common sense beliefs enjoy some degree of epistemic justification since they would seem to enjoy already *some* degree of coherence and justification. *If* coherence is valued because it is seen as a source of epistemic justification, then why should the naturalist sidestep the question of their epistemic status?

In sum, I don't think we should view the common sense tradition as an expression of Strawsonian or Humean naturalism. If it is true that some of the propositions common sense philosophers take as data are natural, original, ineradicable convictions, it seems that some – for example, our epistemic beliefs – are not. Moreover, the attitude of naturalism toward the epistemic status of our framework beliefs seems, from the standpoint of the common sense tradition, unacceptably noncommital. In contrast, the common sense tradition takes these beliefs to have a positive epistemic status, and typically holds them to be instances of knowledge.[21]

---

21 I will simply note here that the positive epistemic status that Reid, Moore, and Chisholm attribute to many common sense propositions also distinguishes them from Wittgenstein and his followers. I think Wittgenstein would accept many common sense propositions as "hinge" propositions, and regard them as being in *some* sense foundational or basic for inquiry, as being exempt from doubt. Still, Wittgenstein is, at best, very reluctant to count as knowledge many of the things that Reid, Moore, and Chisholm would count as knowledge, or to count them as knowledge in the context of philosophical inquiry. Wittgenstein writes, "It can't be said of me at all (except perhaps as a joke) that I *know* I am in pain. What is this supposed to mean – except perhaps that I *am* in pain?" *Philosophical Investigations* translated by G. E. M. Anscombe (New York: Macmillan, 1958), paragraph 246. Again, concerning the things Moore claims to know in his "A Defence of Common Sense," Wittgenstein writes, "I should like to say: Moore does not *know* what he asserts he knows, but it stands fast for him, as also for me; regarding it as absolutely solid is part of our *method* of doubt and enquiry." *On Certainty* translated by Denis Paul and G. E. M. Anscombe (New York: Basil Blackwell, 1969), paragraph 151. Of course, Moore, Reid, and Chisholm would say that

The sort of Strawsonian or Humean naturalism considered here may be viewed as a way of avoiding epistemic objections insofar as it focuses on the irresistibility of our framework beliefs rather than their epistemic character. Indeed, it would suggest that the worries about the epistemic status of such beliefs are "idle." But I take the common sense tradition embodied in Reid, Moore, and Chisholm to hold that various common sense beliefs are known and justified, and that this makes it reasonable for us to take them as data. It is their epistemic character, rather than their irresistibility, that confers upon them this status. Given this stance, it seems they cannot take refuge in a Strawsonian or naturalistic strategy of avoidance. A defense of the common sense tradition must take the epistemic objections of its critics seriously.

they *know* these things. Given that Wittgenstein does *not* think one can be said to know that one is in pain and does not want to say that Moore knows what he asserts in his "Defence," I would not include Wittgenstein and his followers among members of the common sense tradition. If one denies that I can know that I am in pain or that I do not know that there are other people, then I would not say that he is a common sense philosopher.

2

Common Sense and Reliability I

In this chapter, I consider one line of criticism of the common sense tradition. This objection holds that (1) perceptual and mnemonic knowledge require that one know that one's perception and memory are reliable, (2) the only epistemically satisfactory way to know that they are reliable is through a "non-circular" argument, and (3) the common sense philosopher has no such argument. If this objection were sound, then the common sense philosopher would not know what he thinks he knows. Many of the beliefs he takes as "data" would lack the positive epistemic status he takes them to have. In this chapter and the next, I will defend the view that we may reasonably reject both (1) and (2).

In the first section, I consider some of the assumptions that underlie this objection. In the second section, I consider the views of William Alston and Ernest Sosa concerning our knowledge of the reliability of our ways of forming beliefs. Sosa argues, roughly, that when it comes to knowing that our ways of forming beliefs are reliable, we cannot escape epistemic circularity; however, he holds that this fact does not prevent us from knowing that our ways of forming beliefs are reliable. I think Sosa's view is right, and that it provides a way in which the common sense philosopher might respond to this objection.

2.1 TWO ASSUMPTIONS

Here are two assumptions:

A1 Both perceptual and mnemonic knowledge require that one know or be justified in believing that perception and memory are reliable.

A2   The only epistemically satisfactory way to know or to be justified in believing that perception and memory are reliable is on the basis of a non-circular argument.

Let us consider the implications of these views for the common sense tradition. If both A1 and A2 are true, then the position of the common sense philosopher seems quite problematic. This is so for at least two reasons. First, it is not clear what the relevant non-circular argument would be. Common sense philosophers such as Reid, Moore, and Chisholm have not offered us any non-circular argument for the reliability of perception and memory. In the absence of such arguments, given these assumptions, their claims to perceptual and mnemonic knowledge are simply false, and so, too, are their higher-order claims to know that they know various things based upon perception and memory. Second, the common sense tradition holds that the vast majority of people have perceptual and mnemonic knowledge. Thus, even if the common sense philosopher can come up with a non-circular argument for the reliability of perception and memory, that would not be a source of knowledge for the reliability of those faculties for the vast majority of people. Thus, if we accept these assumptions, the vast majority of people will simply not have the perceptual and mnemonic knowledge that the common sense tradition attributes to them. Therefore, a defense of the common sense tradition requires that we reject either A1 or A2 or both.

Let us begin by considering A1. Before we consider some reasons in favor of A1, let us consider one objection to it. A1 seems too strong since it would seem to preclude children and animals from having perceptual and mnemonic knowledge. Children and animals do not seem capable of forming the requisite meta-belief about the reliability of their faculties and do not seem capable of knowing or being justified in believing that their faculties of perception and memory are reliable. Yet it seems plausible that children and animals might have much in the way of perceptual and mnemonic knowledge without knowing or being justified in believing much, if anything, *about* perception and memory. Here too we might think about knowledge based on testimony. Children, I assume, acquire much knowledge by way of testimony. But should we hold that knowledge based on testimony requires that one know or be justified in believing that such testimony is reliable? It is doubtful that children who accept much of what they are told are capable of forming the belief that testimony is reliable or that they are in a position for that belief to be one that is justified for them. Just as A1 would appear to deny children perceptual and mnemonic knowledge, so too a principle concerning testimony analogous to A1 would imply that they lack knowledge based on testimony.

Let us, however, pause to consider this criticism a bit more closely. A1 tells us that perceptual and mnemonic knowledge requires *either* that one know that perception and memory are reliable *or* that one be justified in believing that perception and memory are reliable. For the sake of simplicity, let us focus just on perceptual knowledge. We may note that there is a certain ambiguity in the requirement that one be justified in believing that perception is reliable. This can mean either that one actually *believes* justifiedly that perception is reliable or that one is justified in believing that perception is reliable whether or not one actually does believe it. Taking account of this ambiguity, then, we may say that A1 can be interpreted as making either of the following claims about perceptual knowledge:

A1a Perceptual knowledge requires that one know that perception is reliable.
A1b Perceptual knowledge requires that one believe justifiedly that perception is reliable.
A1c Perceptual knowledge requires that one be justified in believing that perception is reliable (whether or not one does actually believe it).

Now let us consider the following objection. "We may grant that A1a and A1b are false. We may agree that they would incorrectly preclude children and animals from having knowledge because they are not able to form the *belief* that perception is reliable. Still, that would not show that A1c is false. Couldn't it be that perceptual knowledge requires that one be justified in believing that perception is reliable, even if one does not in fact believe it?" In response, I would say that one is justified in believing a proposition only if one can grasp and consider it. I assume that just as children and animals are not able to believe the proposition that perception and memory are reliable, so too they cannot grasp or consider it. Consequently, I would hold that they are not justified in believing it. If this is right, then I would say that A1c rules out perceptual knowledge in children and animals every bit as much as A1a and A1b, and therefore it too should be rejected. Each of these interpretations rules out perceptual knowledge in children and animals, and so I think they should all be rejected. For the same reason, I think we should reject analogous principles pertaining to memory and testimony.

Still, let us consider some reasons why one might think that A1 is true. There are three sorts of reasons I shall consider. These are (1) the view that perceptual and mnemonic knowledge are inferential, (2) an appeal to the "generalizability thesis," and (3) considerations about "epistemic irresponsibility." Let us begin with the view that perceptual and mnemonic knowledge are inferential.

Suppose one thought that perceptual and memory beliefs essentially depend for their justification and status as knowledge on an inference from some general proposition to the effect that such sources are reliable. One might hold, for example, that perceptual knowledge that p is based on an inference of the following sort: (1) Perceptual beliefs are highly likely to be true; (2) my belief that p is a perceptual belief; therefore (3) my perceptual belief that p is highly likely to be true. Given such a view, if one did not know (1), then one would not have perceptual knowledge. Furthermore, if there is no way to know that perception is a reliable source, then one cannot have perceptual knowledge.

However, the view that perceptual and mnemonic beliefs are based on an actual inference of this sort does not seem very plausible. Our perceptual and mnemonic beliefs are not based on inferences from general principles about the reliability of those faculties. Indeed, they do not seem to be based on *any* sort of inference. My perceptual belief that there is a book on the desk does not seem to be based on any inference. It seems cognitively spontaneous and non-inferential. I simply look at the desk and form the belief that there is a book there. No reasoning appears to be involved. Similarly, when I remember what I had for breakfast or where I live, no reasoning or inference seems to be involved. I just remember such things. Chisholm, Reid, and Moore too, at one stage of his career, deny that perceptual and mnemonic knowledge are inferential. If Reid, Moore, and Chisholm are right in holding that perceptual and mnemonic beliefs are not based on inference, and I think they are, then one cannot support or defend A1 by appealing to the inferential nature of such beliefs.

I think many other philosophers would join in rejecting the view that perceptual and mnemonic knowledge are inferential. Traditional foundationalists, for example, would hold, roughly, that in order for one to have perceptual knowledge that p, one must have a true belief that p and one must have the right sort of perceptual experiences. Reliabilists would hold that one's true belief that p must be produced or sustained by a reliable faculty of perception. Coherentists would hold that one's true belief that p must belong to a (sufficiently broad and comprehensive) coherent body of beliefs. None of these approaches is committed to the view that perceptual and mnemonic knowledge must be based on actual inferences from general principles about the reliability of one's faculties.

I do not think that one can plausibly support A1 by appealing to the inferential nature of perceptual and mnemonic knowledge. Still, even if the inferential view is false, that does not imply that A1 is false. A1, after all, does not imply that perceptual and mnemonic knowledge is based on such an inference. It simply tells us that they require that one know or be justified in believing that perception and memory are reliable.

Let us turn to a second way of supporting A1. One might seek to defend A1 by appealing to what Chisholm calls "the generalizability thesis." Chisholm asks us to consider the following view:

> You cannot *know* that any given proposition *p* is true unless you also know two other things. The first of these things will be a certain more *general* proposition *q*; *q* will not imply *p* but it will specify the conditions under which propositions of a certain type are true. And the second thing will be a proposition *r*, which enables you to *apply* this general proposition to *p*. In other words, *r* will be a proposition to the effect that the first proposition *p* satisfies the conditions specified in the second proposition.[1]

The generalizability thesis tells us that in order to know that *p* is true, we must know that our belief that *p* was formed in a certain way such that beliefs formed in that way are likely to be true. The generalizability thesis tells us that one cannot know *any* proposition *p* unless one also knows that one's belief that *p* is reliably formed. The generalizability thesis itself is much more general than A1 since the latter pertains to only perceptual and mnemonic knowledge. Still, one might see in the generalizability thesis, or something close to it, a reason for accepting A1. But Chisholm argues that we should reject the generalizability thesis. He points out that if the generalizability thesis is true, then no one knows anything. He observes:

> According to the thesis, if we know *p*, then we know two further propositions – a general proposition *q* and a proposition *r* that applies *q* to *p*. Applying the generalizability thesis to each of two propositions *q* and *r* we obtain four more propositions; applying it to each of them, we obtain eight more propositions; ... and so on *ad indefinitum*. The generalizability thesis implies, therefore, that we cannot know any proposition to be true unless we know all the members of an infinite hierarchy to be true. And therefore it implies that we cannot know any proposition to be true.[2]

Chisholm thinks, therefore, that we should reject the generalizability thesis since it would imply a thoroughgoing skepticism. Indeed, the

---

1 Roderick Chisholm, *Theory of Knowledge*, 2nd edition, pp. 48–9.
2 *Ibid.*, p. 49.

generalizability thesis seems to be self-refuting in the sense that if it is true, no one could know it to be true since one would not know the infinite series of propositions it requires for knowledge. I do not think, therefore, that one could reasonably claim to support A1 by appealing to the generalizability thesis or its close kin. I do not think that one can plausibly support A1 either by appealing to the alleged inferential nature of perceptual and mnemonic beliefs or to the generalizability thesis. Further, we may wonder that if we reject the view that *every* belief must meet the sort of requirement the generalizability thesis imposes, why then impose it on *any*?

Perhaps the strongest considerations favoring A1 are those that involve the notion of "epistemic irresponsibility." The notion of epistemic irresponsibility is central to BonJour's discussion of the hypothetical case of Norman the clairvoyant. BonJour asks us to imagine the following case:

Norman, under certain conditions which usually obtain, is a completely reliable clairvoyant with respect to certain kinds of subject matter. He possesses no evidence or reasons of any kind for or against the general possibility of such a cognitive power or for or against the thesis that he possesses it. One day Norman comes to believe that the President is in New York City, though he has no evidence either for or against this belief. In fact the belief is true and results from his clairvoyant power under circumstances in which it is highly reliable.[3]

Now let us consider the following three propositions:

1. The President is in New York City.
2. I have a reliable power of clairvoyance.
3. My belief that 1 is the result of such a power.

BonJour deliberately leaves open in his example as to whether Norman *believes* 2 and 3. Yet BonJour thinks that whether or not Norman believes 2 and 3, his belief in 1 is epistemically unjustified and does not amount to knowledge. Suppose, for example, that Norman *does* believe 2 and 3. Suppose further that his beliefs in 2 and 3 contribute to Norman's acceptance of 1 in the sense that if Norman were to give up his belief in 2 and 3, he would also give up his belief in 1. Now, BonJour points out that since Norman has *no* evidence for 2 and 3, he is not justified in accepting them. Thus, if Norman's acceptance of 1 is based on his belief in 2 and 3, we should conclude that his acceptance of 1 is epistemically unjustified

3 Laurence BonJour, *The Structure of Empirical Knowledge* (Cambridge, MA: Harvard University Press, 1985), p. 41.

and does not amount to knowledge. On the other hand, suppose that Norman *does not* believe 2 and 3. In this case, BonJour asks why does Norman continue to believe that the President is in New York City? "Why isn't the mere fact that there is no way, as far as he knows, for him to have obtained this information a sufficient reason for classifying this belief as an unfounded hunch and ceasing to accept it? And if Norman does not do this, isn't he being epistemically irrational and irresponsible?"[4] BonJour suggests that without believing that 2 and 3 are true, Norman's acceptance of 1 is epistemically irresponsible, and he would not be epistemically justified in accepting 1. So we see that BonJour poses a dilemma. If Norman's belief about the President's whereabouts depends on his beliefs in 2 and 3, then his belief in 1 is unjustified. If, on the other hand, he does not believe 2 and 3, then his belief in 1 must be, from his perspective, no better than a hunch, and his acceptance of it is again epistemically irresponsible and unjustified.

Norman seems unjustified in his belief about the President's whereabouts, and his belief does not seem to amount to knowledge. He seems to be unjustified because he lacks justified belief about the source of his belief and about its reliability. But if Norman's clairvoyant belief fails to be justified, and an instance of knowledge because he lacks such a justified meta-perspective, then shouldn't we say that such a justified meta-perspective is required for perceptual and mnemonic knowledge? In other words, shouldn't we affirm A1 after all?

I don't think so. Central to BonJour's assessment of Norman's case is the notion of epistemic irresponsibility. The main idea seems to be that if one is epistemically irresponsible in believing that p, then one does not know that p. Now what would make one epistemically irresponsible in believing something? One answer would be this:

ER (Epistemic Responsibility)   If either (1) one is justified in withholding belief that one's belief that p is reliably formed, or (2) one is justified in believing that one's belief that p is *not* reliably formed, then one is epistemically irresponsible in believing that p.

ER seems plausible enough. For the sake of argument, let's suppose it's true. Since Norman is, *ex hypothesi*, justified in withholding belief that his belief about the President's whereabouts is reliably formed, his continuing to hold that belief is epistemically irresponsible, and for that reason, we might hold, it fails to be knowledge. But it is important to see that ER

---

4   *Ibid.*, p. 42.

does *not* imply that the perceptual and mnemonic beliefs of children and animals are epistemically irresponsible. Since children and animals cannot form the relevant meta-beliefs, I think it is false to say that they are justified in either holding them, withholding them, or rejecting them. Thus, children and animals do not satisfy the antecedent of ER, and ER does not imply that their beliefs are epistemically irresponsible. Again, we may say that children and animals are not justified in believing that their faculties are reliable, but it does *not* follow that they are therefore justified in withholding or rejecting the proposition that their faculties are reliable. It does not follow because they are incapable of grasping or considering that proposition. In sum, if Norman's belief about the President's whereabouts is epistemically irresponsible, the same need not be true for children and animals, who are incapable of adopting the sort of self-reflective stance that Norman takes and that we may expect of *him*. ER does not imply that their beliefs are epistemically irresponsible or support the view that they lack perceptual and mnemonic knowledge because they lack knowledge or justified belief about the reliability of perception and memory. Thus, even if we accept ER, we are not committed to accepting A1. We can explain why Norman lacks knowledge without holding that children and animals lack knowledge and still reject A1.

To support the view that the perceptual and mnemonic beliefs of children and animals are epistemically irresponsible because they do not know or are not justified in believing perception and memory are reliable, one would need some principle other than ER. Such a principle might be the following:

ER′   If one is not justified in believing that one's belief that p is reliably formed, then one is epistemically irresponsible in believing that p.

If epistemically irresponsible beliefs don't amount to knowledge, and if ER′ is true, then one cannot have knowledge that p without being justified in believing that one's belief that p is reliably formed. Such a combination of views would lend support to A1. But is ER′ plausible? I don't think so. ER′ seems no more plausible than the following moral principle:

M (Moral Principle)   If one is not justified in believing that one's action is morally permissible, then one is morally irresponsible in performing it.

Children and animals, as well as some adults with profoundly diminished mental capacities, are not justified in believing, I assume, that their actions are morally permissible. But it would be a mistake to hold that they are morally irresponsible in acting as they do. We hold that they are "not responsible" rather than "irresponsible." The latter is a criticism and a charge of a different sort than the former. To say that someone is acting irresponsibly is to imply that the person is somehow blameworthy. But that sort of implication does not follow from the claim that one is not responsible for his action. Now, ER′ implies that children and animals are epistemically irresponsible in their beliefs. And if the charge of irresponsiblity implies blameworthiness, it implies that they are somehow blameworthy. But that seems too harsh. Consider the child who accepts much on the basis of testimony, but who is not justified in believing that testimony is reliable. ER′ implies that such beliefs are irresponsibly formed and that one is somehow blameworthy. But these consequences are implausible. The perceptual and mnemonic beliefs of children and animals and the beliefs that children form on the basis of testimony are not formed irresponsibly. Should we say then that they believe and form their beliefs responsibly? I suggest rather that we say they form their beliefs in a way that is simply not responsible.

We may agree, then, with BonJour, and hold that Norman's belief is epistemically irresponsible. We may also agree that epistemically irresponsible beliefs don't amount to knowledge. But to concede this much does not support the view that children and animals lack knowledge and it does not support A1. But suppose it is urged that knowledge requires not only beliefs free of epistemic irresponsibility, but also *responsibly* formed beliefs? Here we might simply have a clash of intuitions. Since it is plausible to hold that children and animals do have perceptual and mnemonic knowledge, as well as knowledge based on testimony, and that such beliefs are not responsibly formed, we should reject the view that knowledge requires responsibly formed beliefs. Furthermore, suppose that some of our beliefs were irresistible, that we simply could not help forming them and could not give them up. Reid suggests that our belief in an external world is like this: "My belief is carried along by perception, as irresistibly as my body by the earth."[5] Perhaps our belief that we are in pain, when we are in pain, is such a belief. Perhaps the beliefs that we think or exist are such beliefs. Perhaps there are other beliefs that are what Strawson calls ineradicable framework beliefs. If such beliefs are really not in our power to give up, if they are irresistible, then it is false that we are "responsible" for having them or that we form them responsibly. We would be no more responsible for such beliefs than we are responsible for having been born

5   Thomas Reid, *Inquiry and Essays*, p. 83.

or for being carried along in the orbit of the earth. But neither would it be right to say that we were irresponsible in holding such beliefs. Rather, we should say that we are simply not responsible for such beliefs. Now, if such beliefs were indeed irresistible for us, and we were not responsible for them, it would not follow that they would not be instances of knowledge. So, again, I do not think knowledge requires responsibly formed beliefs.

In sum, I do not think that A1 can be supported by appealing to the inferential character of perceptual and mnemonic beliefs, to the generalizability thesis, or to considerations about epistemic irresponsibility. I think we may reject A1 because it implies that children and animals lack perceptual and mnemonic knowledge. Moreover, an analogous principle about testimony would imply incorrectly, I believe, that children lack knowledge based on testimony.

Yet even if we reject A1, I do not think that the common sense philosopher can simply ignore the question of the reliability of his faculties. Suppose philosophical reflection convinces us that one knows that *p* only if the source of one's belief that *p* is reliable. We must, of course, distinguish this requirement that the source *be* reliable from the requirement in A1 that one *know* or *be justified in believing* that the source is reliable. What might lead us to accept the requirement that the source be reliable? Suppose, for example, that someone generally deceived by an evil demon forms the perceptual belief that there is a table before him (*p*). Suppose that his belief that *p* is supported by his (unreliable) perceptual experience, and further that his belief that *p* coheres with the rest of his (largely false) beliefs. Now let us suppose that his belief that *p* is, by chance, true – that there really is a table before him. Even if his belief is true, it would not seem to be an instance of knowledge given the general unreliability of his faculties. So, again, it seems plausible to think that one has perceptual knowledge only if one's perceptual faculties are, in fact, reliable. Similarly, we might hold that beliefs rooted in memory, introspection, and rational intuition are instances of knowledge only if those faculties are reliable. Suppose such reflection supports the view that reliable faculties are necessary for knowledge.

But now consider the position of one who accepts (1) I know that I have perceptual knowledge, (2) I know that I have perceptual knowledge only if perception is reliable, and (3) I do not know whether perception is reliable. The common sense philosopher and most of those not skeptical about perception will accept (1). Philosophical reflection on the nature of knowledge might convince us that (2) is true. But consider the position of one who accepts (1), (2), and (3). Is there not something deeply incoherent with such a view? It would be like holding (i) I know this is a snake, (ii) I know this is a snake only if it is a reptile, and (iii) I do not know that this is a reptile. Thus, even if we deny that one knows that *p* only if one knows that *p* issues from a reliable source, denying that we have knowledge of the reliability of our source comes with a heavy price. To avoid this sort of incoherence, we could of course, deny either (1) or (2). But that would seem to many to be a rather high price to pay for coherence.

Furthermore, we might consider what Sosa calls the "Principle of Exclusion" (PE):

PE (Principle of Exclusion)   If one is to know that *p* then one must exclude (rule out) every possibility that one knows to be incompatible with one's knowing that *p*. (Where "excluding" means "knowing not to be the case".)[6]

Note that PE does not require that one exclude every possibility that is incompatible with one's knowing that *p*. It requires only that one exclude those possibilities that one *knows* to be thus incompatible. Note further that PE does not imply that A1 is true. A1 requires more than PE. A1 tells us that no one has perceptual or mnemonic knowledge in the absence of knowing those sources to be reliable. PE, in contrast, tells us that once one sees or recognizes that the unreliability of perception and memory are incompatible with one's having perceptual and mnemonic knowledge, then one must exclude those possibilities. So, whereas A1 would deny perceptual and mnemonic knowledge to animals and small children who lack the relevant notions of reliability and perhaps even a distinct notion of faculties such as perception and memory, PE does not have that consequence. But once one leaves the stage of such intellectual innocence and recognizes that the unreliability of perception is incompatible with one's knowing that *p* on the basis of perception, PE implies that knowledge that *p* requires that one exclude that possibility. It requires that one know that perception is reliable. So, for those reflective enough to recognize the incompatibility, PE requires that one must know that one's way of forming beliefs is not unreliable. We are led back then to the problem of how we might know that perception and memory are reliable.

But how is such knowledge to be had? A2 tells us that the only epistemically satisfactory way to know that perception and memory are reliable is on the basis of a non-circular argument. It must be an argument that does not depend on perceptual and mnemonic beliefs and one that does not

---

6 See Ernest Sosa, "Reflective Knowledge in the Best Circles," *Knowledge, Truth, and Duty,* ed. Matthias Steup (Oxford: Oxford University Press, 2001), p. 188.

use the faculties of perception and memory. In order to support the view that perception and memory are reliable, we must "get outside" those sources. BonJour, for example, writes:

Since what is at issue here is the metajustification of an overall standard of empirical knowledge, rather than merely an account of some particular region of empirical knowledge, it seems clear that no empirical premises can be employed. Any empirical premise employed in such an argument would have to be either (1) unjustified, or (2) justified by an obviously circular appeal to the very standard in question, or (3) justified by appeal to some other standard of empirical justification (thereby implicitly abandoning the claim that the standard in question is the correct overall account of epistemic justification for empirical beliefs). Thus, the argument will apparently have to be purely *a priori* in character, and it is certainly far from obvious how such an *a priori* argument might go.[7]

Details aside, BonJour argues that we cannot use empirical beliefs, such as our perceptual and mnemonic beliefs, to show that our ways of forming empirical beliefs are reliable. So we must go outside our empirical beliefs and appeal to non-empirical *a priori* beliefs. But as BonJour notes, it is not clear how such an *a priori* argument would go.

It is worth noting that BonJour does not impose the same requirements on *a priori* knowledge that he imposes on empirical knowledge. Empirical knowledge, he holds, requires a meta-justification, some non-circular argument, that our ways of forming empirical beliefs are reliable. But he rejects such requirements for *a priori* knowledge. He writes, "Obviously, no *argument* can be used to show that reasoning is trustworthy without implicitly begging the question."[8] He points out that any argument for the reliability of reason must use reason insofar as one must see *a priori* that the conclusion of the argument follows from the premise. Since one cannot give a non-circular argument for the reliability of one's *a priori* beliefs, BonJour denies that one's *a priori* beliefs must meet requirements analogous to A1 and A2. But if *a priori* knowledge does not require a non-circular argument for the reliability of reason, why should we impose such a requirement on perceptual and mnemonic knowledge? If *a priori* knowledge does not require that one know that one's way of forming *a priori* beliefs is reliable, why impose this requirement on perceptual and mnemonic knowledge? Why treat these types of knowledge and their sources differently?

7 Laurence BonJour, *The Structure of Empirical Knowledge*, p. 10.
8 *Ibid.*, p. 195.

It is, of course, *possible* that our perceptual and mnemonic way of forming beliefs are often unreliable. Yet this would not be a good reason for treating perceptual and mnemonic knowledge differently from *a priori* knowledge. This is so simply because it is also *possible* that our rational faculties and our rational intuitions are often unreliable. Sometimes our *a priori* intuitions conflict with one another and sometimes they conflict with those of others. Sometimes our *a priori* intuitions are simply mistaken. Our *a priori* ways of forming beliefs and our *a priori* intuitions are fallible. It seems *possible* that our *a priori* ways of forming beliefs, like our perceptual and mnemonic faculties, could be more unreliable than they actually are.[9]

Some philosophers agree with BonJour that it is epistemically unacceptable to use beliefs of kind K to support the view that K is a reliable source. Consider the follow remarks by Richard Fumerton:

You cannot *use* perception to justify the reliability of perception! You cannot *use* memory to justify the reliability of memory! You cannot *use* induction to justify the reliability of induction! Such attempts to respond to the skeptic's concerns involve blatant, indeed pathetic, circularity.[10]

Like BonJour, Fumerton apparently thinks that any epistemically satisfactory attempt to support the reliability of perception and memory must not rely on those sources. BonJour and Fumerton, then, would endorse A2. Now, if A2 is true, and a non-circular argument is not available, then we cannot know that perception and memory are reliable. And this would not be a happy consequence for the common sense philosopher. So let us consider in the next section whether the only way to know that one's faculties are reliable is on the basis of a non-circular argument.

2.2 THE PROBLEM OF CIRCULARITY: ALSTON AND SOSA

In this section, I consider two sorts of responses to the problem of epistemic circularity. The first response is offered by Alston. He argues that epistemic circularity does not prevent us from forming epistemically justified beliefs and from knowing that our ways of forming beliefs are reliable. Yet Alston thinks we need something more "discriminating" than epistemically circular arguments, and instead defends the "practical reasonableness" of our ways of forming beliefs. The second response is that

---

9 I discuss the *a priori* in more detail in Chapter 7.
10 Richard Fumerton, *Metaepistemology and Skepticism* (Lanham, MD: Rowman and Littlefield, 1995), p. 177.

offered by Sosa. Sosa raises some objections to Alston's defense on the grounds of practical reasonableness. He instead argues that while epistemic circularity is unavoidable, it does not preclude knowledge that one's ways of forming beliefs are reliable.

The problem of knowing whether one's faculties are reliable has been addressed with care and subtlety by Alston. To begin, let us consider his discussion of the following "track record" argument for the reliability of perception:

At t_1, I formed the perceptual belief that p and p.
At t_2, I formed the perceptual belief that q and q.
At t_3, I formed the perceptual belief that r and r.
    (And so on)

Conclusion: Perception is a reliable source of belief.[11]

In a track record argument for the reliability of perception, we reason inductively from a wide sampling of perceptual beliefs, noting that the vast majority have been true, and conclude that perception is reliable. Now, in this argument, the conclusion does not appear as a premise in the argument. So the argument is not logically circular. Still, Alston says that the argument is "epistemically circular." According to Alston, epistemic circularity "consists in assuming the reliability of a source of belief in arguing for the reliability of that source. That assumption does not appear as a premise in the argument, but it is only by making that assumption that we consider ourselves entitled to use some or all of the premises."[12] How in this track record argument are we "assuming" the reliability of perception? Consider the second conjunct of each premise. How do I know that it is true? On the basis of sense perception itself. It is only by *using* sense perception or *relying* on it that I can know the truth of the premises.

As we have seen, BonJour and Fumerton reject such circular arguments as epistemically unsatisfactory in supporting the reliability of one's faculties. Alston, however, does not think epistemic circularity renders an argument epistemically useless. He writes, "Contrary to what one might suppose, epistemic circularity does not render an argument useless for justifying or establishing its conclusion. Provided that I can *be* justified in certain perceptual beliefs without already being *justified* in supposing

11   Cf. William Alston, "Epistemic Circularity," *Epistemic Justification: Essays in the Theory of Knowledge* (Ithaca, NY: Cornell University Press, 1989), p. 327.
12   William Alston, "A 'Doxastic Practice' Approach to Epistemology," *Empirical Knowledge*, 2nd edition, ed. Paul K. Moser (Lanham, MD: Rowman and Littlefield, 1996), p. 271.

perception to be reliable, I can legitimately use perceptual beliefs in an argument for the reliability of sense perception."[13] To see how this is so, suppose that our perceptual beliefs are immediately evident. They might be evident in virtue of the character of our sensory experience, as the foundationalist suggests, or perhaps they are evident in virtue of their origin in a reliable faculty of perception. If our perceptual beliefs are thus immediately evident, then the second conjunct of each premise is immediately evident. But if it is immediately evident, then it is not based on any other justified belief, including the belief that sense perception is reliable. Our justification and knowledge of the premises would not be based, therefore, on our knowing or being justified in believing the conclusion. We may grant that if knowledge of the premises is based on knowledge of the conclusion, then knowledge of the premises could not *confer* justification on its conclusion. But that is not how track record arguments must be construed. If knowledge of the premises is not based on knowledge of the conclusion, such as when the premises are immediately evident, then a track record argument won't have *that* flaw. Of course, we may also note that the argument won't have that flaw even if knowledge of the premises is not immediate, provided, of course, that knowledge of the premises is not at some point based on knowledge of the conclusion.

Still, in spite of this concession, Alston thinks that epistemically circular arguments, including track record arguments, are not satisfactory ways of discriminating between reliable and unreliable sources of belief. But why not? What is the problem that he sees with epistemically circular arguments? Alston tells us:

If we are entitled to use beliefs from a certain source in showing that source to be reliable, then any source can be validated. If all else fails, we can simply use each belief twice over, once as testee and once as tester. Consider crystal ball gazing. Gazing into the crystal ball, the seer makes a series of pronouncements: p, q, r, s . . . Is this a reliable mode of belief formation? Yes. That can be shown as follows. The gazer forms the belief that p, and using the same procedure, ascertains that p. By running through a series of beliefs in this way, we discover that the accuracy of this mode of belief formation is 100%! If some beliefs contradict others, that will reduce the accuracy somewhat, but in the absence of massive internal contradiction the percentage of verified beliefs will be quite high. Thus, if we allow the use of mode of belief-formation M to determine whether the beliefs formed by M are true, M is sure to get a clean bill of health. But a line of argument that will validate any mode of belief formation, no matter

13   *Ibid.*, p. 271.

how irresponsible, is not what we are looking for. We want, and need something much more discriminating. Hence the fact that the reliability of sense perception can be established by relying on sense perception does not solve our problem.[14]

One can support the reliability of sense perception through track record arguments and by using sense perception. In this respect, we may say that sense perception is "self-supportive." However, the problem with such epistemically circular arguments in Alston's view is that clearly unacceptable procedures, such as gazing, can also be supported *via* a track record argument. So a track record argument is not, he thinks, a satisfactory way of discriminating between reliable and unreliable ways of forming beliefs. Alston thinks we need to find a better way of discriminating between reliable and unreliable ways of forming beliefs.

In order to get around this problem, Alston favors a different approach. He favors appeals to the "practical rationality" of our way of forming beliefs. He argues that it is "practically rational" for us to rely on our ways of forming beliefs, our "doxastic practices." How does this argument go? In brief, Alston points out that many of our ways of forming beliefs are firmly established. It does not seem to be in our power (easily) to avoid forming beliefs on the basis of those practices. Though there are alternative practices we might try to take up, it would be very difficult to do so. Moreover, the very same problems of epistemic circularity that beset our attempts to support the reliability of our practices would confront these alternatives. So, given these facts, Alston concludes that it is practically rational for us to continue engaging in our own firmly established doxastic practices. Suppose we take Alston's argument to be something like the following:

1. We have various ways of forming beliefs – doxastic practices, sense perception, memory, reason, introspection – that are firmly established. So firmly established that we cannot help forming beliefs in these ways.
2. It would be enormously difficult for us to abandon these ways of forming beliefs and to take up others.
3. One cannot support the reliability of these alternative ways of forming beliefs without facing the same problems of epistemic circularity that beset attempts to support the reliability of sense perception, memory, reason, and introspection.
4. Therefore, it is reasonable for us to continue forming beliefs in the way we standardly do on the basis of sense perception, memory, reason, and introspection.

---

14 *Ibid.*, pp. 271–72.

But does this argument avoid epistemic circularity any more than a track record argument? It would seem not. Aren't we using or relying on memory, reason, and introspection, in accepting the premises and reaching the conclusion? Suppose one asks how do we know that the premises of this argument are true? Why should we accept, for example, the premise that memory and introspection are firmly established practices? How do we know that? Suppose we say that we believe that they are firmly established on the basis of introspection and memory. In offering that answer, are we not using memory, reason, and introspection to support the conclusion that it is reasonable for us to form beliefs in those ways? If epistemic circularity is a vice that makes track record arguments unsatisfactory, then how can it be any less of a vice here? Again, concerning track record arguments for the reliability of sense perception, Alston writes:

[If] I were to ask myself why should I accept the premises, I would, if I pushed the reflection far enough, have to make the claim that sense perception is reliable. For if I weren't prepared to make that claim on reflection, why should I, as a rational subject, countenance perceptual beliefs? Since this kind of circularity involves a commitment to the conclusion as a presupposition of our supposing ourselves to be *justified* in holding the premises, we can properly term it 'epistemic circularity'.[15]

In response to Alston's argument concerning the practical rationality of forming beliefs on the basis of perception and memory, Ernest Sosa asks, "If we push reflection far enough with regard to why we should accept the premises of *this* argument, don't we find ourselves appealing precisely to *its* conclusion? And, if so, is not this argument then just as circular, and in a similar way, as the track record argument in favor of the reliability of [sense perception]?"[16]

Furthermore, Sosa notes that Alston rejects track record arguments because they are not sufficiently discriminating. The crystal ball gazer, for example, can appeal to gazing to argue for the reliability of those sources. But isn't there an analogous problem with the sort of argument that Alston advances? Couldn't the gazer appeal to gazing to argue that it is a firmly established way of forming beliefs? He looks in his crystal and "sees" that it is. He then argues that since gazing is firmly established, and that any other way of forming beliefs will face the problems of epistemic circularity, it is,

15 William Alston, *The Reliability of Sense Perception* (Ithaca, NY: Cornell University Press, 1993), p. 15.
16 Ernest Sosa, "Philosophical Scepticism and Epistemic Circularity," *Empirical Knowledge*, 2nd edition, p. 315.

therefore, practically rational for him to continue to form beliefs on the basis of gazing. Given that the gazer can reason in an analogous way for the practical rationality of his way of forming beliefs, how would Alston's appeal to firm establishment provide a more discriminating approach? If we are to reject track record arguments because gazers can use that form of argument to support the reliability of their practices, then shouldn't we also reject Alston's appeal to being firmly established insofar as the gazer can appeal to gazing to argue that it is firmly established and thus reasonably engaged in?[17]

Now, one might argue that the difference between the gazer's reasoning and Alston's is that perception really *is*, unlike gazing, firmly established. But if it is *actually* being firmly established as opposed to being merely *believed* to be so that makes the difference, then why not simply say that it is *actually* being reliable as opposed to being merely *believed* to be reliable that makes the difference between the perceivers and the gazers? Why not simply point out that the relevant difference between the perceivers and the gazers is that perception really is a reliable source and gazing is not? What would make the position of the perceivers epistemically superior to that of the gazers would not be the logical structure of their arguments; these, after all, are parallel. Neither would the epistemic difference between them be a matter of mere coherence, for we might suppose that the body of beliefs of the gazers could be as coherent. What would make the position of the perceivers epistemically superior is that their belief in the reliability of their way of forming beliefs actually is rooted in reliable faculties.

Let us now consider Sosa's own approach to the problem of circularity. To appreciate Sosa's approach, we need to introduce some important distinctions he makes. First, Sosa distinguishes between the "aptness" of a belief and its "justification." He writes:

The "justification" of a belief B requires that B have a basis in its inference or coherence relations to other beliefs in the believer's mind – as in the "justification" of a belief derived from deeper principles, and thus "justified," or the "justification" of a belief adopted through cognizance of its according with the subject's principles as to what beliefs are permissible in the circumstances as viewed by that subject.

The "aptness" of a belief B relative to an environment E requires that B derive from what is relative to E an intellectual virtue, i.e., a way of arriving at

17   *Ibid.*, pp. 317–18.

beliefs that yields an appropriate preponderance of truth over error (in the field of propositions in question, in the sort of context involved).[18]

Sosa suggests that we distinguish between the "justification" of a belief B, which he treats as a matter of B's cohering with other beliefs, including beliefs about what it is permissible or reasonable to believe, and the "aptness" of B, which is a matter of the intellectual virtue that yields B. Conceivably, a belief might have much in the way of justification, and fail to be apt. Consider the victim of the evil demon to whom nothing seems amiss. He forms perceptual beliefs and believes (mistakenly) perception to be a reliable source. He may even reason brilliantly from his false perceptual beliefs to mistaken conclusions about the world around him and about the nature of his own perceptual faculties. But although his perceptual beliefs might have much in the way of justification, they fail to be apt, since relative to his demonic environment, perception is no virtue, failing to yield much that is true. Conversely, a belief might be apt, and yet fail to be justified. Thus, one suddenly and unknowingly gifted with a reliable faculty of clairvoyance might form apt beliefs, but given his belief that he has no such power, his clairvoyantly formed beliefs might well fail to be justified.

Sosa also introduces a distinction between "animal knowledge" and "reflective knowledge." He says, "For animal knowledge one needs only belief that is apt and derives from an intellectual virtue or faculty. By contrast, reflective knowledge always requires belief that not only is apt but also has a kind of justification, since it must be belief that fits coherently within the epistemic perspective of the believer."[19] Thus, on Sosa's view, we may attribute animal knowledge to small children and animals, who lack the concept of reliability and who are incapable of forming a perspective on their own intellectual powers and lack the capacity to evaluate their beliefs against standards of what are permissible or acceptable ways of forming beliefs. Animal knowledge does not require a justified meta-perspective about one's way of forming beliefs. Reflective knowledge, in contrast, requires reasons that support and sustain one's belief. These reasons must be beliefs of the subject, though they may be largely implicit and not consciously entertained. They form the subject's

---

18 Ernest Sosa, "Reliabilism and Intellectual Virtue," *Knowledge in Perspective* (Cambridge: Cambridge University Press, 1991), p. 144.

19 *Ibid.*, p. 145; Cf. Ernest Sosa, "Knowledge and Intellectual Virtue," *Knowledge in Perspective*, p. 240.

meta-perspective about his beliefs that support the beliefs in question. The notion of a meta-perspective must, I think, allow for degrees of complexity. There is no reason to insist that reflective knowledge require the sort of deep and detailed view to which philosophers may aspire. The web of beliefs that forms a perspective can grow and become more complex over time, increasing in sophistication with reflection and experience.

To illustrate the distinction between animal and reflective knowledge, consider a child who forms the belief that there is an apple before him. His belief is formed on the basis of the intellectual virtue of perception. The child's father might also form the belief that there is an apple before him on the basis of perception, but the father has, in addition, a vast body of background beliefs, much of which is perhaps implicitly held, that he sees the apple, that he can easily tell in ordinary circumstances what is an apple and what isn't, that he has been able to pick out apples for many years. He might hold further that perception is reliable, that he and many others have that reliable faculty, that nothing is amiss in his present conditions that would make perception unreliable. The father's belief is not only aptly formed, his belief that there is an apple before him is also part of a coherent body of beliefs that support what he believes on the basis of perception. The child's belief may amount to mere animal knowledge, but the father's belief amounts to reflective knowledge backed, as it is, by the availability of reasons from within his own perspective.

Let us return to Sosa's views on epistemic circularity. Sosa concedes that any reasoning for the reliability of our ways of forming beliefs will, if reflection is pushed far enough, exhibit epistemic circularity. This is so if only because any reasoning for the reliability of our faculties must rely on or use reason itself. As BonJour has pointed out, we cannot give an argument for the reliability of reason that is free of epistemic circularity. Epistemic circularity seems inescapable.

But must our inability to give arguments free of epistemic circularity preclude our knowing that our ways of forming beliefs are reliable? Sosa thinks not. Suppose, he suggests, that W is our total way of forming beliefs. Suppose we use W, and W assures us that it is reliable. Suppose also:

1. "W *is* reliable (and suppose, even that, given our overall circumstances and fundamental nature, it is the *most* reliable overall way we could have)."
2. "We are *right* in our description of W; it *is* exactly W that we use in forming beliefs; and it is of course (therefore) W that we use in forming the belief that W is our way of forming beliefs."

3. "We *believe* that W *is reliable* (correctly so, given [1] above), and this belief, too, is formed by means of W."[20]

In this situation, what more do we need for an epistemically satisfactory understanding of ourselves and our own reliability? Of course, our belief that W is reliable is itself formed by means of W. We have not, therefore, avoided epistemic circularity. But our belief that W is reliably formed is (1) true, (2) reliably formed by our best intellectual procedures, and (3) fits coherently in our view of ourselves and our intellectual endowments. Though we have not avoided epistemic circularity, in what way do we fall short? Sosa concludes that the mere presence of epistemic circularity would not preclude our knowing ourselves to be reliable. We can achieve an epistemically satisfactory understanding of the reliability of our ways of forming beliefs in spite of it.

Again, Sosa asks, what exactly is the problem with epistemically circular arguments? Why should we think that they are epistemically unacceptable ways of supporting the reliability of our faculties? Recall Alston's complaints about track record arguments. Alston objects that someone with decidedly unreliable ways of forming beliefs might be able to support the reliability of his ways of forming beliefs with a coherence equal to our own. The ball gazer, it is urged, might be able to reach a view of his powers that is as well supported by such an inference as is our view about the reliability of our powers of perception, memory, and the like. However, Sosa argues that though the ball gazer might be able to achieve a coherent view about the reliability of gazing, we need to distinguish justification that is merely a matter of internal coherence from the aptness of beliefs. The gazer's beliefs, based as they are on gazing, fail to be *apt*. We need not hold, therefore, that the gazer's beliefs, though supported from his perspective by a track record argument, are epistemically on a par with our own. Though enjoying the internal justification of coherence, the gazer's conclusions fall short insofar as they rest on reasoning from premises that fail to be apt.

Consider the cartoon character, Mr. Magoo, whose perceptual faculties are terribly unreliable. Magoo might reason brilliantly from his flawed perceptual beliefs, and his beliefs might enjoy a level of coherence comparable to our own. But Magoo's view of the world is flawed by epistemic

---

20 Ernest Sosa, "Philosophical Scepticism and Epistemic Circularity," *Empirical Knowledge*, 2nd edition, p. 318.

44

vice, and fails to manifest overall virtue. The point is that while coherence is a good thing epistemically, it is not the only epistemic virtue. We should not hold that if two bodies of belief enjoy equal coherence, then they enjoy equal epistemic status, nor conclude that if someone can support the reliability of his flawed ways of forming beliefs through arguments that mirror our own in terms of structure and coherence, that his premises or conclusions are as good epistemically. So Alston's fear that the use of epistemically circular arguments by the gazer will yield a view that is epistemically on a par with our own is unfounded once we take into consideration the aptness of one's ways of forming beliefs. We are not forced to accept the view that the gazer's conclusion about the reliability of gazing is epistemically on a par with our beliefs about the reliability of perception and memory.

In discussing epistemic circularity, Sosa also calls our attention to a passage from Descartes's third meditation:

I am certain that I am a thinking being. Do I not therefore also know what is required for my being certain about anything? In this first item of knowledge there is simply a clear and distinct perception of what I am asserting; this would not be enough to make me certain of the truth of the matter if it could ever turn out that something which I perceived with such clarity and distinctness was false. So I now seem to be able to lay it down as a general rule that whatever I perceive very clearly and distinctly is true.[21]

Descartes grants that a powerful enough being could deceive him even about those things that seem most manifest, and he grants that this doubt must be blocked if he is to be certain by intuiting something as clear and distinct. So he launches into his theological reflections to support the existence of a non-deceiving God. Still, Descartes takes himself to have some positive justification even without the proof of a non-deceiving God. He is certain that he thinks, and he takes it to be his clear and distinct perception that the fact he thinks is that which gives him such certainty. But he reasons that his clear and distinct perception would not yield such certainty if it were less than perfectly reliable. So, he concludes that his clear and distinct perception *is* perfectly reliable. Sosa calls our attention to Descartes's inference: "So I now seem to be able to lay it down as a general rule that whatever I perceive very clearly and distinctly

21 Descartes, René. *The Philosophical Writings of Descartes*, ed. J. Cottingham, R. Stoothoff, and D. Murdoch (Cambridge: Cambridge University Press, 1985), vol. 2, p. 24.

is true." Sosa suggests that we might take Descartes's reasoning to be:

(1) I know with a high degree of certainty that I think.
(2) I clearly and distinctly perceive that I think, and that is the only, or anyhow the best, account of the source of my knowledge that I think.
(3) So my clear and distinct perception that I think is what explains why or how it is that I know I think.
(4) But my clear and distinct perception could not serve as a source of that knowledge if it were not an infallibly reliable faculty.
(5) So, finally, my clear and distinct perception must be an infallibly reliable faculty.

Sosa suggests "the move from (1) and (2) to (3) is an inference to an explanatory account that one might accept for the coherence it gives to one's view of things in the domain involved."[22] How does Descartes know that he is certain that he thinks? Would he not explain how he knows this because he clearly and distinctly perceives it? But even though Descartes is using or relying on his clear and distinct perception in order to know the premises, he thinks that by reasoning in this way he can support the reliability of his clear and distinct perceptions.

Sosa suggests that one can fashion a similar argument, one modeled after its Cartesian predecessor, for the reliability of sense perception. Such an argument has been labeled the "Neo-Moorean" argument:

1. I know I have a hand.
2. I can see and feel that here is a hand, and that is the only, or anyhow the best, account of the source of my knowledge that here is a hand.
3. So my perception that here is a hand explains why or how it is that I know here's a hand.
4. But my perception could not serve as a source of that knowledge if perception were not a reliable faculty.
5. So perception must be a reliable faculty.

In this argument, one accepts 3 because it is the best explanation of how it is that one knows "here's a hand." One then notes that perception would not yield that knowledge if perception were generally unreliable, and so one concludes that it is reliable. The conclusion may be accepted for the boost in comprehensive coherence it gives to one's view of oneself as to how one knows. Such an argument, according to Sosa, does not differ "in any fundamental respect from the procedure followed by Descartes."[23] Of

---

22 Ernest Sosa, "Reflective Knowledge in the Best Circles," *Knowledge, Truth, and Duty*, p. 192.
23 *Ibid.*, p. 192.

course, such an argument is epistemically circular insofar as it is by using sense perception that Moore knows that here's a hand. But, again, Sosa denies that such epistemic circularity is vicious or that it prevents Moore from acquiring reasons to believe that perception is reliable.

We have seen that if A1 and A2 are true, then the position of the common sense philosopher is deeply problematic. Sosa holds, plausibly, that A1 is false, at least in an unqualified form. Animal knowledge does not require knowledge or justified belief that one's faculties are reliable. Reflective knowledge, on the other hand, does require a meta-perspective on one's way of forming beliefs, a perspective that includes reasons that support one's belief. Sosa also argues that A2 is false. He rejects the view that the only satisfactory way to know that one's perception and memory are reliable is through a non-circular argument. Epistemic circularity is inescapable, but it does not prevent our knowing that our ways of forming belief are reliable. I think the common sense philosopher may reasonably reject both A1 and A2, the problematic assumptions with which we began this chapter. Therefore, one should not reject the position of the common sense philosopher on the basis of those assumptions. But in the next chapter, I consider in more detail some objections to the views defended here, including objections to track record arguments and to the Neo-Moorean argument.

3

Common Sense and Reliability II

In Chapter 2, we considered Sosa's view that epistemic circularity does not prevent us from knowing that our faculties are reliable. We looked at both track record arguments and the Neo-Moorean argument for the reliability of our faculties. In this chapter, we consider some objections raised by Richard Fumerton and Jonathan Vogel to the use of both sorts of arguments and, more generally, to the view that one may use a faculty or source of belief in order to know that it is reliable. We conclude with some further reflections on the value of track record and Neo-Moorean arguments.

3.1 FUMERTON'S OBJECTIONS

As we saw in Chapter 2, Fumerton claims that one cannot use memory to justify the reliability of memory or use sense perception to justify the reliability of sense perception. Consider the following objection raised by Fumerton:

If a philosopher starts wondering about the reliability of astrological inference, the philosopher will not allow the astrologer to read in the stars the reliability of astrology. Even if astrological inferences happen to be reliable, the astrologer is missing the point of a *philosophical* inquiry into the justifiability of astrological inference if the inquiry is answered using the techniques of astrology . . . If I really am interested in knowing whether astrological inference is legitimate, if I have the kind of philosophical curiosity that leads me to raise this question in the first place, I will not for a moment suppose that further use of astrology might help me to find the answer to my question. Similarly, if as a philosopher I start wondering whether perceptual beliefs are accurate reflections of the way the world really is, I would not dream of using perception to resolve my doubt. Even if there is some sense in which the reliable process of perception might yield justified beliefs about the reliability of perception, the use of perception could never satisfy a *philosophical curiosity* about the legitimacy of perceptual beliefs.[1]

We might compare Fumerton's complaint with that leveled against someone checking the reliability of a newspaper against other reports from that same paper. He finds that the paper reports that *p*, then checks that report against back issues and finds that they also report that *p*, and then concludes that the paper is reliable. Would this not be an unacceptable procedure? And would not relying on astrological readings to support the reliability be similarly unsatisfactory? If so, then would not the same complaint be appropriately raised against using perceptual reports to support the reliability of perception?

In response, Sosa suggests, "What is wrong in the newspaper case, even as a case of simple reasoning is, it now appears, the narrowness of one's purview in judging the newspaper reliable simply on the basis of a set of data one knows to be remediably and relevantly too narrow; namely, the reports of that very newspaper accepted at face value."[2] We know that appealing only to the newspaper reports is not our only option, though Sosa notes that it might be the only option for someone in jail. We know that we can move beyond the narrowness of our limited data, bringing in other sources that seem relevant to the matter at hand. Here we might also think of the detective who has available to him a dozen eye witnesses to a crime, but chooses to interview only one. We would not think the detective's procedure satisfactory since he fails to take into account further relevant and easily accessible evidence.

Might not the same be said for the astrological case? Fumerton is right in thinking that no philosopher would be content to rest simply with the reports of astrology that confirm its own reliability. But what is wrong with such an approach need not be the appeal to that very source. We might fault such an approach because we can make use of other sources such as perception, memory, and reason in evaluating the reliability of astrology. We can widen the body of data against which the claims of astrology might be judged, and see how astrological reports fare against these other sources. The appeal to the reports of astrology alone is, we know, remediably too narrow and, for us, a poor intellectual procedure. In contrast, in assessing the reliability of memory, sense perception, introspection,

---

1 Richard Fumerton, *Metaepistemology and Skepticism*, p. 177.
2 Ernest Sosa, "The Coherence of Virtue and the Virtue of Coherence," *Knowledge in Perspective*, p. 202.

and reason, we can consider the extent to which the testimony of these sources conflicts with the others. Our assessment of their reliability need not display that sort of unacceptable narrowness.

Still, I think Fumerton would object not to the narrowness of appealing *only* to astrological readings, but to one's appealing to a source to support the reliability of that source. But here I think Fumerton leaves himself open to a *tu quoque* on the part of the common sense philosopher. Fumerton, for example, defends the view that "acquaintance" is a source of non-inferential justification. Acquaintance, according to Fumerton, is a *sui generis* relationship that holds between a self and a thing, property, or relation. It is not, in his view, another intentional state, like belief, to be construed as a non-relational property of the mind. Fumerton writes, "My suggestion is that one has noninferentially justified belief that *P* when one has the thought that *P* and one is acquainted with the fact that *P*, the thought that *P, and* the relation of correspondence holding between the thought that *P* and the fact that *P*."[3] For Fumerton, a belief that *P* can be non-inferentially justified on the basis of a complex set of several relations of acquaintance, such as being acquainted with the thought that *P*, the fact that *P*, and the correspondence between the thought that *P* and the fact that *P*. The details of this account need not concern us. But suppose we ask two questions. First, how do we know that the belief that *P* is likely to be true when we have this complex set of relations of acquaintance? Second, how do we know that we ever bear this set of relations of acquaintance to anything? With respect to the first question, Fumerton writes, "If my being acquainted with the fact that *P* is part of what justifies me in believing that *P* and if acquaintance is a genuine relation that requires the existence of its relata, then when I am acquainted with the fact that *P, P* is true."[4]

According to this view, the complex state of acquaintances that is the source of one's non-inferential justification for believing that *P* is an *infallible* source of justification for believing that *P*. But how do we know that it is thus infallible and thus perfectly reliable? How do I know that when I am acquainted with *P*, *P* is true? Would not our answer be that we are acquainted with the relation of acquaintance itself? Would not this knowledge about the perfect reliability of this source rest ultimately on non-inferentially justified belief about the nature of acquaintance? But where would such justification come from if not through acquaintance

3   Richard Fumerton, *Metaepistemology and Skepticism*, p. 75.
4   *Ibid.*, p. 76.

itself? On reflection, it seems that it is direct acquaintance that assures us that direct acquaintance is perfectly reliable. As for our second question, how do we know that we ever bear the complex set of relations of acquaintance that would, in Fumerton's view, be a source of non-inferential justification? Fumerton answers, "If I am asked what reason do I have for thinking that there is any such relation as acquaintance, I will, of course give the unhelpful answer that I am acquainted with such a relation. The answer is question-begging if it is designed to convince someone that there is such a relation, but if the view is true it would be unreasonable to expect its proponents to give any other answer."[5]

The point I am making is not that there is no such relation as acquaintance. It is rather to note that Fumerton himself appeals to acquaintance as his source of justification for believing that he is acquainted with things, and he must appeal to acquaintance ultimately as his source of justification for believing that acquaintance is reliable. Yet that fact does not prevent Fumerton from taking acquaintance to be a source of non-inferential justification. Why then should we object *in principle* to one's using memory and perception to support the view that memory and perception are reliable?[6]

Fumerton objects that we cannot satisfy a "philosophical" curiosity about perception and memory by using perception and memory. If what is required to satisfy such a curiosity is an argument free of epistemic circularity, then such a curiosity cannot be satisfied. But that would imply as well that we cannot satisfy a philosophical curiosity about reasoning itself. As BonJour points out, it is obvious that any argument to show that reasoning is reliable must make use of reasoning itself. Moreover, we could not satisfy a philosophical curiosity about the reliability of direct acquaintance either. If a philosophical curiosity about the reliability of our faculties could only be satisfied by an argument free of epistemic circularity, then it would seem to be a mark of philosophical wisdom to accept the fact that that cannot be done. But why think that the only way to satisfy a philosophical curiosity about the reliability of our faculties requires arguments free of epistemic circularity? As Sosa argues, epistemic circularity does not prevent us from knowing that our faculties are reliable. Could not a curiosity, even a philosophical one, about the reliability of our faculties be satisfied by the knowledge that they are in fact reliable?

5 *Ibid.*, p. 77.
6 A similar point is made by Michael Bergmann in "Externalism and Skepticism," *The Philosophical Review* vol. 109 (April) 2000, pp. 171–72.

The fact that we cannot support the reliability of our faculties except ultimately by using them does not commit us to skepticism about their reliability. And it does not imply that one's use of those sources must exhibit the same flaws exhibited in the newspaper case or the narrow appeal to astrological readings.

Suppose, further, we think that some externalist reliability condition must be met for a belief to be knowledge. Or suppose we think, perhaps less plausibly, that a belief must be reliably produced in order to be justified. Some philosophers object to such a requirement because it would take the question of the epistemic status of our beliefs out of the hands of philosophers and put them into the hands of cognitive scientists. Fumerton writes:

If externalist metaepistemologies are correct, then normative epistemology is an inappropriate subject matter for philosophy. Philosophers as they are presently trained have no special *philosophical* expertise enabling them to reach conclusions about which beliefs are or are not justified. Since the classical issues of skepticism fall under normative epistemology, it follows that if externalism is correct, then philosophers should stop addressing the questions raised by the skeptic. The complex causal conditions that determine the presence or absence of justification for a belief are the subject matter of empirical investigations that would take the philosopher out of the easy chair and into the laboratory.[7]

Fumerton is concerned here with the notion of *justification*, but I think his remarks apply as well to other epistemic notions such as knowledge for which we might think an externalist reliability requirement must be met. Fumerton writes as though the question whether a belief is justified can only be answered by either a philosopher *via* his philosophical expertise or the expertise of the laboratory scientist. But why think that knowledge of epistemic facts is a matter of either sort of special expertise? One need not be an auto mechanic to know that one's car is reliable, and one need not be an electronics expert to know that one's television set is reliable. So too it does not seem that one need be either a philosopher or a cognitive scientist to know that one's perception and memory are reliable. Of course, just as the mechanic or the electronics engineer can explain in a detailed way why one's car or television is reliable, so too the cognitive scientist might be able to explain why perception or memory is reliable. Such expertise might deepen our understanding of our own reliability. Furthermore, just as the mechanic might be able to tell us under what conditions our

---

7 Richard Fumerton, *Metaepistemology and Skepticism*, p. 171.

car is not reliable, so too the cognitive scientist might be able to tell us under what conditions perception and memory are not reliable. But some general knowledge of the reliability of cars and perception does not seem to require the expertise of either sort of specialist. Moreover, if justification or knowledge is a property that attaches to beliefs in virtue of complex causal conditions, why does it follow that the question of whether a belief has that property must be answered in the laboratory? Headaches and toothaches are the products of complex causal conditions, but surely one need not go to a laboratory to learn whether one has them. It is far from clear that an externalist requirement on knowledge or justification commits one to the view that knowledge of epistemic facts requires the expertise of the cognitive scientist. Ordinary people can know that they know many things and they can know that perception and memory are reliable, at least in cases of ordinary employment. Who but a philosopher would think that such knowledge was the sole purview of the philosopher?

3.2 VOGEL, ROXANNE, AND THE NEO-MOOREAN ARGUMENT

Jonathan Vogel raises some interesting problems about the use of our faculties to know that they are reliable. He gives an interesting argument against what he calls "Neighborhood Reliabilism" (NR). The neighborhood reliabilist holds that a belief is reliable "just in case it turns out to be true whenever it is held in a neighborhood N of worlds not too far away from the actual world; a process is reliable just in case it yields (mostly) true beliefs in a neighborhood of worlds not too far away from the actual world."[8] Roughly, according to NR, S knows that p just in case S's belief that p is true and S's belief that p is reliable or produced by a reliable process. Vogel criticizes what he calls a "bootstrapping" procedure for defending the reliability of one's way of forming beliefs.

Vogel begins by asking us to consider an example first suggested by Michael Williams:

Williams describes himself driving a car with a working, highly reliable gas gauge. Williams does not know, however, that the gauge is reliable. Let us stipulate that he has never checked it, he has never been told anything about its reliability, and he does not even have any background information as to whether gauges like his

8   Jonathan Vogel, "Reliabilism Leveled," *The Journal of Philosophy* vol. 97 (Nov.) 2000, p. 604.

are likely to be working. He never takes any special steps to see whether the gauge is going up or down when it ought to be. Rather, without giving the matter a second thought, Williams simply goes by what the gauge says. The gauge reads 'F', and Williams believes that his gas tank is full. According to NR, he *knows* that his tank is full. He has this knowledge because his belief results from a reliable process, that is, going by a well-functioning gas gauge. But Williams does not *know that he knows* that his tank is full. To have this higher-level knowledge, he would need to know that the gauge reliably registers the level of gas in his tank, and we have stipulated that he has no such information.[9]

As Vogel notes, it is hard to imagine how Williams could fail to have *any* background information about the reliability of his gas gauge. Indeed, it is hard to imagine. Are we to assume, for example, that Williams does not know that there are tens of millions of cars that do have reliable gas gauges, that there are thousands of other cars of the same model as his that do have reliable gauges, that tens of millions of people successfully operate their cars using their gas gauges, that if gas gauges were generally unreliable, then there would be widespread consumer complaints and many stranded motorists? If Williams had these sorts of background beliefs, which I assume the typical driver has, then it seems Williams would have reasons to believe that his gas gauge is reliable. In any case, Vogel suggests that we should not be distracted by the details of the case. Vogel then asks us to consider another driver, Roxanne, who is similarly situated to Williams in the previous example. Roxanne has a well-functioning gas gauge, believes implicitly what her gas gauge says without knowing that her gas gauge is reliable, and, we may also assume, lacks any background beliefs about the reliability of gauges like hers and has never taken any special steps to see whether the gauge is going up or down as it ought. She looks at the gauge often, and forms a belief about how much gas is in her tank. She also, however, takes note of the state of the gauge itself. So when the gauge reads 'F' she believes the tank is full and she also believes that the gauge reads 'F'. Roxanne combines these beliefs and accepts the following:

1. On this occasion, the gauge reads 'F' and *F*.

Vogel says that the perceptual process by which Roxanne forms the belief that the gauge reads 'F' is a reliable one. Moreover, we are assuming that her belief that the tank is full is also reached by a reliable process. So, Vogel

9   *Ibid.*, p. 612.

says, according to NR, Roxanne knows 1. From 1, Roxanne deduces:

2. On this occasion, the gauge is reading accurately.

Since deduction is a reliable process, it seems that NR would imply that Roxanne knows 2 as well. Now suppose that Roxanne repeats this procedure many times. She reads that the gauge says 'X' and forms the belief that the tank is X. Given NR, she comes to know on each of these occasions that the gauge was reading accurately. Then, putting these bits of information together, she concludes by induction that

3. The gauge reads accurately all the time.

As Vogel notes, reliabilists generally hold that induction is a reliable process, and so they should concede that Roxanne knows 3. From 3, Roxanne infers that

4. The gauge is reliable.

Vogel suggests that NR is committed to the view that Roxanne knows 4. But Vogel claims Roxanne does not know 4. He concludes that NR is false. He concludes this because NR in conjunction with various steps of inductive and deductive reasoning imply incorrectly that Roxanne knows that her gas gauge is reliable. But note that Vogel writes:

> This extraordinary procedure, which I shall call *bootstrapping*, seems to allow one to promote many, if not all, of one's beliefs that were formed by reliable processes into *knowledge* that those beliefs were formed by a reliable process. I assume that bootstrapping is illegitimate. Roxanne cannot establish that her gas gauge is reliable by the peculiar reasoning I have just described. The challenge to NR is that it may go wrong here. On the face of things, it does improperly ratify bootstrapping as a way of gaining knowledge.[10]

Vogel assumes that bootstrapping is illegitimate. Clearly, Roxanne's reasoning for the reliability of her gauge resembles the track record argument for perception we considered in the last chapter. So we may ask if Roxanne's bootstrapping procedure fails to yield knowledge that her gauge is reliable, does a track record argument for the reliability of perception also fail to yield knowledge? If Roxanne's procedure is unacceptable, then should we reject all track record arguments?

But it is not only track record arguments that are in jeopardy. Vogel also thinks that Roxanne's case also poses a problem for the Neo-Moorean

---

10   *Ibid.*, p. 614–15.

argument developed by Sosa and presented in the last chapter. Vogel suggests that the Neo-Moorean argument resembles Roxanne's poor reasoning. He suggests that we might formulate the former as follows:

A. You know you have a hand.
B. You know that it appears to you as though you have a hand.
C. Therefore you know that your appearance of having a hand is veridical.
D. Therefore you know that you are not a deceived brain in a vat.

Vogel suggests that we can compare the Neo-Moorean reasoning with the following:

A′. Roxanne knows her tank is full.
B′. Roxanne knows the gas gauge reads 'F'.
C′. Therefore Roxanne knows that, on this occasion, her gas gauge is reading accurately.

Vogel thinks that since Roxanne's bootstrapping procedure is unacceptable, so too is the bootstrapping procedure that we find in the Neo-Moorean argument. He writes, "Thus, the reliabilist version of Moore's refutation of skepticism sanctions the same kind of inference that created problems in connection with the gas-gauge case. Suppose we grant that the reliabilist is able to evade those problems by denying, either for principled reasons or by fiat, that bootstrapping can lead to knowledge. The upshot will be that reliabilism cannot provide a satisfactory response to skepticism along the lines provided."[11] Again, if we reject Roxanne's reasoning, must we also reject the Neo-Moorean argument? If not, why not?

In considering these matters, I think we should agree with Vogel that NR is false. NR says:

NR S knows that p if and only if S's belief that p is true and S's belief that p is produced by a reliable process.

There are good reasons for rejecting NR quite apart from Vogel's argument. First, suppose that one forms the belief that p on the basis of a reliable process and p is true. Yet suppose that one has defeating evidence for p and yet ignores this evidence. In such a case, one does not know that p is true. Suppose, for example, that Jones perceives a red object before him, and suppose that there is in fact a red object before him. But suppose further that Jones is told by an otherwise trustworthy source that

---

11   *Ibid.*, p. 619.

the object is really white and that there is a red light shining on it. Still, Jones ignores this piece of defeating evidence and persists in believing that the object before him is red. In such a case, it does not seem that Jones knows that the object is red even though his belief has been formed on the basis of a reliable process and is true. The mere fact that one has a true belief reliably produced is not therefore sufficient for knowledge. Jones's ignoring defeating evidence would seem to preclude his knowing that the object before him is red even though his belief that it is red is formed by a reliable process. Second, it would seem that not just *any* reliable process is sufficient for turning a true belief into knowledge. Suppose that my colleague, Marcia, has lost her dog. She looks for the dog, and far in the distance sees something she takes to be her dog, and forms the belief, "That's my dog." Let us suppose Marcia's belief is true, but the dog is just too far away for her perceptual experience to justify her belief. But now consider a process of belief-formation that makes reference to the identity of the perceiver, the precise time, and the location at which she spots her dog: *Marcia visually perceiving a dog at 3:15 pm on June 15, 2001, next to the water tower.* This process type has only one instantiation, and it turns out to be perfectly reliable. But though Marcia has a true belief that is produced by a reliable process, her belief is not an instance of knowledge.[12]

So we have good reasons for rejecting NR. But we need to distinguish Sosa's virtue account from NR. Sosa's virtue account is *not* committed to the view that just any reliable way of forming beliefs is a source of knowledge, animal or reflective. A virtue-based approach need not hold that every true belief that is formed by a reliable process manifests an intellectual virtue. The subject who ignores defeating evidence might have beliefs produced by a reliable source, but in ignoring defeating evidence fails to manifest overall intellectual virtue. Moreover, the narrowly defined process that Marcia uses in forming her belief about the whereabouts of her dog does not count as a virtue. For one thing, a virtue must be some way of forming beliefs that is repeatable, and the process that Marcia follows is not.

Let us return to Vogel's criticism of bootstrapping. Let us consider what a virtue-based approach to knowledge, such as Sosa's, might say about Roxanne's bootstrapping procedure. Such an account is not committed to endorsing Roxanne's procedure, since a virtue-based approach may deny that Roxanne has knowledge of her first premise and thus she has

---

12   This example is taken from Matthias Steup, *Contemporary Epistemology* (Upper Saddle River, N. J.: Prentice-Hall, 1996), p. 166.

no bootstraps on which to pull. It may deny that Roxanne's belief in 1 (referred to earlier at the beginning of the gas-gauge discussion) is knowledge because she does not know her gas gauge is reliable and, furthermore, it fails to manifest the overall intellectual virtue expected of someone capable of monitoring and assessing her beliefs.

A defender of a virtue-based approach may argue that the competent use of instruments such as gas gauges in a way that yields knowledge is for creatures like us a *derived* virtue or competence. A derived virtue is one that is acquired and sustained through the use of more fundamental virtues such as perception, memory, testimony, and inductive inference.[13] The virtues or competencies involved in reading a text, understanding a language, or using an instrument such as a gas gauge are derived virtues. Whether beliefs formed on the basis of such derived virtues amount to knowledge depends on the subject's having certain sorts of background knowledge. In order for the use of instruments to yield knowledge, one must have background knowledge about the reliability of those instruments, including beliefs about their reliability in the environment in which they are employed. In the case of using an instrument, we may require that the background knowledge include knowledge that the instrument is working reliably (or at least, perhaps, that the instrument is relevantly similar to others that one knows to be reliable). In this case, one's knowledge that p formed on the basis of using an instrument, I, would be based on one's knowing that I was indeed reliable. Now, in Roxanne's case, she lacks this sort of background knowledge concerning the reliability of her gauge, and for this reason we may hold that she does not know 1, she does not know that her tank is full. She has no bootstraps on which to pull and thus to reach the conclusion that her gauge is reliable.

In responding to the Roxanne case in this way, we assume that the virtuous use of instruments in a way that yields knowledge requires some background knowledge about the reliability of those instruments. However, from the fact that knowledge involving the use of instruments must be based on background knowledge about the reliability of the instruments employed, it does *not* follow that *all* knowledge must be based on background knowledge about the reliability of one's way of forming beliefs. Indeed, Vogel himself makes a similar point concerning justification:

Suppose, in general, justification for believing that X always requires justification for the belief that the process by which you came to believe that X is reliable.

13 Enest Sosa, "Intellectual Virtue in Perspective," *Knowledge in Perspective*, p. 278.

It apparently follows that justification for believing any belief will require an endless hierarchy of further beliefs of level $(N + 1)$ as to the reliability of the way one's belief at level N was formed. But to say that justification *sometimes* requires reason to believe that one's belief-forming process is reliable, as it does in Roxanne's situation, does not imply that justification *always* requires such higher-level support or supplementation. It is this second stronger claim that creates the regress, and one can refuse to agree to it.[14]

The view that Vogel rejects here is very similar to the generalizability thesis that Chisholm rejects. As we saw in the last chapter, Chisholm rejects the general view that knowledge that p requires that one know that one's belief that p was formed in a way such that beliefs formed in that way are likely to be true. Here, Vogel denies that justified belief that p always requires that one be justified in believing that one's belief that p is formed reliably. Vogel points out that we can avoid the problematic regress by denying that justified belief that p always requires a meta-belief to the effect that one's way of forming the belief that p is reliable. By the same token, it seems open to the proponent of a virtue-based theory to hold that the beliefs based on the basic virtues of perception, memory, and the like do not need to be based on such meta-beliefs about the reliability of those ways of forming beliefs.

If this is right, then we may say that there is a relevant difference between the sort of bootstrapping procedure Roxanne employs and that which might be involved in the sort of track-record argument for the reliability of perception described by Alston. Roxanne's belief that her tank is full fails to be knowledge in the first instance because she does not know that her gauge is reliable. The use of that instrument to yield knowledge depends on, and must be based on, her knowing that the gauge is reliable. In a track-record argument of the sort Alston describes for perception, one's knowledge of the premises of that argument does *not* depend on knowledge of the reliability of perception. One's beliefs in the premises of a track record for perception have some epistemic merit in virtue of their origin in the basic virtue of perception that Roxanne's instrument-based beliefs about the state of her gas tank simply do not have.

Again, if we reject Roxanne's bootstrapping procedure, must we reject the Neo-Moorean argument? It seems to me the answer is "no." The first premise of Roxanne's parallel argument, A′, is false. But the first premise of Moore's argument is not. Roxanne's knowledge that her tank is full

14   Jonathan Vogel, "Reliabilism Leveled," p. 622.

must be based on her knowledge that her gauge is reliable. But the same requirement need not be met in order to have perceptual knowledge that one has a hand. Again, we may say that there is a crucial difference between what is required in the way of background knowledge for (1) derived virtues and intellectual competencies and (2) the fundamental intellectual virtues.

3.3 FURTHER REFLECTIONS AND REFLECTIVE KNOWERS

I do not think that reflection on the case of Roxanne shows us that Alston's track record argument or the Neo-Moorean argument are as poor as Roxanne's bootstrapping procedure. Still, I want to consider further some issues pertaining to the track record and Neo-Moorean arguments. Suppose we grant that knowledge of the reliability of one's ways of forming beliefs is not necessary for all cases of knowledge. We might be willing to concede, for example, that children and brute animals can know much on the basis of perception and memory without knowing or having justified beliefs about the reliability of perception and memory. Children and brute animals lack the cognitive sophistication to consider the reliability of their faculties. They cannot grasp or consider the proposition that their perception and memory are reliable. In their case, a meta-perspective about the reliability of their ways of forming beliefs is not required for knowledge. In contrast, mature reflective adults such as we can ask ourselves whether our ways of forming beliefs are reliable. Now, suppose we think that in the case of reflective beings such as ourselves, knowledge that p does require that one have some justification for believing that one's belief that p is reliably produced. Such a requirement has seemed plausible to some philosophers. BonJour, for example, seems to hold that such a requirement is needed for knowledge, and Sosa seems to hold that such a requirement is necessary for "reflective knowledge." Suppose that we accept the following requirement:

RK (Reflective Knowledge)   A reflective being knows that p only if he has some justification for believing that his belief that p is reliably produced.

RK does not require that a reflective being actually form the meta-belief that one's belief that p is reliably produced. It requires only that one have some justification for believing that one's belief that p is reliably formed, whether or not one actually does believe it. Assuming that belief is necessary for knowledge, we may also note that since RK does not require belief about the reliability of one's way of forming belief, it does not require that one *know* that one's way of forming beliefs is reliable. Requiring that one actually form the meta-belief would seem too high a requirement on knowledge even for reflective believers such as ourselves, since in general we do not form such meta-beliefs. In ordinary cases of perceptual knowledge, for example, I form beliefs such as the book is on the desk, but I don't form the meta-belief that my belief that the book is on the desk is reliably formed.

Suppose we accept RK. If we accept RK, then perhaps we can point to a further difference between Roxanne's bootstrapping procedure and those of reflective thinkers such as ourselves engaged in track record and Neo-Moorean reasoning for the reliability of perception. Roxanne, who is old enough to drive, is a reflective being capable of assessing whether her beliefs are reliably formed. But when she first forms the belief that her tank is full, she has *ex hypothesi* no background beliefs and nothing else that supports or serves as a justification for the proposition that her belief that her tank is full is reliably formed. So given RK, Roxanne does not know in the first instance that her tank is full. She does not know her first premise. So not only does she fail to have the sort of background knowledge we require for the knowledge-yielding use of instruments, she fails to satisfy the requirements of RK.

In contrast, consider someone (let's call him "Moore") reasoning in the manner of the Neo-Moorean argument. Moore might have a great deal of background knowledge that supports for him the proposition that his belief that he knows here's a hand is reliably formed. He knows, for example, that many other human beings know they have hands, that he has for years been able to recognize hands, that he knows a great deal about human anatomy, and so on, and so on. The proposition that his belief that he knows here's a hand is reliably formed is supported by a coherent web of beliefs that is in turn supported by the basic virtues of perception and memory. The same is true, we may suppose, of reflective thinkers engaged in track record reasoning. They would already know a great deal that would support and justify them in believing that their belief in the premises of the track record argument were reliably formed. For example, they might know that they and others have formed a great many true perceptual beliefs over many years, and this would support the proposition that their beliefs in the premises of the track record argument were reliably formed. These background beliefs would also be supported by the basic virtues of perception and memory. So, unlike Roxanne, reflective thinkers such as Moore or ourselves already have much in the way of background knowledge that supports the proposition that our beliefs are reliably formed. We and Moore do satisfy the requirements imposed by RK when we accept the premises of the track-record and Neo-Moorean arguments.

"Still," one might object, "even if we think that Roxanne lacks background beliefs when she *first* forms her belief that her tank is full, couldn't she acquire them over time? Couldn't she follow her procedure, amassing beliefs about what her gauge reads and forming corresponding beliefs about the state of her tank, so that after a while, she has a set of coherent beliefs about what her gauge reads and about the state of her tank? Even if she does not initially satisfy the requirements of RK, couldn't she do so eventually?" But note here that one is suggesting that Roxanne's beliefs about the state of her tank and the reliability of her gauge are justified in virtue of their cohering with one another. Now *if* coherence is a source of justification, and if we are prepared to grant that Roxanne's belief about the state of her tank and the reliability of her gauge are justified in virtue of such coherence, then surely one who engages in track record or Neo-Moorean reasoning will enjoy at least as much coherence. Perhaps by appealing to coherence one will avoid the objection that Roxanne fails to satisfy the requirements of RK, but then on what ground are we to hold that one cannot be justified or know that sense perception is reliable? After all, the point behind rasing the Roxanne example in the first place is to suggest that track record and Neo-Moorean reasoning cannot yield justification or knowledge that perception is reliable. But if the coherence enjoyed by Roxanne's premises and her conclusion can justify her in believing that her gauge is reliable, then the equally coherent beliefs of a track record or Neo-Moorean reasoner will do the same. If coherence alone is a source of justification, then we have found no reason to think that the track-record or Neo-Moorean reasoning is as *bad* as Roxanne's.

Let us think further about RK. If RK is true, then a reflective thinker knows the premises of the track record or Neo-Moorean argument only if he is justified in believing that his belief in those premises is reliably formed. Suppose also that the following counterfactual is true: If a reflective thinker were not justified in believing that his belief in the premises was reliably formed, then he wouldn't know them. Now, one might object, "Doesn't this mean that one's knowledge of the premises is *based* on one's knowledge of the conclusion after all? Wouldn't this show that track-record and Neo-Moorean arguments exhibit a clearly unacceptable form of epistemic circularity?"

I don't think so. As a first response, one might point out that the conclusion of Alston's track record argument and the Neo-Moorean argument is that *perception* is reliable. All that RK requires is that one be justified in believing that one's belief in the premises be reliably formed. It does not tell us that one must know *how* they are formed or *what* the source of one's beliefs must be. Strictly speaking, RK does not tell us, therefore, that one must know or be justified in believing the conclusion of the track-record or the Neo-Moorean argument in order to know the premises. Second, and more important, RK does not claim or imply that knowledge of the premises must be *based* on knowledge that one's beliefs are reliably formed. In other words,

RK   A reflective being knows that p only if he has some justification for believing that his belief that p is reliably produced

does not imply either that

1. A reflective being's knowledge that p must be *based* on the proposition that his belief that p is reliably produced, or
2. A reflective being's knowledge that p must be *based* on his knowledge that his belief that p is reliably produced.

In general, the fact that one knows that p only if one is justified in believing q does not imply that one's knowledge that p is based on one's knowledge that q or that q is one's reason for believing that p. To see this, let $p = $ I think and $q = $ someone thinks. Suppose that I know p only if I am justified in believing that q. From this fact it does not follow that my knowledge that p must be *based* on my knowledge that q. My knowledge that I think is immediate, non-inferential knowledge. That someone thinks is not my reason for believing that I think, and my knowledge that I think is not based on my knowledge that someone thinks. Again, even if it were true that were I not justified believing that someone thinks, that I would not know that I think, it does not follow that my knowledge that I think is based on my knowledge that someone thinks or that the proposition that someone thinks is my reason for believing that I think. Moore (the real Moore), I think, recognized this point. He writes:

Obviously, I cannot know *that* I know the pencil exits, unless I do know the pencil exists; and it might, therefore, be thought that the first proposition can only be mediately known – known *merely* because the second is known. But it is, I think, necessary to make a distinction. From the mere fact that I should not know the first, *unless* I knew the second, it does not follow that I know the first *merely* because I know the second. And, in fact, I think I do know *both* of them immediately.[15]

Moore is clear that the fact that one knows that *p* only if one knows that *q* does not imply that one knows that *p* because one knows that *q*. Items of knowledge or justified belief might be linked in this way without it being the case that one knows the one on the basis of knowing the other. (On the basis of similar considerations Moore might hold, for example, that he knows he has hands only if he is justified in believing that there are external objects, without holding that his knowledge that he has hands is based on his knowledge that there are external objects or that the proposition that there are external objects is his reason for believing that he has hands.)

Still, we might wonder that if RK is true and if a reflective being knows the premises of a track record argument only if he is justified in believing that his belief in the premises is reliably produced, then what is the value of such arguments? It does not seem that it is track record or Neo-Moorean reasoning that *produces* in a mature reflective thinker a justification for believing that his belief in the premises is reliably produced *when he had none before.* Does this make track record and Neo-Moorean reasoning pointless? No. Again, we might note that the conclusion of Alston's track-record argument and the Neo-Moorean argument is not simply that one's belief in the premises is reliably formed. It is rather that *perception* is reliable. So one could note that one does acquire through such reasoning a justification for believing *something* in addition to what RK requires. Just as Descartes, through his reasoning, might have come to see that his clear and distinct perception was (infallibly) reliable, one might hold that one acquires a justification for believing that perception is reliable. Perhaps this is right, but it seems likely that most mature reflective thinkers running through a track record or Neo-Moorean argument already have sufficient background knowledge that justifies them in believing that conclusion before their track record or Neo-Moorean reasoning.

Still, suppose we grant that for most mature reflective thinkers, track-record and Neo-Moorean reasoning does not produce a justification for believing that their belief in the premises is reliably formed or even that perception is reliable where they had none before. We might hold, nonetheless, that such reasoning does give them something of epistemic merit. Seeing how their belief in the reliability of perception is supported

---

15 G. E. Moore, "Hume's Theory Examined," *Some Main Problems of Philosophy* (New York: Collier Books, 1953), p. 142.

by premises, premises that are not themselves based on knowledge of the conclusion, might provide a further degree of support for their belief in the conclusion. Seeing how things coherently "hang together" epistemically enhances one's belief in the premises and in the conclusion. Both become, we may say, "better known" when we can see the relations of support of which we might not have taken reflective note before.

Reid probably recognized this when he wrote about beliefs based on testimony in children and adults:

I believed by instinct whatever they told me, long before I had the idea of a lie, or thought of the possibility of their deceiving me. Afterwards, upon reflection, I found that they had acted like fair and honest people, who wished me well. I found that, if I had not believed what they told me before I could give a reason for this belief, I had to this day been little better than a changeling. And though this natural credulity hath sometimes occasioned my being imposed upon by deceivers, yet it has been of infinite advantage on the whole; therefore, I consider it as another good gift of Nature. And I continue to give credit, from reflection, to those whose integrity and veracity I have had experience, which before I gave from instinct.[16]

As a child, one does not need to know or be justified in believing that testimony is reliable in order to have knowledge on the basis of testimony. But our confidence in the trustworthiness of testimony can be enhanced by reflection, so that beliefs accepted on the basis of a basic intellectual virtue can also become backed by reasons that we now reflectively recognize as such. The same is true in the case of perception and memory. As children, we need not know or be justified in believing that perception is reliable in order to have knowledge on the basis of perception. As reflective adults, we enjoy much in the way of background knowledge that justifies us in believing that various perceptual beliefs are reliably formed. But our confidence in the reliability of perception can be enhanced by reflection, so that our perceptual beliefs can also become backed by reasons that we now reflectively recognize as such. And that would seem to be, epistemically, a good thing.

I conclude that the common sense philosopher may reasonably reject both A1 and A2, the problematic assumptions introduced at the beginning of the last chapter. I do not think the considerations advanced by Fumerton or Vogel should lead us to think that we cannot use the beliefs of a source in order to know that that source is reliable or that we should

---

16 Thomas Reid, *Essays and Inquiry*, p. 87.

reject track record and Neo-Moorean arguments. Still, the issue of the reliability of our ways of forming beliefs looms large in Reid, and it is relevant as well to Moore's proof for an external world and to his treatment of skepticism. In the next two chapters, we shall examine their views on this and related issues. I think we can still learn much by reflecting carefully on what they had to say about these matters, and that we can learn as well from their occasional missteps. In the next chapter, we will examine further Reid's views on our knowledge of the reliability of our faculties.

4

Reid, Reliability, and Reid's Wrong Turn

In this chapter, I consider the views of Thomas Reid concerning our knowledge of the reliability of our faculties. Reid holds that it is a "first principle" that perception and memory and, indeed, all of our natural cognitive faculties are reliable. Yet, in several places, he seems to endorse ways of supporting the reliability of our faculties that seem to be epistemically circular. In the first section, I shall examine some of these passages. In the second section, I shall consider a brief yet important criticism Reid makes of Descartes. Reid argues that Descartes's argument that his faculties are reliable is question-begging. If Reid's criticism of Descartes is sound, then it seems that any reasoning for the reliability of our faculties must also be question-begging. I will argue, however, that Reid's charge that Descartes begs the question rests on a mistaken view of what knowledge requires. It also seems to be a view that is inconsistent with positions that Reid endorses elsewhere. Reid's endorsement of this mistaken view seems to be a lapse on his part.

4.1 REID ON OUR KNOWLEDGE OF THE RELIABILITY OF OUR FACULTIES

Kant is among the most prominent critics of the common sense tradition, at least as it is represented by Reid. In Kant's view, it is an appeal to the opinion of the multitude, of which a real philosopher ought to be ashamed. In one blistering passage, Kant writes:

It is indeed a great gift of God to possess right or (as they now call it) plain common sense. But this common sense must be shown in action by well-considered and reasonable thoughts and words, not by appealing to it as an oracle when no rational justification for one's position can be advanced. To appeal to common sense when insight and discovery fail, and no sooner–this is one of the subtle discoveries of modern times by which the most superficial ranter can safely enter the ranks of the most thorough thinkers and hold his own. But as long as one particle of insight remains, no one would think of having recourse to this subterfuge. Seen clearly, it is but an appeal to the opinion of the multitude, of whose applause the philosopher is ashamed, while the popular charlatan glories and boasts in it.[1]

In this passage, Kant seems to be raising two criticisms of the common sense tradition. First, he complains that the appeal to common sense is nothing more than an appeal to the opinion of the multitude. Second, he objects to the appeal to common sense "when no rational justification for one's position can be advanced."

I am not quite sure in what way Kant takes the common sense philosopher to be appealing to the multitude. Perhaps he takes the common sense philosopher to be reasoning like this: (1) Whatever is widely believed (accepted by the multitude) is likely to be true, (2) p is widely believed, therefore (3) p is likely to be true. Now, if this is what appealing to the multitude amounts to, then, contrary to Kant's suggestion, the common sense philosopher *does* give an argument for his views even though it might not strike us as an especially good one. In any event, there is no reason to think that the common sense philosopher is committed to an argument like this or that he appeals to the opinion of the multitude in this way. Certainly there is no reason to think that this is the position of later philosophers such as Moore or Chisholm. Even Reid, who is clearly one of Kant's targets, does not take the positive epistemic status of his common sense beliefs to depend on such an argument.

Kant's more important charge is that the common sense philosopher takes for granted various propositions without giving any argument for them, and to Kant this seems no better than the appeal to an oracle. Perhaps Kant's point is that in the absence of an argument or "rational justification," we can have no reason, no justification, for believing the propositions that the common sense philosopher takes for granted. Why should we accept the view that the only way in which a proposition can be known or justified for a person is on the basis of an argument? Why must we think that the only way one can be justified in believing, for example, that there are other people who have bodies and talk, is on the basis of an argument? Could there not be sources of justification for such

---

1   Immanuel Kant, *Prolegomena to Any Future Metaphysics* (Indianapolis: Bobbs-Merrill, 1950), p. 7.

beliefs other than reasoning or rational argument, such as their origin in sources like perception and memory? The view that the only way a proposition can be justified is on the basis of an argument would rule out the possibility of immediate knowledge, and this is something that Kant himself would not accept.

We might, however, see the Kantian complaint as claiming that it is reasonable to accept the testimony of such sources only if we have some reason to believe that such sources *are* reliable or trustworthy. In the absence of some argument or reasons for believing that such sources are reliable or trustworthy, are we not relying on them the way one might rely on an oracle? Oracles might be quite reliable, but in the absence of reasons for believing that they are reliable, accepting their testimony would not seem to be justified, and true beliefs based on their testimony would not amount to knowledge. In the absence of any argument for the reliability of our sources, how can we treat their deliverances or output as knowledge or justified?

Perhaps we might view the Kantian complaint as reflecting the assumption considered in the last two chapters – namely:

A2   The only epistemically satisfactory way to know or to be justified in believing that perception and memory are reliable is on the basis of a non-circular argument.

To someone who endorses A2, Reid's failure, and the failure of later philosophers such as Moore and Chisholm, to give such an argument will seem a crippling deficiency. But, as we have seen in the last two chapters, Sosa holds both (1) that we cannot give such an argument, and (2) that this does not preclude our knowing that our faculties are reliable. Reid, too, I think, would reject A2. Let us consider his views more closely.

Reid holds that we have immediate, non-inferential knowledge of various simple logical truths or axioms and of our own mental states, of our own beliefs and sensations. My knowledge that $2 = 2$ and that I am thinking about Boston are instances of immediate knowledge. I know such things without inferring them from anything else that I know. Yet what we know immediately is not confined to simple logical truths and the testimony of introspection. Reid extends the sphere of what is known immediately to both memory and perception. He tells us that memory is a source of immediate, non-inferential knowledge: "It is by memory that we have an immediate knowledge of things past."[2] He takes a similar

---

2   Thomas Reid, *Essays on the Intellectual Powers of Man*, Essay III, Chapter 1, p. 324.

view with respect to sense perception:

> If the word *axiom* be put to signify every truth which is known immediately, without being deduced from any antecedent truth, then the existence of the objects of sense may be called an axiom. For my senses give me an immediate conviction of what they testify, as my understanding gives me of what is commonly called an axiom.[3]

For Reid, the testimony of memory and sense perception is immediate. Our perceptual and mnemonic beliefs are not known on the basis of reasoning. I do not infer, for example, that I had breakfast today from any other propositions. Thus, I do not infer that I had breakfast today from the propositions (1) memory beliefs are likely to be true, and (2) I have a memory belief that I had breakfast today. Similarly, I do not, on Reid's view, infer the existence of external material objects from what I know about the nature of my sensations. I do not infer them from what I know about my "sense data." Nor do I infer the existence of material objects from other propositions that I know such as (1) beliefs formed on the basis of perceptual experiences are likely to be true, and (2) my belief that there is a table before me is formed on the basis of perceptual experience. Yet Reid does hold that we have knowledge of the reliability of perception and memory. How do we know that they are reliable?

In his *Essays on the Intellectual Powers of Man*, Reid presents a variety of "first principles" concerning the reliability of our faculties. He offers a principle concerning memory: "That those things did really happen which I distinctly remember."[4] He offers a principle concerning sense perception: "That those things do really exist which we distinctly perceive by our senses, and are what we perceive them to be."[5] He offers us a general principle to the effect that "the natural faculties, by which we distinguish truth from error, are not fallacious."[6] In taking these propositions to be first principles, Reid holds that they are incapable of proof and that they do not depend epistemically on other things that we know. In this respect, Reid suggests that the general principle about the reliability of our faculties and the principle about perception and memory are immediately evident. Reid held that we do know that perception, memory,

---

3   *Ibid.*, Essay II, Chapter 20, p. 294.
4   *Ibid*, p. 625.
5   *Ibid.*, p. 630.
6   *Ibid.*, p. 630.

and, more broadly, all of the cognitive faculties by which we distinguish truth from error are reliable. But since he held that such knowledge is immediate knowledge, he rejects A2, the view that the only epistemically satisfactory way to know that perception and memory are reliable is on the basis of a non-circular *argument*. Since such knowledge is, in Reid's view, immediate knowledge, it does not depend on any argument whatever. But it is also important to note that Reid does not seem to accept the view that one cannot know on the basis of some faculty that it is itself reliable. This seems implicit insofar as he holds it to be immediately evident that our natural faculties are reliable. Would it not, after all, be on the basis of some natural faculty that we believe such a principle? Such an immediately evident conviction would itself be, for Reid, the testimony of some natural faculty itself, some faculty "vouching" for itself.

Now, Reid's view that we know immediately that perception and memory are reliable has, to put it mildly, not been universally accepted. Perhaps this is because the claims that perception and memory are reliable seem to be general propositions. I think many philosophers would hold that what we know immediately are either (1) *particular* propositions about one's own existence or about one's own mental states such as I am in pain or I want a boat, or (2) they are *general* propositions that are necessary truths such as all red things are colored and all squares are rectangles. The propositions that perception and memory are reliable, however, are not necessary truths. We have seen that Reid would reject (1) insofar as he holds that we have immediate knowledge of the past through memory and immediate knowledge of external objects through perception. So, too, Reid seems to be denying (2) that our immediate knowledge of general truths is confined to those that are necessary. Still, such a stance has not seemed plausible to many.

In any event, though Reid holds that we have immediate knowledge of the reliability of those faculties, he does *not* reject other sources of evidence for their reliability. He does not reject something like the track-record arguments we considered in the last chapter. Consider, for example, what he says about memory:

Perhaps it may be said, that the experience we have had of the fidelity of memory is a good reason for relying upon its testimony. I deny not that this may be a reason to those who have had this experience, and who reflect upon it. But I believe that there are few who ever thought of this reason, or who found any need of it. It must be some very rare occasion that leads a man to have recourse to it; and in those who have done so, the testimony of memory was believed before the experience of its fidelity; and that belief could not be caused by the experience which came after it.[7]

Reid does not deny that such a track-record argument can be a reason for believing in the reliability of memory even though such an argument would employ memory itself. Still, Reid makes two points about such an argument. First, he notes that one who reasons in this way has already accepted the testimony of memory – that is, formed particular memory beliefs, before the experience of the fidelity of memory or before going through a track record argument. Prior to accepting the argument, one accepts as true the testimony of memory in particular cases, and in those cases, memory supplies one with evidence of the truth of such beliefs. The role of memory as a source of evidence is therefore not dependent on one's first going through a track record argument. Second, Reid suggests that few have ever found any need of such an argument. I take Reid to hold not only that we don't need such an argument in order for memory to be a source of evidence for particular memory beliefs – their origin in memory suffices for that – but also to hold that the conviction that memory is generally reliable does not arise from such a track record argument. I assume that for Reid, the belief that memory is generally reliable is not based on such reasoning. It is for him a first principle that is immediate and not based in reasoning. Still, it is worth pointing out that here again Reid does not assume that one cannot know on the basis of a faculty F that F is reliable. Again, he does not endorse A2, but seems to reject it. It is true that Reid thinks our knowledge of the reliability of memory is immediate, yet we should note that one may consistently claim that one has immediate knowledge that p and also that one has additional evidence in the form of reasons or reasoning that support p. One's evidence for p can in this way be epistemically over-determined.

We might also consider what Reid writes in connection with his principle concerning the reliability of our senses. Reid writes, "How came we at first to know that there are certain beings about us whom we call father, and mother, and sisters, and brothers, and nurse? Was it not by the testimony of our senses?"[8] Though Reid is here asking questions, rather than formulating an argument, he clearly seems to be pointing to

---

7 *Ibid.*, Essay III, Chapter 2, p. 329. For an excellent discussion of this passage and Reid's views on circularity, see James Van Cleve, "Reid on the First Principles of Contingent Truths," *Reid Studies* vol. 3 (Autumn) 1999, pp. 3–30.

8 Thomas Reid, *Essays on the Intellectual Powers of Man*, Essay VI, Chapter 5, pp. 625–26.

a reliable faculty of perception as the best explanation for our knowing what we take ourselves to know. Could we not take Reid here to be reasoning that (1) I know that this man is my father and that woman is my mother, and (2) the best explanation of how we have this knowledge is through sense perception, (3) unless perception were reliable I would not have such knowledge, and therefore, (4) perception is reliable? The conclusion that perception is reliable could be justified for us in virtue of its explaining for us how we have the knowledge that we take ourselves to have. Our belief in the reliability of our senses would thus have some degree of justification for us in virtue of its cohering with and explaining what we take ourselves to know about other people. Such an argument resembles closely the Neo-Moorean argument that we considered in the last chapter.

Is this argument epistemically circular? Let us assume that an argument is epistemically circular if one uses a source to support the reliability of that source. Now is one using perception in this argument? It might seem that the answer is "no." Note that the argument takes as its first premise the particular epistemic proposition that I know this is my father rather than the proposition, this is my father. The latter proposition seems to be something that would be known on the basis of sense perception, but the epistemic proposition is not the *object* of sense perception. I do not see that I know this is my father the way I see that this is my father. Still, in a case where I see my father and I know that I know this is my father, my knowledge of the epistemic fact is dependent on the use of sense perception. It is, after all, only through the use of sense perception that I do know that this is my father. We should concede, then, that the argument is epistemically circular in the sense that it is only by using perception that Reid knows the first premise. If we do attribute such reasoning to Reid, then again we should hold that Reid rejects A2.

We find Reid taking a similar view elsewhere. In his *Inquiry*, for example, Reid considers the skeptic's claim that we should withhold belief in the testimony of our senses. To this claim, Reid makes three responses. First, he replies that he will not do such a thing because he cannot do it. "My belief is carried along by perception, as irresistibly as my body by the earth."[9] Second, he suggests that it would not be prudent for him to do so. "But what is the consequence? I resolve not to believe my senses. I break my nose against a post that comes my way; I step into a

---

9 Thomas Reid, *Inquiry and Essays*, p. 85.

dirty kennel; and, after twenty such wise rational actions, I am taken up and clapped into a mad-house."[10] In both of these responses, we find the roots of Alston's approach to dealing with the problem of epistemic circularity. We find Reid pointing to the great difficulty in giving up our perceptual way of forming beliefs and to its being imprudent or *practically* irrational to do so. But Reid does not confine himself to such considerations. He offers a third line of reasoning, which it is worth quoting in full.

I gave implicit belief to the informations of Nature by my senses, for a considerable part of my life, before I had learned so much logic as to be able to start a doubt concerning them. And now, when I reflect upon what is past, I do not find that I have been imposed upon by this belief. I find that without it I must have perished by a thousand accidents. I find that without it I should have been no wiser now than when I was born. I should not ever have been able to acquire that logic which suggests these skeptical doubts with regard to my senses. Therefore, I consider this instinctive belief as one of the best gifts of Nature. I thank the Author of my being, who bestowed it upon me before the eyes of my reason were opened, and still bestows it upon me, to be my guide where reason leaves me in the dark. And now, I yield to the direction of my senses, not from instinct only, but from a confidence and trust in a faithful and beneficent Monitor, grounded upon the experience of paternal care and goodness.

In all this, I deal with the Author of my being, no otherwise than I thought it reasonable to deal with my parents and tutors. I believed by instinct whatever they told me, long before I had the idea of a lie, or thought of the possibility of their deceiving me. Afterwards, upon reflection, I found that they had acted like fair and honest people, who wished me well. I found that, if I had not believed what they told me before I could give a reason for my belief, I had to this day been little better than a changeling. And though this natural credulity hath sometimes occasioned my being imposed upon by deceivers, yet it hath been of infinite advantage on the whole; therefore, I consider it as another good gift from Nature. And I continue to give that credit, from reflection, to those of whose integrity and veracity I have had experience, which before I gave from instinct.

There is a much greater similitude than is commonly imagined between the testimony of nature given by our senses, and the testimony of men given by language. The credit we give to both is at first the effect of instinct only. When we grow up, and begin to reason about them, the credit given to human testimony is restrained and weakened, by the experience we have of deceit. But the credit given

---

10   *Ibid.*, p. 86.

to the testimony of our senses, is established and confirmed by the uniformity and constancy of the laws of nature.[11]

If Reid's first two answers pre-figure Alston's approach to the problem of circularity, then I suggest that this third response reflects that suggested by Sosa. We begin, according to Reid, by accepting on instinct the testimony of our senses and memory just as we naturally accept the testimony of others. We begin with what Sosa calls "animal knowledge" rooted in "apt" faculties of perception and memory. But we do not stay confined to the level of animal knowledge. We can ascend to the level of "reflective knowledge" by developing a coherent epistemic perspective on our cognitive faculties. We recognize that our faculties of perception and memory are the sources of much that we know, that without them we should be "no wiser" than when we were born, and that our faculties have saved us from perishing by a "thousand accidents." Our acceptance of the reliability of perception and memory is, for Reid, supported by such beliefs, so that our acceptance of the testimony of perception and memory is supported not merely by instinct, as when we were children, but by a fuller epistemic perspective supported by reflection. The development of such a reflective perspective does, of course, rely on the use of perception and memory. Reid notes that the credit given to the testimony of our senses is supported by the uniformity and constancy of the laws of nature. Such confirmation would seem to depend on the use of perception and memory. But, as Sosa has argued, and Reid himself seems to accept, that in itself does not make it epistemically unacceptable or illicit. Even if, for Reid, our belief in the reliability of perception and memory does not have its origin in such reasoning, even if the belief that such faculties are reliable is a first principle known immediately, it seems, nonetheless, that our belief in the reliability of such faculties can be supported by such aptly formed beliefs. Here again, I suggest, Reid rejects A2.

Reid, I conclude, at least implicitly, rejects A2. He rejects the view that the only epistemically satisfactory way to know that perception and memory are reliable is through an argument free of epistemic circularity. He holds that knowledge of the reliability of perception and memory can be known immediately, and thus need not depend on any reasoning. Furthermore, he implicitly rejects the view that one cannot know on the basis of a source that that source is reliable. In holding that we know immediately that the natural faculties by which we distinguish truth from

11   *Ibid.*, pp. 86–87.

error are not fallacious, Reid is of course using his natural faculties. It is some natural faculty by which he knows this first principle. Finally, Reid seems to endorse a variety of reasons and arguments for the reliability of his faculties, none of which is itself free from epistemic circularity. So if the Kantian complaint were merely that the common sense philosopher offers no argument for the reliability of his ways of forming beliefs, we can see that, on the contrary, Reid *does* offer such arguments. If, however, the Kantian complaint is rather that the common sense philosopher offers no argument for the reliability of faculties that is free from epistemic circularity, then of course Kant is right. Reid does not offer such arguments. But, as we saw in the last two chapters, it would be impossible to do so if reflection is pushed far enough. Still, as Sosa argues, epistemic circularity does not prevent one from knowing that one's faculties are reliable. That view, I think, is also endorsed at least implicitly by Reid.

4.2 REID'S WRONG TURN

Unfortunately, Reid's position is rather more complicated. Or so it seems. Let us consider what Reid says elsewhere in his *Essays*. Let us consider the following passage.

Another first principle is, that the natural faculties, by which we distinguish truth from error, are not fallacious. If any man should demand a proof of this, it is impossible to satisfy him. For suppose it should be mathematically demonstrated, this would signify nothing in this case; because, to judge of a demonstration, a man must trust his faculties, and take for granted the very thing in question.

If a man's honesty were called into question, it would be ridiculous to refer it to the man's own word, whether he be honest or not. The same absurdity there is in attempting to prove, by any kind of reasoning, probable or demonstrative, that our reasoning is not fallacious, since the very point in question is, whether reasoning may be trusted.

If a skeptic should build his skepticism upon this foundation, that all our reasoning, and judging powers are fallacious in their nature, or should resolve at least to withhold assent until it be proved that they are not; it would be impossible by argument to beat him out of this strong hold, and he must be left to enjoy his skepticism.

Des Cartes certainly made a false step in this matter; for having suggested this doubt among others, that whatever evidence he might have from his consciousness, his senses, his memory, or his reason; yet possibly some malignant being had given him those faculties on purpose to impose upon him; and therefore, they are not to be trusted without a proper voucher: to remove this doubt, he endeavours to prove the being of a Deity who is no deceiver; whence he concludes, that the faculties he had given him are true and worthy to be trusted.

It is strange that so acute a reasoner did not perceive, that in this reasoning there is evidently a begging of the question.

For if our faculties be fallacious, why may they not deceive us in this reasoning as well as in others? And if they are to be trusted in this instance without a voucher, why not in others?

Every kind of reasoning for the veracity of our faculties, amounts to no more than taking their own testimony for their veracity; and this we must do implicitly, until God give us new faculties to sit in judgment upon the old; and the reason why Des Cartes satisfied himself with so weak an argument for the truth of his faculties, most probably was, that he never seriously doubted of it.

If any truth can be said to be prior to all others in the order of nature, this seems to have the best claim; because in every instance of assent, whether upon intuitive, demonstrative, or probable evidence, the truth of our faculties is taken for granted, and is, as it were, one of the premises on which our assent is grounded

How then come we to be assured of this fundamental truth on which all others rest? Perhaps evidence, as in many other respects it resembles light, so in this also, that as light which is the discoverer of all visible objects, discovers itself at the same time: so evidence which is the voucher for all truth, vouches for itself at the same time.[12]

There is much here that requires comment. Is Reid endorsing the view that we cannot know on the basis of a source that that source is reliable? Is he, in effect, endorsing A2? Reid writes that "if a man's honesty were called into question, it would be ridiculous to refer it to the man's own word, whether he be honest or not." One could read this as holding that one cannot take the testimony of a source as evidence for the reliability of that source. If so, then Reid would be endorsing the sort of view that we found Fumerton taking, that one cannot use memory to justify that memory is reliable.

But is this how we should take Reid's comment? I don't think so. First, as we have seen, Reid himself *does* seem to use testimony of various sources to support the reliability of those sources. He does this in the sorts of epistemically circular arguments considered earlier. Second, as we have noted, Reid holds that it is immediately evident that our natural

---

12 *Ibid.*, Essay VI, Chapter 5, pp. 630–32.

77

faculties are reliable, and this claim is itself the product of some natural faculty. Third, note that in the final cryptic passage, Reid suggests that "evidence" can "vouch" for itself. It is hard to know what Reid means by this remark, but he does suggest that some things can vouch for themselves. We should not, then, take Reid as holding as a general principle that nothing can vouch for itself or that nothing can supply evidence for its own trustworthiness or reliability. Furthermore, we should note that Reid says that it would be ridiculous to take a man's own word for his honesty *if* his "honesty were called into question . . .". Perhaps what Reid means is that it would be ridiculous to take a man's word for his own honesty *when we have positive grounds for doubting it on some particular occasion.* When we do have evidence pointing to the fact that a man is dishonest, then in the absence of any further evidence, his own testimony to the contrary would not make it reasonable to believe that he is trustworthy. But with respect to the senses, memory, and reasoning, we are not in *that* situation. We do not have positive grounds for thinking that they are generally unreliable. On the contrary, as Reid suggests in the passage from the *Inquiry* just quoted, we have lots of evidence that they have not been generally unreliable even though this evidence comes from those sources themselves.

Second, Reid notes that it would be impossible to beat the skeptic out of his position if he held that his judging powers are fallacious or if he should resolve to withhold assent until it is proved that they are not. But this point need not be read as holding that we cannot know that a source is reliable by using that source. Rather I take Reid to be pointing out that if one mistrusts his faculties, and thus refuses to accept their testimony, or won't use them until it is first proved to him that they are reliable, then one cannot prove to him that they are reliable. For proving such a thing to a person would require that he use his faculties and that he accept their testimony. Perhaps this is also the point behind Reid's comment that "if any man should demand a proof of this, it is impossible to satisfy him." It is not impossible to satisfy a demand for proof or an argument for the reliability of our faculties if we allow ourselves to use epistemically circular arguments, since we can in fact give such arguments. Indeed, Reid, I think, endorses such arguments. It is impossible to satisfy a demand for a proof or an argument for the reliability of our faculties that *does not depend on the use of our faculties.* In order to have anything proved to you, you must use your faculties and accept their testimony, at least with respect to the premises. As Reid points out, "Every kind of reasoning for the veracity of our faculties amounts to no more than taking their own testimony for their veracity."

Still, the previous remarks notwithstanding, there is a serious problem raised by Reid's remarks. Reid is critical of Descartes's attempt to prove that his faculties are reliable. Reid charges that Descartes's reasoning is "question-begging." But how exactly is it question-begging? Reid seems to explain the charge by asking, "For if our faculties are fallacious, why may they not deceive us in this reasoning as well as in others? And if they are to be trusted in this instance without a voucher, why not in others?" But how does this show that Descartes's reasoning is question-begging?

Perhaps Reid is claiming that (1) Descartes holds that we ought not to trust the testimony of our faculties without a proper voucher, without a non-circular argument that they are reliable, and (2) Descartes does accept the testimony of his faculties in arguing for the existence of a non-deceiving God. If this is so, then Descartes is guilty of inconsistency in first endorsing a kind of normative epistemic principle and then proceeding to violate it. But how would this make his reasoning question-begging? Being inconsistent is one sort of flaw and begging the question is another.

Perhaps Reid is pointing out that Descartes accepts the testimony of some faculties, such as reason and introspection, without a non-circular proof of their reliability while he insists on such a proof for the reliability of others, such as perception and memory.[13] This would also point to a kind of inconsistency, but again, this sort of inconsistency would not appear to be begging the question.

Perhaps Reid thinks Descartes begs the question insofar as Descartes argues for the conclusion that his faculties are reliable by using the testimony of his faculties. But why should that be a problem with Descartes's reasoning? Reid's claim to know immediately that his natural faculties are reliable is itself based on his natural faculties, as are the epistemically circular arguments he appears to endorse.

I think we can glean a better sense of the charge that Descartes begs the question if we consider what Reid writes a few lines later. He says, " . . . in every instance of assent, whether upon intuitive, demonstrative, or probable evidence, the truth of our faculties is taken for granted, and is, as it were, one of the premises on which our assent is grounded." Here we *might* take Reid to hold that whenever we know anything, our knowledge

---

13 Reid makes this criticism of some skeptical positions in the *Inquiry*. For example, "Reason, says the skeptic, the only judge of truth, and you ought to throw off every opinion and every belief that is not grounded on reason. Why sir, should I believe the faculty of reason more than that of perception? – they both came out of the same shop, and were made by the same artist; and if he puts one piece of false ware into my hands, what should hinder him from putting another?" *Inquiry and Essays*, pp. 84–85.

of it is based on our knowledge that our faculties are reliable. This is one way in which we might understand the allusion to "premises on which our assent is grounded." Suppose, then, we take Reid to be endorsing the following argument:

1. If one knows that *p*, then one's knowledge that *p* must be based on one's knowing that one's faculties are reliable.

Now we might take the argument to run:

2. If Descartes knows the premises of his argument for the reliability of his faculties, then his knowledge of the premises is based on his knowing that his faculties are reliable, on his knowing the conclusion of the argument, and this reasoning begs the question.
3. Therefore, if Descartes knows the premises of his argument for the reliability of his faculties, then his reasoning begs the question.

This objection employs a clear sense of begging the question. In this case, knowledge of the premises would be based on knowledge of the conclusion. And this would seem to be an unacceptable form of begging the question. Knowledge of the premises would not be a source of knowledge of the conclusion. Further, this problem would seem to confront not only Descartes's reasoning, but *any* reasoning for the reliability of one's faculties insofar as the knowledge from which we might reason to the conclusion that our faculties are reliable would be based on our knowing that our faculties are reliable.

But does Reid really accept 1? Does he, for example, really think that every proposition that we believe is literally inferred from the proposition that our faculties are reliable? Does he believe that every belief is actually based on reasoning from that premise? Surely not. He insists that perceptual, mnemonic, and introspective beliefs are immediate, that they are not based on reasoning. Moreover, I think that 1 is inconsistent with what Reid himself holds elsewhere. Accepting 1 is, for example, inconsistent with what Reid writes about self-evident propositions and first principles:

But there are other propositions which are no sooner understood than they are believed. The judgment follows the apprehension of them necessarily, and both are equally the work of nature, and the result of our original powers. There is no searching for evidence; no weighing of arguments; the proposition is not deduced or inferred from another; it has the light of truth in itself, and has no occasion to borrow it from another.

Propositions of this last kind, when they are used in matters of science, have commonly been called *axioms*; and on whatever occasion they are used, are called *first principles, principles of common sense, common notions, self-evident truths.*[14]

Reid holds that there are self-evident propositions. "I take it for granted that there are self-evident principles. Nobody, I think, denies it."[15] I assume that in the case of a self-evident proposition, it is possible that our knowledge of it is *not* based on knowledge of some other proposition. Otherwise, it would not be "self" evident. As Reid puts it, " . . . it has the light of truth in itself, and has no occasion to borrow it from another." Furthermore, concerning the reliability of "consciousness" or introspection, Reid writes:

If I am asked to prove that I cannot be deceived by consciousness, to prove that it is not a fallacious sense; I can find no proof. I cannot find any antecedent truth from which it is deduced, or upon which its evidence depends. It seems to disdain any such derived authority, and to claim my assent in its own right.[16]

Here Reid denies that this first principle depends on any other proposition for its evidence. It disdains "any such derived authority" and claims his assent "in its own right." Again, concerning the first principle that "the thoughts of which I am conscious, are the thoughts of a being which I call *myself*, my *mind*, my *person*."[17] Reid writes, "If any man asks a proof of this, I confess I can give none: there is an evidence in the proposition itself which I am unable to resist."[18] Reid finds that there is an evidence in the first principle *itself* that he is unable to resist. The principle is not based on our knowing some other proposition as 1 would require.

Premise 1 conflicts with Reid's comments about other first principles. Reid cannot consistently accept both these claims and 1. So, if 1 is the basis of Reid's charge of question-begging, then we may note that is seems inconsistent with the plausible claims that Reid says elsewhere. It would be a wrong turn on Reid's part. Moreover, how would we understand our knowledge of the first principle that our faculties are reliable? If 1 is true, then our knowledge of that principle must itself be based on itself. It is

14   Thomas Reid, *Essays on the Intellectual Powers of Man*, Essay VI, Chapter 4, p. 593.
15   *Ibid.*, p. 594.
16   *Ibid.*, Chapter VI, Chapter 5, p. 617.
17   *Ibid.*, p. 620.
18   *Ibid.*, p. 621.

hard to see how that would be possible and hard to see how knowledge of that principle would avoid the same sort of vicious circularity that Reid is attributing to Descartes.

However, perhaps Reid is not endorsing 1. Perhaps he is not claiming that whenever one knows a proposition, p, one knows that p on the basis of knowing that one's faculties are reliable. Perhaps Reid is endorsing rather some view such as the following:

1′. Whenever anyone assents to a proposition, p, he assumes, at least implicitly, that his belief that p is reliably produced.

There is some reason to think that Reid would accept 1′ at least in the case of reflective adults. He writes:

When a man in the common course of life gives credit to the testimony of his senses, his memory, or his reason, he does not put the question to himself, whether these faculties may deceive him; yet the trust which he reposes in them supposes an inward conviction, that, in that instance at least, they do not deceive him.[19]

Also, as we have seen Reid writes, "[S]uppose it should be mathematically demonstrated [that our natural faculties are reliable], this would signify nothing in this case; because, to judge of a demonstration, a man must trust his faculties, and take for granted the very thing in question." Perhaps we may take Reid to be claiming that in reasoning for the reliability of one's faculties, one must assent to the premises, yet in assenting to the premises one is assuming, at least implicitly, that one's faculties are reliable.

Let us suppose that Reid does accept 1′. How would this support the view that Descartes's argument is question-begging? Could Reid have reasoned this way?

Argument A

1. Whenever anyone assents to a proposition, he assumes, at least implicitly, that his belief in that proposition is reliably produced.
2. In attempting to prove that some of his beliefs are reliably produced, Descartes assents to various propositions (say, p, q, and r).
3. Therefore, in attempting to prove that some of his beliefs are reliably produced, Descartes assumes that some of his beliefs are reliably produced.
4. But the conclusion of the argument is that some of his beliefs are reliably produced.
5. Therefore, in assenting to the premises of his argument, Descartes assumes the conclusion.

---

19 *Ibid.*, p. 633.

6. Therefore, Descartes, in attempting to prove that some of his beliefs are reliably produced, begs the question.

But does Argument A point to a fatal defect in Descartes's reasoning? I think the answer is "no." At most, Argument A shows that Descartes cannot believe the premises of his argument without believing that his faculties are reliable or that some of his beliefs are reliably produced. Yet it is far from clear why this should be a fatal flaw in Descartes's reasoning. Even if a belief in the reliability of his faculties *accompanies* his acceptance of the premises, it would not follow that knowledge or justified belief of the premises is epistemically *based* on that belief. On the contrary, Descartes might hold that knowledge of that accompanying belief is had through his reasoning from q, r, and s. What confers the epistemic status is not the belief in the conclusion but the knowledge of the premises in the argument. Suppose, for example, that Descartes knows immediately the premises of his argument p, q, and r and infers from them the conclusion that his faculties are reliable or that some of his beliefs are reliably produced. In that case, Descartes's assenting to the premises of the argument is not based on his accepting the conclusion. It would not follow that Descartes knows the premises only in virtue of knowing the conclusion. His argument would not be question-begging in the sense that knowledge of the premises is based on knowledge of the conclusion. If we think that "begging the question" involves knowing or having justified belief in the premises in virtue of knowing or having justified belief in the conclusion, then we should say that 6 does not follow from 5.

Consider the following. Reid holds that the proposition that his faculties are reliable (R:F) is something he knows immediately. But if 1' is true, then he assents to (R:F) only if he assumes that his belief in (R:F) is reliably produced. But his knowledge that (R:F) is *not* based on his knowing that his belief (R:F) is reliably produced. His knowledge that (R:F) is immediate knowledge, at least according to Reid. Therefore, it is not based on his knowing any other proposition, including the proposition that his belief (R:F) is reliably produced. He has some other source of knowing (R:F) – namely, reason or that branch of reason he calls common sense. Now consider the analogous case for Cartesian or other forms of reasoning concerning the reliability of one's faculties. Suppose one knows some propositions p, q, and r from which one infers the conclusion that his faculties are reliable. Suppose that he knows p, q, and r immediately – perhaps they are known immediately on the basis of reason or clear and distinct perception. (Or even perception and memory, in the case of the track-record and Neo-Moorean arguments.) Could it not be that one's knowing p, q, and r, and seeing that they imply that his faculties are reliable, is a source of knowledge for that conclusion? Could one not in this way support his belief that his faculties are reliable in a way that is no more viciously question-begging than Reid's supposedly immediate knowledge? Of course, given $1'$, he accepts the premises only if he accepts that his belief in the premises was reliably produced. Still, that does not imply that his knowing the premises, and seeing that they imply the conclusion, is not itself a source of knowledge for the conclusion. That would not follow in Descartes's case any more than it would follow for Reid's allegedly immediate knowledge.

Even if we accept $1'$, it does not seem that Reid has shown us that Descartes's reasoning is question-begging in the sense that Descartes's knowledge of his premises must be based on his knowledge of the conclusion. Moreover, we have seen no reason to think that one cannot know that a source of belief is reliable by using that source. Still, if $1'$ is true, then it is not through Cartesian reasoning that one comes to believe that one's beliefs are reliably produced. For one would already have that belief, at least implicitly, in accepting the premises. Perhaps it is also true that one who did not already have the belief that his faculties were reliable would not accept the premises of the argument. Thus, a skeptic who did not already implicitly assume that his faculties were reliable would not accept the premises of the argument. Then, as Reid says "it would be impossible to beat him out of his strong hold, and he must be left to enjoy his skepticism." But from the fact that arguments and reasoning, whether Cartesian, track record, or Neo-Moorean are useless for dealing with skeptics of that ilk, it does not follow that they are useless.

What would be the value of such arguments? We considered a question very much like this at the end of the last chapter. I think a similar answer remains appropriate, and that is an answer drawn from Reid – namely, that our confidence in the reliability of our faculties can be enhanced by reflection, so that our acceptance of the testimony of our faculties can be backed with reasons that we now reflectively recognize as such. But what is more, the Kantian complaint that common sense philosophers have not provided a non-circular argument for the reliability of their faculties is unjustified. It is unjustified insofar as such an argument is not needed in order to know that one's ways of forming beliefs are reliable.

5

Moore, Skepticism, and the External World

It is sometimes charged that Moore and other philosophers in the common sense tradition do not take skepticism seriously. Certainly, they do not take skepticism seriously in the sense that they are skeptics. Still, it would be a mistake to hold that they do not address skeptical arguments or positions. Moore's responses to skepticism are well-known, though many philosophers think them unsatisfactory. In the first section of this chapter, I focus on Moore's proof of an external world and the charge that it is question begging. In the second, I look at Moore's response to skepticism and Stroud's criticism of it. In the third, I look at the "sensitivity requirement" prominent in recent relevant alternative and contextualist accounts of knowledge.

5.1 MOORE'S PROOF AND THE CHARGE OF QUESTION-BEGGING

Kant tells us that it is a scandal to philosophy that the existence of things outside of us must be accepted merely on faith. In his "Proof of an External World," Moore gives a simple argument that has perplexed, or vexed, many philosophers. Moore thinks that our belief in external objects is not a matter of mere faith, but something that we know and, as the title of his paper suggests, can be proved. After pages of careful Moorean exploration of such distinctions as "being presented in space" and "being met with in space," Moore offers his proof. It is, in brief:

1. Here is one hand.
2. Here is another hand.
3. Therefore, there are external objects.

Moore claims that his argument meets three conditions for being a proof. First, the premises are different from the conclusion. Second, he knows each of the premises. Third, the conclusion follows from the premises. Moore grants that there might be other conditions that a proof must meet, but he seems to think that his argument would satisfy those conditions as well.

Moore points out that the sort of proof he has offered for his conclusion is similar to proofs that we ordinarily take as "absolutely conclusive proofs." Suppose there were a question as to whether there were three misprints on a page. A believes there are, and B is inclined to doubt it. Moore suggests that A could prove his contention by turning to a certain page and pointing to three separate misprints. Moore says that that is one method by which A might prove his point.

Moore is well aware that many philosophers will think he has not given a satisfactory proof of his conclusion. He says that many philosophers will not think he has given a satisfactory proof because he has given no proof of his premises. He has not offered any proof, for example, of the premise that here is a hand. Moore candidly admits that he does not think he can give a proof of that premise:

How am I to prove now that 'Here's one hand, and here's another'? I do not believe I can do it. In order to do it, I should need to prove, for one thing, as Descartes pointed out, that I am not now dreaming. But how can I prove that I am not? I have, no doubt, conclusive reasons for asserting that I am not now dreaming; I have conclusive evidence that I am awake: but that is a very different thing from being able to prove it. I could not tell you what all my evidence is; and I should be required to do this at least, in order to give you a proof.[1]

Still, Moore insists that he can know things without proof. "I can know things, which I cannot prove; and among the things which I certainly did know, even if (as I think) I could not prove them, were the premisses of my [proof]."[2]

But how does Moore know the premise, "Here is a hand"? Is such knowledge immediate or is it based on an inference? Moore seems to have taken different views about the nature of such knowledge. As we saw in Chapter 3, Moore writes:

Obviously, I cannot know *that* I know that the pencil exists, unless I do know that the pencil exists; and it might, therefore, be thought that the first proposition

1   G. E. Moore, "Proof of an External World," *Philosophical Papers*, p. 149.
2   *Ibid.*, p. 150.

can only be mediately known – known *merely* because the second is known. But it is, I think, necessary to make a distinction. From the mere fact that I should not know the first, *unless* I knew the second, it does not follow that I know the first *merely* because I know the second. And, in fact, I think I do know *both* of them immediately.[3]

Here Moore holds that his knowledge that the pencil exists is immediate knowledge. If one has immediate knowledge that *p*, then one does not know that *p* merely because one has inferred it from some *other* proposition. (Moore is careful to point out, however, that one could have *both* immediate and mediate knowledge of some proposition.) If, as Moore suggests here, his knowledge that the pencil exists is immediate knowledge, then it seems Moore would also be open to the view that his knowledge that here is a hand is also immediately known. It is not known merely because one knows some other proposition.

Elsewhere, however, Moore seems to take a different view about the nature of his knowledge concerning pencils and hands. For example, in his "Four Forms of Skepticism," he writes

Russell's view that I do not know for certain that this is a pencil or that you are conscious rests, if I am right, on no less than four distinct assumptions: (1) That I do not know these things immediately; (2) That they don't follow from any thing or things that I do know immediately; (3) That, *if* (1) and (2) are true, my belief in or knowledge of them must be 'based on an analogical or inductive argument'; and (4) That what is so based cannot be *certain knowledge*. And what I can't help asking myself is this: Is it, in fact, as certain that all these four assumptions are true, as that I *do* know that this is a pencil and that you are conscious? I cannot help answering: It seems to me *more* certain that I *do* know that this is a pencil and that you are conscious, than that any single one of these four assumptions is true, let alone all four . . . I agree with Russell that (1), (2), and (3) *are* true; yet no one even of these three do I feel *as* certain as that this is a pencil. Nay more: I do not think that it is *rational* to be as certain of any one of these four propositions, as of the proposition that I do know that this is a pencil.[4]

Here Moore says that he agrees with Russell that he does *not* know that this is a pencil immediately. Moore tentatively endorses Russell's view that knowledge that this is a pencil must be based on analogical or inductive arguments, including abductive arguments that the best explanation for one's sense experience is that there really is a pencil before one. Still,

3   G. E. Moore, "Hume's Philosophy Examined," *Some Main Problems of Philosophy*, p. 142.
4   G. E. Moore, "Four Forms of Skepticism," *Philosophical Papers*, p. 226.

Moore says that it is not as rational to be as certain of any of Russell's four assumptions as it is of the proposition that he does know that this is a pencil. If one cannot consistently accept all of Russell's assumptions *and* the proposition that I know this is a pencil, then, in Moore's view, we must abandon one or more of Russell's assumptions. Still, it seems that there is some ambivalence in Moore's writing's about the nature of his knowledge concerning pencils and hands, at least with respect to whether such knowledge is immediate. Yet Moore is clear *that* he knows this is a pencil or here is a hand even if he may be less clear about *how* he knows these things. Such a stance is consistent with that which Moore takes elsewhere.[5]

It is sometimes charged that Moore's proof of an external world "begs the question." There are different ways in which this objection might be understood. Suppose, for example, one took begging the question to involve taking as a premise some proposition that someone else denies. More precisely, one might hold that A's argument for *p* begs the question against B if A takes as a premise some proposition that B denies. Now, Moore takes as a premise the proposition, here's a hand, a real flesh and blood hand and not a mere sense datum of a hand. Now, some philosophers might deny Moore's proposition that here's a hand, and thus Moore's proof may be said in this respect to beg the question against those philosophers. But if this is what is involved in begging the question, then it is not clear that this amounts to a serious defect in Moore's proof or in his reasoning. To use Moore's own example, suppose B maintains that there are no misprints on a certain page, and A argues that there are by taking as premises "here's one misprint on the page" and "here's another." Even though A takes as premises propositions that B denies, it does not seem that there is anything wrong with A's proof. We often do accept such arguments as proofs of their conclusions. Certainly A would be entitled to believe the conclusion that there are misprints on the page given his knowledge of the premises. The mere fact that his proof begs the question in this sense against B would not change that fact. So if Moore does beg the question in this sense, it is not clear that it represents a serious defect and it is not clear that he is not entitled to believe his conclusion on the basis of his proof.

We might, however, understand the charge of begging the question in a different way. Suppose we say that an argument begs the question if

---

5   Cf. Moore's comment from "A Defence of Common Sense" that "We are all, I think, in this strange position that we do *know* many things, with regard to which we *know* further that we must have had some evidence for them and yet we do not know *how* we know them, i.e. we do not know what the evidence was." *Philosophical Papers*, p. 44.

knowledge of a premise is based on knowledge of the conclusion. In the last chapter, this is how I suggested we understand Reid's objection that Descartes begged the question. Does Moore's proof beg the question in this sense?

Suppose one held that perceptual knowledge that here's a hand is based on one's one's knowing both (1) perceptual experience is a reliable indicator of the external world, and (2) there is an external world. If we accept this view about what is required for perceptual knowledge, then it does seem that Moore's argument would beg the question. For in that case, Moore's knowledge of his premise, which is presumably a bit of perceptual knowledge, would be based on his knowing (2) that there is an external world, and that (2) is the conclusion of the argument. If this view of perceptual knowledge is right, then Moore's knowledge of his premises would be based on his knowledge of the conclusion, and his proof would beg the question.

In his defense, however, Moore may, correctly I think, deny the underlying assumption about the nature of perceptual knowledge. There is, as we have seen, good reason for denying that perceptual knowledge depends upon knowing both (1) and (2), for that would preclude children and animals from having perceptual knowledge. Moreover, as we have seen, Moore holds in "Hume's Theory Examined" that his perceptual knowledge that this is a pencil is something that he knows immediately. Here Moore, like Reid before him, holds that perceptual knowledge is not based on one's knowing some other proposition. Furthermore, Moore's claim that he knows, but cannot prove, his premises would support the view that Moore takes his knowledge that here's a hand is something he knows immediately. If this is so, then his knowledge is not based on his knowing (1) and (2). But further, even if one held that perceptual knowledge was *not* immediate, it is not obvious that it must be based on (1) and (2). In other words, even if one held that perceptual knowledge is based on one's knowing some other propositions, it is not clear that it must depend upon one's knowing (1) and (2). Thus, even if Moore held with Russell that perceptual knowledge involved some sort of inductive inference, it is not clear that the inductive conclusion that, for example, there is a pencil, must be based on one's knowing (1) and (2). So, since I think Moore can correctly deny the underlying assumption about the nature of perceptual knowledge, I think he may correctly deny the charge that his knowledge of his premises is based on his knowledge of the conclusion, and thus the charge that his proof is in this sense question-begging.

Still, let us consider the following objection that Moore's proof is question-begging. "Perceptual experience does not give one a reason to believe 'Here's a hand' as opposed to mere sense data unless one has a reason to believe that perceptual experience is a reliable indicator of the external world. One has no reason to believe that perception is reliable if one does not believe or has no reason to believe that there is any external world to be reliable about. But that is just the conclusion."[6] The charge is that Moore's proof is question-begging because he has a reason to believe his premise only if he has a reason to believe his conclusion. His belief in his premises is not epistemically independent of his belief in the conclusion.

In assessing this objection, I think it is important to bear in mind the distinction Moore makes in the passage from "Hume's Theory Examined." As we noted in Chapter 3, Moore denies that the proposition "S knows that p only if S knows that q" implies "S knows that p because S knows that q." From the fact that one knows that p only if one knows that q it does not follow that one knows that p on the basis of one's knowing that q or that q is one's reason for believing that p. Again, to use an example from Chapter 3, we may say that I am justified in believing that I think only if I am justified in believing that someone thinks. If these justified beliefs are linked in this way, it does not follow that the proposition "someone thinks" is my reason for believing that I think or that my knowledge that I think is *based* on my knowledge that someone thinks. Let us distinguish two senses in which one proposition can be "epistemically dependent" on another. In the first sense, p is epistemically dependent$_1$ on q just in case one is justified in believing (or knows) p only if one is justified in believing (or knows) q. The proposition "I think" is epistemically dependent$_1$ on the proposition "someone thinks." But in a second sense, p is epistemically dependent$_2$ on q just in case one is justified in believing (or knows) p on the basis of one's being justified in believing (or knowing) q. The proposition "I think" is *not* epistemically dependent$_2$ on the proposition that "someone thinks." Now, it seems that Moore might concede both that:

1. One has a reason to believe that here's a hand as opposed to mere sense data only if one has a reason to believe that there is an external world.

6 Walter Sinnott-Armstrong, "Begging the Question," *Australasian Journal of Philosophy* vol. 77 (June) 1999, p. 184.

2. One is justified in believing that here's a hand as opposed to mere sense data only if one is justified in believing that there is an external world.

Moore might grant that each is true, at least for a reflective being such as himself, who is capable of considering the proposition that there is an external world. Moore might say, "If I have *no* reason to believe there is an external world, then I certainly have no reason to believe that I have hands as opposed to mere sense data." He might concede that the proposition "here's a hand" is epistemically dependent$_1$ on the proposition "there is an external world." Still, he could consistently deny that the former proposition is epistemically dependent$_2$ on the latter. That is, he could consistently deny that his knowledge of the former proposition is *based* on his knowledge of the latter, and deny that the latter proposition is his reason for believing the former.

Now, if an argument begs the question when one's knowledge of a premise is based on knowledge of the conclusion, Moore could simply deny that his knowledge of the premise "here's a hand" or even "here's a hand as opposed to mere sense data" is *based* on his knowledge of the conclusion. Since he may hold that his knowledge of such premises is immediate knowledge, he may deny that knowledge of them need be based on his knowing or his being justified in believing any other proposition. He could consistently deny this even if he grants 1 and 2 and grants that his premise is epistemically dependent$_1$ on his conclusion. "But," one might object, "Moore's premises *are* epistemically dependent$_1$ on his conclusion, and *that* makes his proof question-begging." But that is not so clear. Suppose one reasons, "I think, therefore, someone thinks." It is not clear that such an argument is question-begging even though it exhibits epistemic dependence$_1$ or, more importantly, that there is anything unacceptable with such reasoning. So, in Moore's defense, even if he concedes that his premises are epistemically dependent$_1$ on his conclusion, he might deny that this makes his argument question-begging or that it implies that there is anything unacceptable about his reasoning.

5.2 MOORE'S RESPONSE TO SKEPTICISM AND STROUD'S OBJECTION

In any event, Moore continued to reflect on skeptical arguments. In his Howison lecture, "Certainty," he considered the skeptical hypothesis that he might be dreaming. The skeptic argues, "If you don't know that you are not dreaming, then you don't know that you are standing up; you don't know that you are not dreaming; therefore you don't know that you are standing up." But Moore characteristically replies:

I agree, therefore, with that part of this argument which asserts that if I don't know now that I'm not dreaming, it follows that I don't *know* that I am standing up, even if I both actually am and think that I am. But the first part of this argument is a consideration which cuts both ways. For, if it is true, it follows that it is also true that if I *do* know that I am standing up, then I do know that I am not dreaming. I can therefore just as well argue: since I do know that I am standing up, it follows that I do know that I am not dreaming; as my opponent can argue: since you don't know that you're not dreaming, it follows that you don't know that you're standing up. The one argument is just as good as the other, unless my opponent can give better reasons for asserting that I don't know that I'm not dreaming, than I can give for asserting that I do know that I am standing up.[7]

Let us consider a version of the skeptic's argument, one that focuses on our Moorean knowledge of hands, and a Moorean counter-argument. Suppose the skeptic argues:

The Argument from Ignorance
1. If you do not know that you are not dreaming, then you do not know that you have hands.
2. You do not know that you are not dreaming.
3. Therefore, you do not know that you have hands.

Moore's counter-argument accepts the same first premise as the skeptic's argument, but it takes as its second premise the negation of the skeptic's conclusion:

Moore's Counter-Argument
   1. If I do not know that I am not dreaming, then I do not know that I have hands.
Not-3. I do know that I have hands.
Not-2. Therefore, I do know that I am not dreaming.

Clearly, Moore *does* agree with the skeptic's premise that if he does not know that he is not dreaming, then he does not know that he has hands. Why does he accept this premise? Perhaps this is because Moore accepts "the principle of exclusion" (PE):

PE   If one is to know that p, then for every q such that one knows that q is incompatible with one's knowing that p, one must exclude q (rule out q or know that not q).

7   G. E. Moore, "Certainty," *Philosophical Papers*, p. 247.

Given that Moore recognizes that his dreaming would be incompatible with his knowing that he has hands, PE requires that Moore know that he is not dreaming. But Moore thinks he does know that he is not dreaming. For as we have seen, he says in his "Proof of an External World" that he has conclusive evidence that he is awake, though he cannot say what all the evidence is.

Many philosophers have found the Moorean response unsatisfactory. In *The Significance of Philosophical Scepticism*, Barry Stroud questions the adequacy of this response and Moore's general strategy of appealing to particular examples of knowledge in his replies to skepticism. Stroud asks us to consider the following sort of case. A master detective and his apprentice have been summoned to investigate the murder of a young duke during a weekend party at the duke's country house.

[The apprentice] gets from the duke's secretary a list of all those who were in the house at the time and with careful research shows conclusively and, let us suppose, correctly that the only one on the list who could have done it is the butler. He then announces to the detective that he now knows that the butler did it. 'No,' the master replies, 'that list was simply given to you by the secretary; it could be that someone whose name was not on the list was in the house at the time and committed the murder. We still don't know who did it.'[8]

Stroud goes on to observe:

This is a successful objection to the apprentice's claim to know. If he has not checked the completeness of the list, we recognize that he has been hasty and does not yet know who committed the murder. It would obviously be absurd at this point for him to try to reject what the detective said by appealing to his "knowledge" that the butler did it. The detective said that even after all the apprentice's valuable work they still do not know who committed the murder, and the apprentice cannot reply by saying 'No. You're wrong because I know the butler did it.'[9]

Suppose the apprentice responds to the master this way:

The Apprentice's Counter-Argument
　　　1. If I do not know the list is complete, then I do not know the butler did it.
Not-3. I do know the butler did it.
Not-2. Therefore, I know the list is complete.

8　Barry Stroud, *The Significance of Philosophical Skepticism* (Oxford: The Clarendon Press, 1984), p. 108.
9　*Ibid.*, p. 109.

The Apprentice's Counter-Argument has a similar structure to Moore's Counter-Argument. Stroud thinks that the apprentice's response is unsatisfactory and thinks that Moore's response is also unsatisfactory. He writes, "If the apprentice did not even check the list, then for all he knows there could have been people in the house whose names were not on the list; he has to show how he knows that that possibility does not obtain. In the same way Moore would have to show how he knows that the dream-possibility does not obtain in his case. He cannot simply deflate the objection by reversing the philosopher's argument in the way he does."[10]

What might we say in defense of Moore against Stroud's criticism? Is Moore's counter-argument to skeptical challenges as bad as that of the apprentice detective? I don't think so. Stroud says that Moore would have to show *how* he knows that the dream-possibility does not obtain. But why would Moore have to show that? Such a requirement does not follow from PE. All that PE requires is that Moore be able to rule out the dream hypothesis to know that it is false. It simply requires that Moore know that he is not dreaming. It does not require that he show or explain *how* he knows it. Moreover, PE does not tell us that in order to know that he has hands he must *first* show *how* he knows that he is not dreaming, or even that he must first show *that* he is not dreaming. PE does not imply that Moore's knowledge that he has hands must be based on his knowing that he is not dreaming.

Of course, the apprentice's response strikes us as unsound. In the example, it seems clear that the apprentice's knowledge that the butler did it must be based on his knowledge that the list is complete. If we assume that the apprentice has not checked whether the list is complete, and really does not know that it is complete, then the apprentice's response is unsound. For in that case, he doesn't know that the butler did it, and the second premise of his counter-argument is false. Stroud is certainly right that if the apprentice does not know the list is complete, then his response is poor indeed. But if we think that the apprentice's counter-argument is poor when he does not know the list is complete, why think Moore's response is just as poor? Moore's response *would* be just as poor *if* the second premise of *his* argument were false if he did not know that he has hands. But unless we have some reason for thinking that Moore's second

10   *Ibid.*, pp. 121–22.

94

premise is false, then we have no reason for thinking that his response is as bad as the apprentice's.

On the other hand, suppose that the apprentice *does* know that the list is complete. Stroud considers the following possibility:

When [the master] pointed out that the apprentice does not know that the list is complete, the apprentice might have been in a position to answer 'No, I checked it, I also examined all the doors and the windows, none of the guests reported seeing anyone else, the trustworthy doorman admitted only those on the list, the social secretary was a reliable servant of the duke . . .', and so on. He might have good reasons for believing that the list is complete. He would thereby meet the detective's challenge and fulfil the condition for knowing by eliminative reasoning that the butler did it. There is nothing in the detective's objection which by itself implies that it cannot be met.[11]

Suppose the apprentice *has* checked the list, examined all the doors and windows, has strong evidence that the doorman and the duke's secretary are loyal servants, and so on. In this passage, the apprentice presents his evidence that the list is complete. He explains how he knows that the list is complete. We might think that this a better, more informative and enlightening response to the master than the apprentice's counter-argument. Still, none of this is required by PE. All that PE requires is that he know that the list is complete. It does not require that he explain how he knows it. But then, if we assume that the apprentice *does* have such evidence and knows that the list is complete, what's wrong with the apprentice's counter-argument? If he does know his premises, would his conclusion not follow? If the apprentice does know his premises, then his counter-argument is sound. But by the same token, we may say that if Moore knows the premises of his counter-argument, then his response is also sound. Of course, we might want Moore to explain how it is that he knows that he is not dreaming and how he knows that he has hands. That would provide us with a better, more informative, and enlightening response to the skeptical challenge. But again PE does not require such an explanation, and Moore need not give one in order to respond soundly to the skeptical challenge.

In sum, if the apprentice does not know that the list is complete, then his counter-argument is unsound and poor. But Stroud has given us no reason to think that Moore's counter-argument is also unsound. If Moore were

---

11 *Ibid.*, p. 122.

to explain how he knows that he is not dreaming, then we would have a more enlightening response to the skeptical challenge than his counter-argument. But such an explanation is not required by PE, and Moore's failure to give one does not show that his counter-argument is unsound or that it is as bad as that of the apprentice who has not checked his list. Still, in the next section we shall consider some reasons for thinking that Moore does *not* know that he is not dreaming. We shall consider some reasons for thinking that Moore cannot exclude this and various other possibilities that he must know in order to know what we ordinarily take ourselves to know.

5.3 THE SENSITIVITY REQUIREMENT AND THE CONTEXTUALIST CRITICISM

The Moorean response to skepticism faces other challenges. Central to many of the more recent challenges is the notion of sensitivity and its relation to knowledge. Let us say that:

D1 S's belief that p is sensitive = Df. If it were not the case that p, S would not believe that p.

The concept of sensitivity figures prominently in various accounts of knowledge, including Nozick's tracking account, various "relevant alternative" accounts, and contextualist theories of knowledge. Given the notion of sensitivity, the following sensitivity requirement on knowledge may seem intuitively plausible:

SRK (Sensitivity Requirement on Knowledge)   One knows that p only if one's belief that p is sensitive.

Many of our beliefs seem to be sensitive. Take, for example, h: I have hands. In those close possible worlds where h is false, I would not believe it. If it were the case that I did not have hands – say, because I'd lost them in an automobile accident – I would not believe that I had hands. So, my belief that h seems both sensitive and to satisfy SRK.

Other beliefs of ours, however, are not sensitive. Consider $\sim d$: I am not a handless brain in a vat being caused to have experiences as though I had hands. This belief is not sensitive insofar as in those possible worlds where $\sim d$ is false, I would still believe $\sim d$. In those closest possible worlds where I am so envatted and deceived, I would still believe that $\sim d$. So my belief that $\sim d$ fails to be sensitive and fails to satisfy SRK. So given SRK, I do not know $\sim d$.

96

But now consider again, PE, which Moore seems to accept. In order for me to know h, I must rule out any proposition that is incompatible with my knowing h. One such proposition is, of course, d – that I am a handless brain in a vat being caused to have experiences as though I have hands. According to PE, in order to know h, I must know that $\sim d$. But, as we have seen, given SRK and the fact that $\sim d$ is not sensitive, I don't know $\sim d$. So if we accept *both* PE and SRK, it seems that I do not know h. If we are not skeptics, this should give us pause. Something seems to have gone wrong. What should we give up?

Some philosophers – those who favor the relevant alternatives approach, relevantists – would have us reject PE in its unqualified form. Knowledge, they would tell us, does not require that we rule out all incompatible alternatives; it simply requires that we rule out all "relevant" alternatives. So instead of PE, they would have us accept instead:

PE′ If one is to know that p, then for every q such that q is relevant to one's knowing that p, and q is incompatible with one's knowing that p, one can exclude q (know that $\sim q$).

The relevantists would suggest that d is not a relevant alternative. So it need not be ruled out. I could thus know I have hands even though I cannot rule out d. Still, I could rule out *some* alternatives that are incompatible with my knowing that I have hands. For example, consider $\sim s$: I do not have stumps at the ends of my arms. The proposition that s is incompatible with my knowing that I have hands. But my belief that $\sim s$ is sensitive. In those close possible worlds, where $\sim s$ is false, I would not believe it. So SRK does not imply that I fail to know $\sim s$, and so I can rule out s.

The relevantist approach may seem attractive. It seems to offer us a way of responding to the skeptic. As we have seen, Moore and the skeptic accept PE. But given both PE and SRK, the skeptic argues that we cannot rule out various skeptical alternatives to Moorean common sense propositions such as I have hands. So the skeptic argues that we do not know such things. The relevantist argues that we should reject PE in favor of PE′. In doing so, he would still accept SRK and allow that we know that we have hands even though we do not know that incompatible skeptical alternatives are false.

The relevantist differs from Moore in rejecting PE. Adopting the relevantist line opens the way for further challenges to the Moorean stance. Consider again Moore's proof of an external world. Moore holds that he knows both that here's a hand (h) and there is an external world (e). But now consider i: there are only immaterial substances and I am having sense data of hands. *i* is incompatible with both *h* and *e*. But suppose one held that *i* is a relevant alternative to *e* but not to *h*. In that case, PE′ requires that to know *e*, one must rule out *i*, but one need not rule out *i* to know *h*. But Moore's belief that ∼*i* fails to be sensitive, for in the closest worlds where *i* is true, Moore would still believe ∼*i*. Thus, given PE′ and SRK, Moore would not know ∼*i* and not know *e*. The relevantist would hold that Moore's proof fails insofar as Moore's knowledge that *h* does not give Moore a basis for knowing *e*. This is so even if the relevantist agrees that Moore does know both *h* and *h implies e*. For the relevantist denies that knowledge is preserved under known implication. So, on these assumptions, Moore's proof fails not because it is question-begging, but because of PE′, SRK, and various assumptions about what counts as a relevant alternative.

Yet there are two problems with the relevantist position. First, what exactly counts as a "relevant" alternative? Why should *s* count as a relevant alternative to *h* that needs to be ruled out but not *d* or *i*? It is not clear that there is any clear and principled way of determining which alternatives are to count as relevant alternatives. Second, the relevantist approach permits what, to many, seems an "abominable conjunction" – namely, that I do not know that I am not a handless brain in a vat being caused to have experiences as if I had hands (∼*d*) *and* that I know I have hands (*h*). The relevantist view implies I can know *h* and further know that *h implies* ∼*d* and yet can't know ∼*d*. Abandoning the view that knowledge is preserved under known implication seems a high price to pay. But it is a price the relevantist is willing to pay to avoid accepting skepticism. But is this our only option?

Contextualist theories of knowledge offer us an alternative. Again, let us consider the following propositions:

1. I know *h* only if I know ∼*d*.
2. I do not know ∼*d*.
3. I know *h*.

As we have seen, Moore accepts 1, 3, and not-2. The skeptic accepts 1, 2, and not-3. The relevantist accepts 2, 3, and not-1. To many, 1, 2, and 3 each seem plausible, but they cannot all be true. One could reject any of the three because it conflicts with the others that one finds more plausible. Thus, Moore would reject 2 because it conflicts with 3 and 1, which he takes to be more reasonable. To some, however, Moore's rejection of 2 seems an unsatisfactory resolution of the puzzle. Keith DeRose suggests, for example, that the Moorean response of denying 2 is not very satisfying.

He writes, "Rejecting something on the grounds that other propositions one finds plausible imply its falsity is not very fulfilling when what one rejects is itself plausible."[12] He suggests that we might hope for a better resolution to the puzzle:

There is an alternative, and perhaps more promising, avenue of possible progress that Moore seems to overlook: One can hope for an *explanation* of how we fell into the puzzling conflict of intuitions in the first place. Perhaps we can explain how premises that together imply a conclusion we find so implausible can themselves seem so plausible to us. Such an explanation can take the form of explaining, for the member of the set that one seeks to deny, why it *seems* to us to be true, though in fact it's false.[13]

What we would like to have, according to DeRose, is a satisfying resolution of our philosophical puzzle, and this would involve some explanation of why 1, 2, and 3 all seem so plausible.

DeRose offers a contextualist solution to the puzzle concerning 1, 2, and 3. As we have seen, the relevantist denies 1. In contrast, contextualists accept 1. In this respect, the contextualist position sides with Moore and the skeptic. According to contextualists such as DeRose, the relevantist account that denies 1 leads to the "abominable conjunction" that one can't know $\sim d$ but one can know h.

However, like the relevantist, DeRose accepts SRK – one knows that p only if one's belief that p is sensitive. In addition, DeRose introduces the notion of the "strength of one's epistemic position." He writes, "The further away one can get from the actual world, while still having it be the case that one's belief matches the fact at worlds that far away and closer, the stronger a position one is in with respect to P."[14] The farther away one can get from the actual world where one's belief that p avoids belief–fact mismatch, the stronger one's epistemic position is with respect to p.

In order to know that p, one must be in a strong epistemic position. But how strong? What determines the relevant standard of strength? The answer is, roughly, that context determines how strong one's position must be in order to know. DeRose introduces the "rule of sensitivity." This tells us, "When it's asserted that S knows (or doesn't know) that P, then,

---

12 Keith DeRose, "Introduction: Responding to Skepticism," *Skepticism: A Contemporary Reader*, eds. by Keith DeRose and Ted A. Warfield (Oxford: Oxford University Press, 1999), p. 6.

13 *Ibid*, p. 6.

14 Keith DeRose, "Solving the Skeptical Problem," in *Skepticism: A Contemporary Reader*, p. 204

if necessary, enlarge the sphere of epistemically relevant worlds so that it includes the closest worlds in which P is false."[15] According to the rule of sensitivity, when someone makes (or denies) a knowledge claim that S knows that p, the truth of that claim depends on whether S would believe that p in the closest or least remote possible worlds where p is false. If S would believe that p in the least remote possible worlds where p is false, then S is not in a strong enough position and S does not know that p.

Now, in skeptical contexts, where skeptical hypotheses such as d are being considered, one must be in a strong enough epistemic position to know that $\sim d$. The standard of strength is quite high. So high in fact that we can't meet it. As the skeptic claims, one is not in that strong position, since one would believe that $\sim d$ in the closest possible worlds where d is true. So, in the skeptical context where d is being considered, one does not know $\sim d$. So, also in the skeptical context where d is being considered, 2 is true. But since, as we have seen, the contextualist holds that 1 is true in every context, it follows that in skeptical contexts where skeptical hypotheses such as d are being considered, one does not know h.

Does this mean, then, that skepticism is true? Not at all, according to the contextualist. For in ordinary contexts where skeptical hypotheses are not being considered, the standards of strength of one's epistemic position are much lower. In ordinary contexts, the rule of sensitivity requires only that we would not believe falsely that we have hands in the least remote possible worlds where we did not have hands. In the close possible worlds where I did not have hands, I would not believe that I did. So, my belief is sensitive with respect to those worlds. Thus, in ordinary contexts, I do know that I have hands. Thus, the skeptic who denies that 3 is true in every context is mistaken.

The key to resolving the puzzle of the intuitive plausibility of 1, 2, and 3, according to the contextualist, is to see that the truth of 2 and 3 is determined by the contextually determined standards of the strength of one's epistemic position. In skeptical contexts, the standards are higher, and one must be in a stronger epistemic position than in ordinary contexts. Given the higher standards of skeptical contexts, where one's belief must be sensitive to more remote possibilities of falsehood, one fails to know $\sim d$ and thus fails to know h. Thus, in skeptical contexts, 1, 2, and not-3 all turn out to be true. But given the lower standards of ordinary contexts,

---

15 *Ibid.*, p. 206.

where one's belief that h must be sensitive to the less remote possible worlds where not-h is true, one can know h, and thus in those non-skeptical contexts 3 is true.

Thus, according to contextualists, Moore's response to the argument from ignorance turns out to be unsound. For in the skeptical context where such a reply is raised, Moore infers that not-2 from the fact that 1 and 3 are true. Yet, according to the contextualists, 1, 2, and not-3 in skeptical contexts all turn out to be true. Further, the contextualists hold that they have, unlike Moore, offered a satisfactory explanation of why 1, 2, and 3 all seem true or plausible. Their answer is that in different contexts, each is true.

In spite of the plausibility and sophistication of the contextualist approach, I think that the Moorean response is superior. As we have seen, both the relevantist and the contextualist approaches accept SRK – that S knows that p only if S's belief that p is sensitive. A defense of Moore should begin by rejecting that requirement. There are serious problems with imposing a sensitivity requirement on knowledge. Ernest Sosa calls our attention to three sorts of problems.[16] First, consider our knowledge of necessary truths. Recall that a belief that p is sensitive only if if p were false one would not believe that p. How are we to understand such counter-factual claims where p is a necessary truth and cannot be false? Since a necessary truth is true in every possible world, there is no world in which it is false. It is hard to see how knowledge of necessary truths could be understood in terms of a sensitivity requirement. Second, consider the propositions, (1) p, and (2) I am not wrong in believing that p. Suppose my belief that p is sensitive and is an instance of knowledge. But what about (2)? My belief that I am not wrong in believing that p fails to be sensitive, for in those close possible worlds where p is false, I would still believe that p. Thus, given the sensitivity requirement, I would not know that I am not wrong in believing that p but I would know that p.[17] This is a counter-intuitive result, as bad perhaps as the abominable conjunction permitted by the relevantist's account. Surely, it seems plausible that if I can know p, then I can also know that I am not wrong in believing that p.

---

16 See Ernest Sosa, "How to Defeat Opposition to Moore," *Philosophical Perspectives* vol. 13 (1999), pp. 145–46.

17 Sosa also makes this point in "Proper Function and Virtue Epistemology," *Warrant in Contemporary Epistemology*, ed. by Jonathan Kvanvig (Lanham, MD: Rowman and Littlefield, 1996), pp. 271–81. Sosa notes that this problem is anticipated by Jonathan Vogel's "Tracking, Closure, and Inductive Knowledge," *The Possibility of Knowledge*, ed. by Steven Luper-Foy (Lanham, MD: Rowman and Littlefield, 1987).

Finally, Sosa suggests the following example. Suppose I drop a trash bag down the chute of my high-rise condominium. Presumably, I know that the bag will soon be in the basement. But what if (incredibly) the bag were not to arrive there, perhaps because it were somehow to be snagged on the way down or because of some other incredibly rare occurrence. My belief that the bag will soon arrive in the basement is not sensitive since if that belief were false (say, because of the snagging), I would still hold it. Still, I do know the bag will soon be in the basement even if that belief fails to be sensitive. I think, therefore, that there are good reasons for doubting SRK, and thus good reasons for rejecting the claim that Moore fails to know $\sim d$ because his belief that $\sim d$ is not sensitive.

In his defense of Moore, Sosa suggests that we should distinguish sensitivity from what he calls "safety." As we have seen, a belief is sensitive just in case had it been false, then one would not have believed it. In other words, S's belief B(p) is sensitive if and only if $\sim p$, then $\sim$B(p). Following Sosa, we may say that a belief is safe just in case were one to believe that p, then p would be true. Let us say S's belief B(p) is safe if and only if B(p), then p. As Sosa, points out, these are *not* equivalent because subjunctive conditionals do not contrapose.[18] If we distinguish sensitivity from safety, we may also distinguish between the sensitivity requirement on knowledge – that S knows that p only if S's belief that p is sensitive – and what Sosa calls "the safety requirement." The safety requirement tells us that S knows that p only if S's belief that p is safe.

One advantage of the safety requirement over the sensitivity requirement is that the former does not seem to face the sorts of problems noted here. My beliefs, for example, that p and that I am not wrong in believing that p could both be safe, even though the latter could not be sensitive. Moreover, the proposition that the dropped trash will soon be in the basement is for me safe, though not sensitive. In those close worlds where I were to believe it, it would be true. Finally, the safety requirement does not face the problem of the sensitivity requirement concerning our knowledge of necessary truths. The requirement of safety does not appear

---

18 For a defense of this claim, see Sosa, "How to Defeat Opposition to Moore." Here is one of Sosa's arguments: Let f = water flows from the faucet. Let o = the main valve is open. Then we have : (a) f → $\sim$(f & o), (b) $\sim$[(f & $\sim$o) → $\sim$f]. Sosa notes that if the subjunctive conditional contraposes, then the following must also be true: (c) (f & $\sim$o) → $\sim$f. But (c) seems intuitively unacceptable. We might also consider the following example. Let g = Tom is not in Gary, Indiana. Let h = Tom is in Indiana. Suppose that Tom hates Gary and would never go there. So we can say: (p) h → g. But the contrapositive is false: (q) $\sim$g → $\sim$h.

to face the problem of what one would believe if some necessary truth were false.

As we have seen, Moore's belief that $\sim d$ (that he is not an envatted brain being caused to have hand experiences) fails to be sensitive and fails to satisfy the sensitivity requirement on knowledge. In contrast, however, his belief that $\sim d$ is safe. For were Moore to believe that $\sim d$, $\sim d$ would be true. In those close possible worlds where Moore *would* believe that he is not an envatted brain, his belief would be true. (This is not, of course, to say that Moore *could* believe he was not so envatted only if it were true.) As Sosa, notes "In the actual world, and for quite a distance away from the actual world, up to quite remote possible worlds, our belief that we are not radically deceived matches the fact as to whether we are radically deceived."[19] Suppose we reject the dubious sensitivity requirement on knowledge, and opt instead for the safety requirement. Moore's claim to know $\sim d$ would meet that requirement.

DeRose thinks that a satisfactory resolution to our philosophical puzzle requires that we explain why 1, 2, and 3 seem so plausible. DeRose's explanation is that in ordinary contexts where we have more relaxed standards, 3 is true. But when skeptical hypotheses are introduced, the standards are raised, and 3, relative to those standards, is false and 2 is true. The Moorean claim to knowledge turns out to be false and the skeptical claim turns out to be true. Sosa, however, proposes a different explanation of our intuitions, and one that does not imply that the skeptic's claims are true. He suggests, "Those who find the skeptic's distinctive premise plausible *on the basis of sensitivity considerations* may thus be confusing sensitivity with safety, and may on that basis assess as correct affirmations of that premise."[20] Sosa suggests that, given the similarity between the requirements of sensitivity and safety, and the fact that they are so easy to confuse, it might be such an error that leads one to endorse the mistaken sensitivity requirement and in turn the claim that one does not know $\sim d$. Perhaps they find 2 plausible because they are confusing SRK with the requirement of safety. But again, Sosa notes, even if there is in fact no such confusion, all one really needs to explain the plausibility of the skeptic's premise is that it follow from something that is itself plausible. If one finds the sensitivity requirement plausible, then the skeptic's premise will also seem plausible. But we can allow that they are both plausible without holding that they are *true*. In short, Sosa suggests that we can explain *why*

19 *Ibid.*, p. 147.
20 *Ibid.*, p. 148.

2 seems plausible without endorsing the *truth* of 2, even in those contexts where skeptical hypotheses are being entertained.

There is a further advantage to Sosa's way of explaining the plausibility of 2 and the sensitivity requirement without endorsing their truth. Sosa reminds us that while we do feel the need to explain the plausibility of 2, there is also a need to explain why it also seems so *implausible*. Many people, after all, feel that it is not plausible to hold that one can never know that one is not a deceived brain in a vat. Many will feel, as Moore felt, that even in the face of skeptical hypotheses and scenarios, one really does know that one has hands and that one is *not* an envatted brain. Given the need to explain these powerful conflicting intuitions as well, it is not clear that the contextualist account is up to the task. For the contextualist view does not explain the powerful intuition that, even in the face of skeptical challenges, one does know, after all, that one is not envatted. One advantage of Sosa's explanation, then, is that it does explain how the skeptical claims can seem plausible yet false and the non-skeptical claims plausible yet true, even when skeptical scenarios are in play. At least that seems an advantage to those who would be sympathetic to the Moorean view that we do know 1 and know that 2 is false even when entertaining the skeptical hypotheses. Sosa's brief on behalf of the Moorean response clearly goes well beyond what Moore himself says on these matters, but it provides a way of vindicating the main points on which Moore himself would insist.

6

Chisholm, Particularism, and Methodism

We have seen that one criticism of the common sense tradition is that it presents no non-circular argument for the reliability of sense perception and memory. It is charged that in the absence of such an argument, one cannot know that those ways of forming beliefs are reliable. I have argued that while it is true that common sense philosophers such as Reid, Moore, and Chisholm fail to give such arguments, this does not preclude one's knowing that sense perception and memory are reliable. In this chapter, I will turn to another sort of criticism. Philosophers in the common sense tradition assume that they can pick out various instances of knowledge and use these to assess and evaluate various epistemic principles. But, according to the line of criticism I will consider, this is to put the cart before the horse. According to this criticism, knowledge of particular epistemic propositions such as "I know I have a body" is epistemically dependent on knowledge of general epistemic criteria or general epistemic principles. This objection holds that common sense philosophers incorrectly assume that they can pick out particular instances of knowledge without knowing the general epistemic criteria.

It will surprise no one that I think that the common sense philosophers are right and that this objection is mistaken. In discussing the views of Reid and Moore, for example, I have assumed that we can pick out instances of knowledge. I have assumed, for example, that small children and animals do know things. I have assumed, with Sosa, that Moore does know that he has hands and even the contextualist critics of Moore assume that, in ordinary contexts, Moore does know such things. But if the current line of objection is sound, then without knowing general criteria of knowledge, neither I nor Sosa nor Moore's contextualist critics do in fact know this. Moreover, the great majority of people who are not epistemologists and who do not know such general principles also fail to know that they know anything at all.

I have divided this chapter into six sections. In the first section, I explain what Chisholm takes to be the problem of the criterion and what he takes to be our options – namely, skepticism, methodism, and, Chisholm's favored option, particularism. In the second section, I look at some reasons for rejecting methodism and say what's wrong with methodism. Some of the reasons that Chisholm gives for rejecting methodism do not seem very good, yet others seem quite sound. In the third section, I will look at an objection to particularism based on the evaluative and supervenient character of epistemic properties. I will argue that the objection fails. The fourth, fifth, and sixth sections deal with a variety of objections to common sense particularism that have been raised by Moser, BonJour, and Butchvarov. Among the objections raised are that Chisholm's common sense particularism stifles epistemological inquiry, begs the question, does not take skepticism seriously, and is dogmatic and intemperate.

6.1 CHISHOLM AND THE PROBLEM OF THE CRITERION

In *The Problem of the Criterion*, Chisholm identifies two main questions in the theory of knowledge:

A. *What* do we know? What is the *extent* of our knowledge?
B. How are we to decide *whether* we know? What are the *criteria* of knowledge?

Chisholm distinguishes three general approaches to these two questions: skepticism, methodism, and particularism. Let us consider briefly what he says about each. He tells us that we can formulate the skeptical view as follows: "You cannot answer question A until you have answered question B. And you cannot answer question B until you have answered question A. Therefore, you cannot answer either question. You cannot know what, if anything, you know, and there is no possible way for you to decide in any particular case."[1] Chisholm's remarks indicate that the brand of skepticism he is considering here is a "second level" skepticism. This sort of skepticism does not deny that we know some things. It holds, rather, that if we do in fact know anything, we cannot know that we know it.

Unlike the skeptic, the methodist assumes that he has an answer to question B, and he then tries to answer question A. In other words, he

---

1 Roderick M. Chisholm, *The Problem of the Criterion* (Milwaukee: Marquette University Press, 1973), p. 14.

begins with a criterion of knowledge and then uses it to determine the extent of his knowledge. Chisholm takes the empiricism of Locke and Hume to be a species of methodism. According to Chisholm, Locke held that in order for a belief to be an instance of knowledge, it had to be related in certain ways to our sensations. Hume followed Locke in adopting the empiricist criterion, and found that when it is applied consistently, we have no knowledge of the physical world or other minds. Indeed, it seems that a consistent application of the empiricist criterion implies that we cannot have any knowledge of the past either. All we can know is that we have certain sensations here and now.

The particularist thinks he has an answer to A, and then he tries to work out an answer to B. Chisholm takes his common sense predecessors, Reid and Moore, to be particularists. Reid saw that Hume's criterion implied that we do not know that there are physical objects and other people, and since, Reid held, we *do* know such things, we know *ipso facto* that Hume's criterion is false. Moore held that he knew a great many things about the world − for example, that there are other people, that they have bodies and think and feel, that he was smaller when he was born, and so forth. And Moore held that he *knew* that he knew these things and that others know similar things. Chisholm says, "I suggest the third possibility is the most reasonable."[2]

Let us consider more closely what is involved in methodism and particularism. Ernest Sosa describes methodism and particularism as follows:

Particularism and methodism are meta-epistemological positions, for they tell us which justifies which of two sorts of *epistemic* knowledge. They tell us whether our knowledge of certain epistemic principles is based on our knowledge that we have certain bits of knowledge of a certain related kind (e.g., of the external world, that I have two hands), or whether, conversely, our knowledge that we have certain bits of knowledge of a particular kind rests on our knowledge of certain related epistemic principles.[3]

Following Sosa, I shall take methodism and particularism to make claims about epistemic dependence. Methodism claims that our knowledge of particular epistemic propositions depends on our knowing general epistemic principles, and particularism says it does not.

2   *Ibid.,* p. 21.
3   Ernest Sosa, "The Foundations of Foundationalism," *Noûs,* vol. 14 (Nov.) 1980, p. 558.

In order to clarify these views, let us consider the following three propositions:

(a) I have hands.
(b) I know I have hands.
(c) I am justified in believing that I have hands.

Propositions (b) and (c), unlike (a), are *epistemic* propositions. Both (b) and (c) make epistemic claims about what I know or am justified in believing. Furthermore, (b) and (c) are *particular* epistemic propositions rather than general epistemic principles or criteria that tell us under what conditions a belief is justified or an instance of knowledge. Methodism tells us that our knowing particular epistemic propositions such as (b) and (c) depends on our knowing some general epistemic principle or criterion. Particularism says that it doesn't. Instead, particularism holds that our knowing general epistemic principles depends on our knowing particular epistemic propositions.

In describing particularism and methodism, Sosa refers to "epistemic principles" and Chisholm to "criteria of knowledge." What sorts of principles or criteria do they have in mind? Presumably these would be principles that tell us under what conditions a belief has some epistemic feature such as being an instance of knowledge or epistemically justified. Such principles would have the following form: "If belief B has F, then B is an instance of knowledge (justified)" or "Belief B is an instance of knowledge (justified) if and only if B has F." Since the methodist holds that knowledge of particular epistemic facts depends on our knowing general epistemic principles, I assume that the relevant sorts of criteria would enable us to pick out particular epistemic facts by picking out non-epistemic facts and properties. Thus, though F might be a very complex property, it won't contain any epistemic properties. If F did contain some epistemic property, then presumably the methodist would hold that we would need some *further* criterion in order to know that some particular belief had F.

The sort of principle I take the methodist to require has its analogue in ethics. Consider, for example, moral principles of the form, "If act A has G, then act A is right." Simple hedonistic utilitarianism holds roughly that if an act A produces at least as much utility as any alternative act, then A is right. This simple form of hedonism attempts to tell us what non-ethical feature of acts – that is, producing a certain balance of pleasure over pain – makes acts right. Kant offers a similar sort of formula in suggesting that one's performing some act is right if and only if in performing that act one treats no one as a mere means. Such criteria in ethics would, if they were true, enable us to pick out right actions by picking out the non–ethical features of actions.

But what about principles of the following form: If belief B has F, then it is *prima facie* an instance of knowledge (justified)? Could methodism be committed only to the more modest view that knowledge of particular epistemic propositions depends on our knowing such *prima facie* principles? I assume, perhaps controversially, that the answer is "no." I take the methodist to hold that we need a criterion or epistemic principle that will tell us when a belief is an instance of knowledge, or justified. Principles of *prima facie* justification can only tell us when a belief is *prima facie* justified or *prima facie* an instance of knowledge. In other words, even if I know a principle of the form, "If belief B has F, then B is *prima facie* justified" and I know that B has F, nothing follows about whether B *is* justified. *Prima facie* principles don't provide the sort of criterion that the methodist thinks we need.

Given what we have said about the relevant sorts of epistemic principles or criteria, we may consider the following two theses. The first we may call "The Dependence of Particular Judgments" (DPJ) and the second, "The Dependence of General Principles" (DGP).

The Dependence of Particular Judgments (DPJ)
One's knowledge, if any, of particular epistemic propositions depends on one's knowing general epistemic principles or criteria.

The Dependence of General Principles (DGP)
One's knowledge, if any, of general epistemic principles or criteria depends on one's knowing particular epistemic propositions.

We may say that methodism accepts the first principle, DPJ. Particularism denies it. Perhaps we might also add that particularism accepts DGP and methodism rejects it.

We have seen that Chisholm thinks that particularism is closely tied to the common sense tradition. But the kind of particularism Chisholm endorses and that he finds in Reid and Moore is a "common sense" particularism that holds that we and others know various facts about the world around us. These include such obvious truisms as that there are other people, they have bodies, they think and feel, and so on. They also include various epistemic propositions – for example, that most people know their own names, they know that they have bodies, they know that there are other people. Common sense particularists deny that our knowledge of particular epistemic facts depends on our knowledge of general epistemic principles of the sort the methodist thinks are needed. And, obviously, they would deny that one's knowledge of various epistemic facts depends on one's knowing some criterion to the effect that "If one believes a common sense proposition, p, then one knows that p."

Still, the common sense particularism that Chisholm endorses and attributes to Reid and Moore seems to be only one species of particularism. There are other possible forms. For example, one might be a "Cartesian" particularist and hold that one's knowledge is confined to one's own existence and mental states, some simple necessary truths, and to the epistemic propositions that one knows such things. Such a Cartesian particularist would hold that he knows that he is thinking, and that he knows that he knows he is thinking. The class of epistemic facts that the Cartesian particularist claims to know is only a small subset of what the common sense particularist knows, but like the latter, the Cartesian particularist holds that his knowledge of these particular epistemic propositions does not depend on his knowledge of general epistemic principles. In contrast with common sense and Cartesian particularism, we can imagine forms of particularism that claim to know a great many more epistemic facts than the common sense particularist claims he knows. Thus, we can imagine someone claiming that his knowledge includes knowing there has been no evolution, knowing that his people have always inhabited the land they now occupy, knowing that he is God's appointed messenger, and so on. Such a person might claim that his knowledge extends well beyond that of the Cartesian or common sense particularist. Yet he would still be a particularist insofar as he held that his knowledge of these particular epistemic facts did not depend on his knowing any general epistemic principles.

Moreover, just as there are different species of particularism, it seems there are also different species of methodism. As we have seen, Chisholm rejects the empiricist methodism of Locke and Hume because it implies that we do not know various things that Chisholm and other common sense particularists think we know. But we may wonder whether there could be a "common sense" methodism that begins with a criterion for justification and knowledge that *is* compatible with our knowing the sorts of things that Chisholm, Moore, and Reid take themselves to know. Could there not be a common sense methodism that begins with a criterion that is such that, when applied, it turns out we *do* know, for example, that we have two hands, that there are other thinking people, and that we know such things? Why should common sense particularism be more reasonable for us to accept than common sense methodism? We shall consider some answers to these questions next.

Chisholm offers a variety of criticisms of methodism. Some of these, however, do not seem compelling. For example, according to Chisholm, the methodist holds that we must begin with a general criterion of knowledge. One line of criticism Chisholm offers is the following, "How can one *begin* with a broad generalization? . . . [The methodist] leaves us completely in the dark so far as concerns what *reasons* he may have for adopting this particular criterion rather than some other."[4] But as Robert P. Amico points out, there are several problems with this objection.[5] First, if Chisholm is objecting to the broadness of the criterion, it is not clear why being broad is a problem. Isn't broadness a desirable feature of a criterion? As Amico suggests, being broad would seem to be a desirable feature of a criterion because it suggests that the criterion would be applicable to many cases.

Furthermore, Chisholm criticizes the methodist because the methodist offers no reasons for his generalization. Perhaps Chisholm's objection is that the methodist gives us no argument as to why one should adopt the methodist's criterion as opposed to some other. But it is not clear that this objection must be fatal to the methodist. Suppose the methodist held that his knowledge of his criterion was basic or direct knowledge, that it was not based on any inference. Perhaps he might hold that his knowledge of his criterion was a matter of direct *a priori* insight. Or perhaps he might hold simply that the criterion is known immediately whether or not it is known *a priori*. He might take it to be akin to a Reidian "first principle." If methodism is not to be rejected because it begins with a broad criterion, or because no reasons or argument are given for the criterion, what's wrong with methodism? What is to be said in favor of Chisholm's common sense particularism?

In reflecting on methodism, we might begin with the following observation by St. Augustine, who wrote, "For he who says 'I know I am alive' says that he knows one single thing. Further, if he says, 'I know that I know I am alive,' now there are two; but that he knows these two is a third thing to know."[6] By being "alive," I take St. Augustine to be referring to being conscious or thinking. More importantly, I take him

---

4 Roderick M. Chisholm, *The Foundations of Knowing*, p. 67.
5 Robert P. Amico, *The Problem of the Criterion* (Lanham, MD: Rowman and Littlefield, 1993), pp. 78–79.
6 St. Augustine, *On the Trinity* in *The Essential Augustine*, ed. Vernon J. Bourke (Indianapolis: Hackett, 1974), p. 35

to hold that we can know that we are conscious or thinking and further that we can know that we know this. But our epistemic knowledge – our knowledge that we know this – is not epistemically dependent on our knowing some general criterion. It is not deduced from such a general epistemic principle. It as not as though St. Augustine suggests that when one says when he knows that he knows he is conscious, he knows *three* things: that he is conscious, that he knows he is conscious, and that he knows some criterion from which the knowledge of the second is deduced.

Along these same lines, we might consider again the following passage from Descartes's third *Meditation*:

I am certain that I am a thinking being. Do I not therefore also know what is required for my being certain about anything? In this first item of knowledge there is simply a clear and distinct perception of what I am asserting; this would not be enough to make me certain of the truth of the matter if it could ever turn out that something which I perceived with such clarity and distinctness was false. So now I seem to be able to lay it down as a general rule that whatever I perceive very clearly and distinctly is true.[7]

Note that in this passage, Descartes begins with a particular epistemic fact – his being certain that he is a thinking being. He then asks, "Do I not therefore also know what is required for my being certain of anything?" The general rule that "whatever I perceive very clearly and distinctly is true" seems to be supported by his recognition of his certainty that he exists. The recognition of the general principle is *not* epistemically prior to the apprehension of the particular epistemic fact. On the contrary, it seems that here, for Descartes, it is the apprehension of the epistemic fact that is epistemically prior to the apprehension of the general principle. In other words, it is *not* as though Descartes argues: (1) Whatever I clearly and distinctly perceive is certain, (2) I clearly and distinctly perceive that I am a thinking being, therefore (3) I am certain that I am a thinking being. It would be closer, I think, to Descartes's view to hold that he begins with the recognition of the particular epistemic fact and then accepts the general principle as the best explanation of that fact. In other words, Descartes begins with the epistemic fact that he is certain that he is a thinking being, and from this he concludes, with the help of some other assumptions about what must be the case to enjoy such certainty, that the

7 Descartes, René. *The Philosophical Writings of Descartes*, vol. 2, p. 24.

general principle is true. If this is right, then we should view Descartes, like Chisholm, as rejecting DPJ.

In reflecting on the views of St. Augustine and Descartes, we should consider our knowledge of our own existence and our own mental states. We do know, each of us, I assume, that we exist and that we are conscious. We also know a great deal about our mental states. We know, for example, that we are happy or sad or thinking about Boston. But not only do we know such things, we *also* know *that* we know them. But our knowing that we know we exist does not seem to be epistemically dependent or based on our knowing some general epistemic principle. I am not sure what the general principle would be. Ordinary people, were they to reflect on the matter, would know that they know they exist. Yet they would be hard pressed to give any epistemic principle on which such knowledge is based. Indeed, it is not clear that reflective epistemologists would all point to the same epistemic principle to explain how they know such a thing. Yet I think they have such higher-order knowledge without having knowledge of the relevant general principles. If this is so, then we should reject DPJ and methodism. Both would rule out our having the sort of epistemic knowledge recognized by St. Augustine and Descartes (and Reid, Moore, and Chisholm).

Of course, the sorts of epistemic knowledge that Chisholm and common sense philosophers take themselves to have is not confined to knowledge about one's own existence and one's own mental states. Their particularism ranges more broadly and includes more. Still, couldn't the common sense particularist argue in a similar way against DPJ and methodism? Consider the strategy that Chisholm's particularist predecessor, Moore, takes in his essay, "Hume's Theory Examined." Moore considers two of Hume's principles that imply, according to Moore, that he doesn't know that this pencil exists. Moore writes:

It seems to me that, in fact, there really is no stronger and better argument than the following. I *do* know that this pencil exists; but I could not know this, if Hume's principles were true; *therefore* Hume's principles, one or both of them are false. I think this argument really is as strong and good as any that could be used; and I think it really is conclusive. In other words, I think the fact that, if Hume's argument were true, I could not know of the existence of this pencil, is a *reductio ad absurdum* of those principles.[8]

---

8 G. E. Moore, "Hume's Theory Examined," *Some Main Problems of Philosophy*, p. 136.

Couldn't Chisholm take a similar strategy in arguing against methodism and skepticism? Consider the following epistemic propositions:

(i) It is beyond reasonable doubt that I was alive five minutes ago.
(ii) I know that I was alive five minutes ago.

Now suppose Chisholm were to argue this way:

Argument A

1. If DPJ is true, then I know (i) and (ii) only if I know the relevant general principles.
2. I don't know the relevant general principles.
3. But I know (i) and (ii).
4. Therefore, DPJ is not true.

Concerning 2, it seems clear that I do not know the relevant general principles. Yet it does seem that 3 is true. I do know (i) and (ii). I am not unique in this respect. Many people do not know the relevant general principles. Indeed, many *philosophers* do not know the relevant general principles. Some philosophers who *think* they know them accept principles that are incompatible with those accepted by other philosophers who also think they know them. But many of those who are thus ignorant of the relevant general principles do know similar epistemic propositions. They know, for example, that they know that they were alive five minutes ago. Just as we might reject DPJ and methodism because it would rule out our having the sort of knowledge that St. Augustine and Descartes point to, so we might reject DPJ and methodism because it is incompatible with our knowing (i) and (ii). What's wrong with DPJ and, thus, methodism and skepticism, is that if it were true, then I and others would not have the sort of epistemic knowledge that we do in fact have.

I think one can find at least the suggestion of a similar argument in Chisholm. He claims that one merit enjoyed by his common sense particularism, but not by methodism or skepticism, is that we do know many things after all, and that his common sense particularism corresponds with what we do know. As Chisholm says, one of the merits of his brand of particularisim is that it is compatible with the fact that "there are many things that, quite obviously, we do know to be true."[9] What Chisholm is telling us is that if methodism and skepticism were true, then we would not know particular epistemic propositions such as (i) and (ii). But since

9 Roderick M. Chisholm, *The Foundations of Knowing*, p. 69.

we do know such things (and since we don't know the relevant principles), methodism and skepticism are false.

"But," one might object, "don't we in fact know at least for (i) the relevant principle? Consider the principle that if S seems to remember that p, and S has no ground for doubting that p, then it is beyond reasonable doubt for S that p. Isn't it the case that one's knowledge of (i) depends epistemically on one's knowing this principle?" The critic might go on to point out that Chisholm himself defends an epistemic principle very much like this one.[10] There are three responses to this objection. First, the principle proposed is not of the right sort for the methodist, since "having no ground for doubt" is itself an epistemic concept. The methodist holds, I assume, that the needed criterion will pick out epistemic properties by picking out non-epistemic features of beliefs. One would need not only the principle in question, but some *further* principle that would tell us what non-epistemic condition must be satisfied in order for S to have no ground for doubting that p. It is far from clear what that additional principle would be. Second, it does not seem that the knowledge that I and others enjoy with respect to (i) is based on knowledge of that principle. Many people know (i) without knowing or believing the principle. Indeed, I knew (i) before I had ever entertained such a principle, and some epistemologists have known (i) without accepting *that* principle.[11] Finally, suppose one did know the principle in question, as, for example, an epistemologist might know it. It would not follow that one's knowledge of the particular epistemic fact was epistemically dependent on that knowledge. It might be that knowledge of the principle would help explain why one's belief was justified, and it might further enhance the justification for the particular epistemic belief even if the latter is not dependent on it.

Chisholm claims that one advantage of his common sense particularism is that it corresponds with what we do in fact know. But one might object that this advantage is not unique to particularism. Couldn't there be a "common sense" methodism that corresponds with what we ordinarily

10 Roderick M. Chisholm, *Theory of Knowledge*, 2nd edition, p. 81.
11 Indeed, Chisholm in the first edition of *Theory of Knowledge* accepts a different principle concerning memory. There he endorsed a more latitudinarian principle that if S seems to remember that p, then p is beyond reasonable doubt for S. Chisholm later rejected this principle for good reason. But at the time he wrote the first edition he did know it was beyond reasonable doubt that he had been alive five minutes ago. But he would not have had such knowledge if his belief had been dependent on his false epistemic principle. His particular epistemic principle was not dependent on his knowing the correct epistemic principle.

think we know? Amico writes, "Chisholm's position does have the merit of corresponding to what we ordinarily take ourselves to know. . . . [but] this merit only sets him apart from the empiricist, not all methodists. There is nothing about methodism that precludes the possibility of its coinciding with our common sense beliefs."[12] We might concede the possibility that someone could know much, if not all, of what the common sense particularist takes himself to know by basing such knowledge on a "common sense" criterion of knowledge. Still, I think this misses the point. The problem with methodism is *not* that it implies that it is *impossible* to know particular epistemic propositions such as (i) and (ii). The problem is rather that from methodism *and* what seems to be our ignorance of, or even justified belief in, the relevant general principles, it follows that we don't in fact know (i) and (ii). Given that we don't know the relevant principles, methodism implies that we don't know the sorts of things we do know. That's what's wrong with methodism.

6.3 SUPERVENIENCE AND PARTICULAR EPISTEMIC BELIEFS

In this section, I will consider an objection to particularism based in part on the view that epistemic properties are evaluative and supervenient properties. This objection holds that given the evaluative and supervenient character of epistemic properties, particularism must be false. Before we take up that line of objection, however, let us begin by considering the following objection:

1. It is reasonable to use particular epistemic propositions as data only if one is justified in accepting them.
2. In order to be justified in believing any proposition, *p*, one must show that *p* is true.
3. The common sense philosopher has not shown that the epistemic propositions he takes as data are true.
4. Therefore, it is not reasonable for him to take such propositions as data.

Now, how is one to show that the particular epistemic beliefs one accepts are true? How would one show, for example, that the proposition "My belief that I have hands is an instance of knowledge" is true? Presumably, this could be done by deducing that proposition from a criterion of knowledge. One might point out, for example, that one's belief had some property F, and then appeal to the general principle that

---

12   Robert P. Amico, *The Problem of the Criterion*, pp. 84–88.

beliefs having F are instances of knowledge. Given the conception of justification embodied in 2, it would be unsatisfactory for the common sense philosopher to take particular epistemic propositions as data without showing that they are true and without showing that his criterion of knowledge is true. If this argument is sound, then the common sense philosopher's claim that he can know various particular epistemic propositions without knowing some criterion of knowledge is simply mistaken. So, a defender of the common sense tradition must reject this argument.

Perhaps a defender of the common sense tradition might reject premise 1. As we saw in Chapter 1, one might defend the taking of various beliefs as data because they are inescapable or irresistible "framework" convictions. One might thus reject 1, denying that it is reasonable to use particular epistemic propositions as data only if they are epistemically justified. But, as I argued in that chapter, our particular epistemic beliefs do not seem to be irresistible framework convictions, and, moreover, philosophers in the common sense tradition *do* take particular epistemic beliefs to be epistemically justified.

I suggest that the common sense philosopher would reject the second premise. Moore, in his "Proof of an External World," held that he can know some propositions that he cannot prove.[13] Similarly, Chisholm and Reid both hold that there are some propositions that one can know without proof. And surely 2 is false. It leads to an implausible infinite regress. In order to be justified in believing any proposition, one would need to justifiably believe premises from which it followed and one would need, in turn, to justifiably believe premises from which those premises followed and so on. As a general conception of justification, 2 is false if we are justified in believing anything at all. Premise 2 would rule out our being justified in believing anything, including the general epistemic principles that the methodist appeals to, as well as the premises of the simple argument just considered. This argument, then, would offer little support for methodism.

Moreover, why should we think that justification through argument is necessary for particular epistemic propositions to have a positive epistemic status? It is not clear that it is necessary if we are careful to distinguish the *state* of being justified from the *activity* of justifying a proposition. Though the activity of justifying a proposition seems typically to involve giving an

---

13   G. E. Moore, "Proof of an External World," *Philosophical Papers*, p. 150.

argument for it, or at least giving reasons why it is true, this is not clearly necessary for one's being justified in believing a proposition.

We should remind ourselves that many prominent approaches to knowledge and justification do not take showing a proposition to be true to be necessary for knowledge and justification. Among these are various forms of foundationalism, coherentism, and externalism. For the foundationalist, some beliefs are justified or known in virtue of their being takings of what is given in experience. For the coherentist, it depends on the belief's belonging to a (sufficiently broad and comprehensive) coherent body of beliefs. For the externalist, whether a belief is known or justified depends on one's belief being the product of a reliable belief-forming process or one's "tracking the truth" of the proposition believed or one's belief being the product of a truth-conducive intellectual virtue. Neither foundationalism, coherentism, nor externalism endorse 2 or hold that knowledge or justification require showing or giving a rational argument for the proposition believed.

Consider again the epistemic propositions that the common sense philosopher takes as data – for example that I know I have hands, that most people know their names. Could not these propositions be known or justified for him at least in part because they are things whose truth he tracks or because his beliefs issue from some truth-conducive reliable process or intellectual virtue of belief acquisition? Furthermore, given his view that many of the things he takes himself to know are the sorts of things that almost everyone knows, his beliefs about what he knows cohere with his views about the cognitive powers of ordinary people. He is not, therefore, in the position of someone who has some reliable cognitive faculty and yet believes or has good reason to believe that no one has that faculty. On this view, the common sense philosopher's epistemic beliefs would be known or justified in part because of his reliability about the beliefs in question and the fact that those beliefs fit coherently into his picture about the cognitive powers of ordinary people. He is reliable about such things, and his belief that he is reliable about such things fits into a broader and coherent conception of the epistemic powers of others and himself.[14]

As a general thesis about justification, 2 is false. But one might think it more plausible when restricted to a particular domain of beliefs – namely,

---

14   I do not mean to imply that only an externalist or reliabilist account of our epistemic knowledge is plausible. For an internalist account, see Chapter 4 of Chisholm's *The Foundations of Knowing*.

the particular epistemic propositions that the common sense philosopher takes as data. One line of thought suggesting this more restricted view involves the plausible assumption that knowledge and justification are *evaluative* concepts or properties like the concepts or properties of right and wrong, good and bad. When one says that a belief is an instance of knowledge or justified, one seems to be making a favorable or positive evaluation of that belief. When one says that a belief is unjustified or unreasonable, one is making an unfavorable or negative evaluation of it. If we think of knowledge and justification in this way, then it is plausible to think that they, like other evaluative properties, supervene on other non-evaluative properties. Thus, if an apple is a good one, then it seems that it is good in virtue of various non-evaluative properties such as being sweet, crisp, and worm-free. The goodness of the apple supervenes on its having these non-evaluative properties. Similarly, if an act is right, it would seem to be so in virtue of its having certain other properties. Different theories of right action will pick out different "right-making" properties. So, for example, act utilitarianism will tell us approximately that an act is right in virtue of its producing a greater balance of pleasure over pain than any alternative act. A Kantian might hold that an act is right in virtue of its treating no one as a mere means.

Suppose, then, one thinks that knowledge and justification are evaluative and supervenient concepts or properties. How might this be thought to support DPJ and methodism? Consider the following passage from R. M. Hare's *The Language of Morals*:

[I]f we knew all of the descriptive properties which a particular strawberry had . . . and if we knew also the meaning of the word 'good', then what else should we require to know, in order to be able to tell whether a strawberry was a good one? Once the question is put this way, the answer should be apparent. We should require to know, what are the criteria in virtue of which a strawberry is to be called a good one, or what is the standard of goodness for strawberries. We should require to be given the major premiss.[15]

In Hare's view, knowledge of the descriptive or non-evaluative properties of a strawberry is not sufficient for one to know it to be good. Knowing that a particular strawberry is good requires or depends on knowing a standard or criterion for the goodness of strawberries. Though Hare refers to our knowledge of the goodness of strawberries, we may take him as making a general claim about our knowing the goodness of other sorts

---

15   R. M. Hare, *The Language of Morals* (Oxford: Oxford University Press, 1952), p. 111.

of particulars. A similar view about our knowledge of right and wrong is suggested, as we noted in Chapter 1, by John Stuart Mill. Mill writes: "A test of right and wrong must be the means, one would think, of ascertaining what is right or wrong, and not a consequence of having already attained it."[16] Mill seems to hold that our knowledge of the rightness or wrongness of particular acts must be epistemically dependent on our knowledge of some general criterion of right and wrong.

In the epistemic sphere, William Alston suggests a similar view about what is required for us to be justified in believing that a particular belief is justified. He writes:

In taking a belief to be justified, we are evaluating it in a certain way. And, like any evaluative property, epistemic justification is a supervenient property, the application of which is based on more fundamental properties . . . Hence, in order for me to be justified in believing that S's belief that p is justified, I must be justified in certain other beliefs, viz., that S's belief that p possesses a certain property Q, and that Q renders its possessor justified. (Another way of formulating this last belief is: a belief that there is a valid epistemic principle to the effect that any belief that has Q is justified.)[17]

Alston suggests that justified belief that a particular belief is justified is epistemically dependent on justified belief in a general principle. Moreover, he supports this view by appealing to the supervenient character of evaluative properties that makes justified attributions of them dependent on our being justified in general principles.

Reflection on the passages by Hare and Alston suggests the following general principle about justified attributions of evaluative properties:

EV(Evaluative) One is justified in believing that x has F (where F is some evaluative property) only if one is justified in believing both that (a) x has some non-evaluative property Q, and (b) whatever has Q has F.

Given EV, justified particular attributions of an evaluative property must meet *two* conditions. First, one must be justified in believing a general evaluative principle. Second, if Q is the property on which the evaluative property supervenes, one must be justified in believing that the thing in question has Q. EV seems to be a rationale for accepting DPJ and methodism.

16 John Stuart Mill, *Utilitarianism*, p. 1979.
17 William Alston, "Two Types of Foundationalism," *The Journal of Philosophy* vol. 73 (April) 1976, p. 170; Cf. "Some Remarks on Chisholm's Epistemology," *Nôus* vol. 14 (Nov.)1980, p. 579.

But is EV true? Does it provide us with any good reason for accepting DPJ? I think the answer to these questions is "no." First, we should not confuse claims about *exemplification* with claims about *application*. In assuming that evaluative properties are supervenient, we assume that they are exemplified in virtue of the exemplification of non-evaluative properties. But this is very different from Alston's claim that the application of an evaluative property is based on the more fundamental properties on which the evaluative property supervenes. That things exemplify evaluative properties in virtue of their having non-evaluative properties does not imply that the application or attribution of evaluative properties must be based on those more fundamental properties or on one's accepting a general criterion that states that connection. Thus, EV does *not* follow from the mere fact that evaluative properties are supervenient. Endorsing the supervenient character of epistemic properties does not commit one to the truth of EV.

Second, it seems plausible that there are justified attributions of supervenient properties that do not depend on justified belief in general principles. Many philosophers hold, for example, that mental properties supervene on physical properties. Thus, the mental properties of being in pain or being conscious supervene on various physical properties, such as various physical properties of one's brain. But does our knowledge that we are in pain depend on our knowing some *other* propositions such as (1) I have F, and (2) whatever has F is in pain? Surely I can know that I am in pain or conscious without knowing what physical properties pain or consciousness supervene on or knowing that I have those properties.

Third, it seems plausible to believe that there are justified attributions of supervenient evaluative properties that do not depend on justified belief in general principles. Consider, for example, someone driving in the mountains and suddenly coming on a spectacular vista. He thinks, "That's beautiful!" It is plausible that such a belief can be justified without one's being justified in believing some general principle about beautiful-making properties. We often form justified beliefs about the beauty of things when we are *struck* by their beauty. In such cases, our beliefs seem based on our experience of the thing, and not on our beliefs that it has some property F and that whatever has F is beautiful. In such a case, it might be that our non-doxastic experience, our seeing or hearing the thing's beauty-making properties, plays a role in justifying our belief that EV mistakenly assigns to beliefs, beliefs we often simply do not have or form.

I conclude that accepting the supervenient character of justification or knowledge does not commit one to accepting principle EV or DPJ. It does not commit one to rejecting the common sense particularism that Chisholm endorses and attributes to Reid and Moore. Still, there remain a variety of objections to common sense particularism that have been raised by very able philosophers. In the next three sections, I will consider some of these criticisms.

6.4 MOSER'S CRITICISM OF PARTICULARISM

Paul Moser raises a variety of objections to Chisholmian particularism. He points out that common sense judgments are sometimes false. He also raises questions about the epistemic status of the particular epistemic judgments that the common sense philosopher takes as data. Finally, Moser expresses doubts about "question-begging" philosophical strategies. In this section, I consider Moser's criticisms.

Moser takes the common sense tradition to hold "that we have pretheoretical access, *via* "intuition" or "common sense," to certain considerations about justification, and these considerations can support one epistemological view over others." Yet, Moser writes,

Intuitive judgments and common sense judgments can, and sometimes do, result from special, even biased, linguistic training. Why then should we regard such judgments as *automatically* epistemically privileged? Intuitive judgments and common-sense judgments certainly can be false, as a little reflection illustrates. Such judgments, furthermore, seem not always to be supported by the best available evidence. Consider, for instance, how various judgments of "common sense" are at odds with our best available evidence from the sciences or even from ordinary perception. It is unclear, then, why we should regard our intuitive or common sense judgments as the basis for our standards for justification.[18]

It is not clear, however, that the class of judgments Moser is picking out as "common sense judgments" is the same as the class of propositions that common sense philosophers such as Reid, Moore, and Chisholm take as data. Perhaps the class of things Moser is calling a "common sense judgment" is much broader than that which the common sense philosopher takes as data or takes as items of common knowledge. Perhaps it is so broad as to include whatever is only a widely held prejudice or widely accepted article of faith. It is hard to say, since Moser doesn't really tell us what is to count as a "common sense belief." As we noted

18 Paul Moser, Epistemological Fission," *The Monist* 81 (1998), p. 364.

in Chapter 1, Moore says that the phrase "common sense judgments" as used by philosophers is vague, and Moore is certainly not willing to defend everything that might be called a common sense judgment.

If Moser's criticisms apply to what he counts as a "common sense judgment," it is not at all clear that those same criticisms apply to the data of the traditional common sense philosopher, such as the propositions that there are other people, that they think and feel, that thay walk and talk. More importantly, it is not clear that they apply to particular epistemic propositions such as "I know I was alive five minutes ago" and "I know there are other people." These claims are not contrary to the best available evidence from the sciences or ordinary perception. Nor are they the products of "biased" linguistic training. Moreover, it seems that some of Moser's criticisms of "common sense judgments" actually presuppose the truth of many of the propositions that the common sense philosopher takes as data. It is hard to see how it might be true, for example, that some people's beliefs are the result of biased linguistic training unless it were also true that there are other people that think and talk and were alive yesterday (that they've been around long enough to be trained). It is hard to see how one could reasonably hold that some people's beliefs are the result of biased linguistic training unless it were also reasonable to hold that there are other people, that they have existed in the past, and so on. In any case, in spite of Moser's criticisms and reservations about what he takes to be "common sense beliefs," I think he has given us no good reason to believe that the propositions that the common sense philosophers take as data are quite the dubious lot he suggests they are. He has given no good reason to think, for example, that it is false that I know I was alive five minutes ago.

Moser also raises a question about the epistemic status of our particular epistemic judgments. He writes:

It is often left unclear what the epistemic status of the relevant preanalytic epistemic data is supposed to be. Such data, we hear, are accessed by "intuitions" or by "common sense." We thus have some epistemologists talking as follows: "Intuitively (or commonsensically), justification resides in a particular case like *this*, and does not reside in a case like *that*." A statement of this sort aims to guide our formulation of a notion of justification or at least a general explanatory principle concerning justification. A simple question arises: is such a statement *self*-justifying, with no need of independent epistemic support? If so, what notion of self-justification can sanction the deliverances of intuition or common sense, but exclude spontaneous judgments no better, epistemically, than mere prejudice or guesswork?[19]

Now, Moser suggests that the common sense tradition holds that these epistemic facts are accessed *via* "intuition" or "common sense." If this means that the common sense tradition holds that we have knowledge of epistemic facts on the basis of a faculty of common sense or intuition, as we have knowledge of the past on the basis of a faculty of memory, I see no reason to accept this claim. There is no reason to think that Moore and Chisholm hold such a view. Though one might be able to make a somewhat stronger case that this is Reid's view, I believe, on balance, that we should not attribute such a view to him either. So, let us set aside the view that particular epistemic propositions are known through a faculty of intuition or common sense.

If particular epistemic propositions do not derive their positive epistemic status by being inferred from general epistemic principles, then are they, as Moser asks, "self-justifying"? Moser wonders what a self-justifying proposition is supposed to be, and finds the notion of self-justification troublesome. Perhaps it is troublesome. How could a belief or a proposition justify itself? But, more importantly, why should we think that the positive epistemic status of a belief must derive either from self-justification or argument (rational justification)? Why must we take these to be the only sources of justification? Is it not plausible to think that various propositions about our immediate surroundings and the past are justified, at least in part, in virtue of their origin in perception and memory? The propositions, for example, that I have hands and that I had eggs for breakfast are evident to me, but they are not self-justifying, nor does their evidence depend on my having inferred their truth. By the same token, it is not clear why we should think that those epistemic propositions the common sense philosopher takes as data must be either inferentially justified from general epistemic principles or self-justifying. It is not clear that those are the only options. Perhaps they are justified in virtue of belonging to a (sufficiently broad and comprehensive) coherent body of beliefs or because they are the product of a reliable faculty or intellectual virtue or because they are appropriately related to what is given in experience. The notion that particular epistemic propositions must either be deduced from general epistemic principles or that they are self-justifying incorrectly excludes other possibilities.

19   *Ibid.*, p. 363.

But what *does* make particular epistemic beliefs justified? That, of course, is an interesting problem for epistemology. Moore wrote, "We are all, I think, in this strange position that we do *know* many things, with regard to which we *know* further that we must have had evidence for them and yet we do not know *how* we know them, i.e. we do not know what the evidence was."[20] Following Moore, we might distinguish between knowing *that* some particular belief is true from knowing *how* we know it or knowing *what* justifies that belief, and hold, in addition, that one can have the former sort of knowledge without the latter. Just as one might know that one has a certain mental property without knowing on what underlying physical property it supervenes, or one might know that some act is wrong without knowing what makes it wrong, so too one might know that one's belief is knowledge or justified without knowing what makes it so. So, in one respect, Moser is right that the epistemic status of these epistemic beliefs is unclear or problematic – namely, it is hard to say, even to the common sense philosopher who makes these judgments, *what* makes these beliefs justified. But from the fact that it is unclear what justifies these beliefs, it does not follow that one cannot know that they are justified. So the common sense philosopher may ask, with Moser, "What justifies particular epistemic propositions?" but we have seen no reason why he cannot answer that question by using his particular epistemic beliefs as data.

Many critics have charged that Chisholm's defense of particularism is "question-begging." Chisholm is aware that his defense of particularism is open to the charge of begging the question. What is his response? Well, he admits it. He holds that his defense of particularism *does* beg the question against those opposing views:

But in all this I have presupposed the approach I have called "particularism". The "methodist" and the "skeptic" will tell us that we have started in the wrong place. If we now try to reason with them, then, I am afraid we will be back on the wheel.

What few philosophers have had the courage to realize is this: we can deal with the problem only by begging the question. It seems to me that, if we do recognize this fact, as we should, then it is unseemly for us to pretend that it isn't so.

---

20   G. E. Moore, "A Defence of Common Sense," *Philosophical Papers*, p. 44.

One may object: "Doesn't this mean that the skeptic is right after all?" I would answer: "Not at all. His view is only one of the three possibilities and in itself has no more to recommend it than the others do. And in favor of our approach is the fact that we *do* know many things after all."[21]

But what is the sort of question-begging that Chisholm admits to here? He is not claiming that his knowledge of particular epistemic propositions is epistemically dependent on his knowing that methodism and skepticism are false. He is not admitting that he has given some argument in which the knowledge of the premises is epistemically dependent on knowledge of the conclusion. But then to what kind of question-begging is Chisholm admitting? I think Chisholm admits that his defense of particularism begs the question in the sense that it assumes to be true what others have denied. Chisholm assumes that we do know some particular epistemic facts without knowing the relevant general epistemic principles. The same, of course, is true of Argument A in Section 6.2. In this respect, both assume what the methodist and the skeptic deny.[22] In this respect, Chisholm's defense of particularism and Argument A beg the question against methodism and skepticism. But Chisholm maintains that in spite of the fact that his defense of particularism begs the question against these opposing views, it is nevertheless more reasonable to accept particularism than the opposing views.

But is such a question-begging defense or response philosophically acceptable? I take it that Chisholm thinks so, but consider the following opposing view expressed by Moser:

Questions under dispute in a philosophical context cannot attract non-question-begging answers from the mere presumption of the correctness of a disputed answer. If we allow such question begging in general, we can support *any* disputed position we prefer. Simply beg the key question in any dispute regarding the preferred position. Given that strategy, argument becomes superfluous in the way that circular argument is typically pointless. Question-begging strategies promote

---

21 Roderick Chisholm, *Theory of Knowledge*, 2nd edition, p. 121.
22 The sort of begging the question that Chisholm admits is that he assumes what the methodist and skeptic deny. Note that this is not a matter of "circular" reasoning, in which one's knowledge of the premises is epistemically dependent on one's knowledge of the conclusion. In Argument A, for example, one's knowledge of the premises is not epistemically dependent on knowledge of the conclusion. It is not as though one's knowledge of the premises is epistemically dependent on knowing that DPJ is false.

an undesirable arbitrariness in philosophical debate. They are thus rationally inconclusive relative to the questions under dispute.[23]

But must a question-begging strategy such as Chisholm's defense of particularism, or a question-begging argument such as Argument A, involve an intellectually unsatisfactory procedure, and must it be "rationally inconclusive"? I don't think so.

Moser assumes that if we allow question-begging arguments, then any position can be supported, and argument in general becomes pointless. Perhaps this is true if one thinks that supporting a position involves nothing more than giving an argument for it. But of course we might hold that there is more to supporting a position than merely giving an argument for it. We might hold that supporting a position involves giving an argument for it that has premises that one knows or that one is justified in believing. In this stronger, "epistemic" sense of supporting a position, it does not follow that one can support every proposition even if we allow question-begging arguments. For some question-begging arguments will have premises that are not known and that one is not epistemically justified in believing. We need not hold, therefore, that if we allow question-begging arguments, then every position can be supported in this stronger epistemic sense. Consequently, we need not hold that if we allow question-begging arguments, then all question-begging arguments are epistemically on a par in terms of the strength of epistemic support that they provide their conclusions.

Further, is it true that question-begging arguments are "rationally inconclusive"? Suppose we take an argument that has premises that are known and that imply the conclusion to be a rationally conclusive argument. It then seems that an argument could be *both* question-begging insofar as it assumes some premise denied by someone *and* rationally conclusive insofar as the argument is valid and the premises are known. If "begging the question" and "rationally conclusive" are understood in this way, then it is false that no question-begging arguments are rationally conclusive. I would say that Chisholm's defense of particularism and Argument A *are* rationally conclusive, since the arguments are valid and many people know the premises, *and* they are question-begging insofar as they assume premises that some have denied. But from the fact that *some* arguments are both question-begging and rationally conclusive,

---

23   Paul Moser and Arnold vander Nat, *Human Knowledge*, 2nd edition, p. 27.

it does not follow that *all* question-begging arguments are rationally conclusive. Some are rationally conclusive and some aren't. Endorsing some question-begging arguments as rationally conclusive does not commit us to endorsing them all or to regarding argument as pointless. Furthermore, I would say that if our aim is to reach the truth about the philosophical questions that concern us, then such "question-begging" is not always intellectually vicious. There is nothing intellectually vicious or unsound in reasoning from premises one knows or taking as data what one knows, even if someone has denied it. On the contrary, reasoning from what one knows would seem to be intellectually sound.

Still, I think that one might admit that Chisholm's defense of particularism and Argument A are in another sense "inconclusive." They are inconclusive in the sense that they will not settle or conclude the debate between the particularist, the methodist, and the skeptic. I doubt that any committed methodists or skeptics will say, "Ooops! I really blundered there!" But why must we judge the merits of Chisholm's defense of particularism or Argument A by how well it settles that debate? Why not judge it instead by its appeal to a rational, yet uncommitted, audience – to a thoughtful and open-minded jury that considers the plausibility of the premises? More importantly, why must we judge the merits of Chisholm's defense or Argument A by how well it settles a dispute? After all, how many good philosophical arguments really enjoy that feature? Indeed, how many good philosophical arguments *don't* beg the question against some other position? In any case, the settlement of disputes is but one possible aim of philosophical reflection and reasoning, and resolving a dispute but one merit or virtue of an argument. Surely there are other aims, such as extending our knowledge and understanding, and other merits or virtues, such as yielding knowledge of the conclusion. From the fact that the argument or reasoning does not settle the debate between the various parties, it does not follow that it yields no knowledge of the conclusion. In Chapter 1, I cautioned against the assumption that the common sense philosopher is engaged in the project of trying to refute or convince the skeptic by arguing from mutually accepted premises. Chisholm, Reid, and Moore take as data what they take themselves to know, and we should view them not as attempting to carry on a debate within the rules of rhetoric, but as attempting to know the answers to the philosophical questions with which they and others are concerned.

Laurence BonJour criticizes Chisholm's particularist approach as "dogmatic" and "question-begging." Concerning particularism, BonJour writes in *The Structure of Empirical Knowledge*:

The main objection is that such an approach has the effect of ruling out even relatively weak versions of skepticism absolutely and conclusively from the very beginning of one's epistemological inquiry in a way that is both question-begging and dogmatic. It may be reasonable to hold on commonsense grounds that there is some *presumption*, perhaps even a relatively strong one, against skepticism and in favor of the thesis that the scope of our knowledge is pretty much what we think it is. But to turn this presumption into an absolute bar against skepticism seems in any case entirely too extreme. If knowledge requires that one be in possession of a good reason for thinking one's beliefs to be true, then the possibility of skepticism cannot be eliminated in this relatively easy way.[24]

Again, more recently, BonJour writes:

[T]o accept commonsense convictions as Moore and other particularists do, does appear to rule out illegitimately even the possibility that skepticism might in fact be true, that common sense might be mistaken. And, equally importantly, if this solution is taken at face value, it would have the effect of stifling or short-circuiting epistemological inquiry at least as effectively as would simply acquiescing in skepticism.[25]

BonJour makes a variety of objections here. Let us begin with the objection that particularism "stifles" epistemological inquiry. Is this true? It depends on what one takes to be involved in epistemological inquiry. It does not seem that particularism stifles the inquiry into the search for criteria of knowledge and justification. On the contrary, Chisholm took the search for such criteria to be one of the principle aims of epistemological inquiry. Even if we assume that we do know various things about the world around us, we might still wonder how we know them. We might still seek philosophical answers to that question. Here the situation seems no different from that which one might find in moral philosophy. We might be convinced that certain actions are morally wrong, and yet

---

24 Laurence BonJour, *The Structure of Empirical Knowledge*, pp. 12–13.
25 Laurence BonJour, *Epistemology* (Lanham, MD: Rowman and Littlefield, 2002), p. 265.

seek to explain why they are wrong. I am convinced, for example, that it would be morally wrong for me now to torture my secretary to death. But is it wrong because it fails to maximize utility, because it fails to treat her as an end in herself, or for some other reason? Even the assumption that we know such actions are wrong need not stifle our attempts at moral inquiry into the criteria of right and wrong. Moreover, even if we assume that we do know the sorts of things that the skeptic denies we do, we need not treat skeptical arguments as "idle" and hold that they ought to be ignored. As we saw in Chapter 1, Strawson takes such a view. But that need not be the position of the common sense particularist. One might adopt a particularist approach and continue to take skeptical arguments seriously, attempting to identify what plausible, yet mistaken, assumptions yield skeptical conclusions. Sosa's treatment of skeptical arguments, and the sensitivity requirement illustrate one way in which one could combine both a particularist approach with careful epistemological inquiry. I do not see, therefore, that particularism stifles epistemological inquiry.

BonJour also objects that particularism appears to rule out illegitimately the possibility that skepticism is true. But here we must be careful. Does particularism rule out the possibility that skepticism is true? Not if the relevant sense of "possibility" is that of "logical possibility." Both Chisholm and Moore admit that it is logically possible that skepticism is true. They grant that it is logically possible that we know nothing or next to nothing about the external world. They grant the possibility of deception by evil demons or dream experiences. Of course, both Chisholm and Moore would deny that skepticism is "epistemically possible" in the sense that, given what we know, it is reasonable to believe that skepticism is true. Both would hold that since we do know that we know much about the external world, it is not reasonable to accept skepticism about the external world. But why should this rule out the possibility of skepticism *illegitimately*?

I think part of the answer according to BonJour is reflected in the following passage:

[T]o have a strong reason to think there is justification for beliefs about the external world is not the same thing as to be actually able to specify such a justification in detail – something that must be possible if it genuinely exists. Thus this presumption can at least in principle be defeated by the long-term failure of epistemologists to actually succeed in specifying the justification in question. Many epistemologists would no doubt want to say that this failure has already been long-term enough to warrant the conclusion that the presumption in favor of common sense is in fact mistaken. The opposing view – which I am inclined to opt for (albeit tentatively) – is that the failure so far is adequately explained by the extreme difficulty and complexity of the issues – and also by the pronounced tendency of philosophers in the twentieth century especially to evade the main issues rather than attempting to deal with them in a direct way.[26]

BonJour's view is that we may assume that there is a presumption in favor of the view that our common sense beliefs are justified and do amount to knowledge. But this presumption is *defeasible*. It can be defeated by the long-term failure of epistemologists to succeed in specifying the nature of the justification for our common sense beliefs. According to BonJour, our common sense beliefs in the event of such a failure are *not* justified and do not amount to knowledge. The problem with common sense particularists is that they do not take this possibility of defeat seriously. In claiming to really know various things about the external world, the common sense philosophers illegitimately ignore this possibility of defeat, and that is why their claims to knowledge illegitimately rule out skepticism.

BonJour tells us that the presumption in favor of our common sense beliefs would be defeated by our long-term failure to specify the justification for those beliefs. What does this mean? What does it mean to "specify such a justification in detail" for our common sense beliefs? In *The Structure of Empirical Knowledge*, it appears to mean providing some argument for the reliability of our ways of forming common sense beliefs that is free from epistemic circularity. To specify such a justification for perceptual and mnemonic beliefs would entail providing some non-circular argument that beliefs formed in those ways are likely to be true. On this reading, then, BonJour is telling us that our common sense beliefs are justified, and amount to knowledge only if it is possible to give a non-circular argument for the claim that they are reliably formed. In other words, our common sense beliefs are justified only if it is possible to give some non-circular meta-justificatory argument for the reliability of our ways of forming common sense beliefs. Again, this seems to be BonJour's point in *The Structure of Empirical Knowledge*, where he writes,

26   *Ibid.*, p. 265–66.

"This presumption is completely defeasible by a failure to find any account of the standards of epistemic justification which yields results in agreement with common sense and which can adequately be defended by philosophical argument – where one main requirement for a satisfactory defense is a metajustification or vindication of the sort discussed above."[27] (The relevant sort of non-circular meta-justification is described in Section 2.1.)

Given what has been said in earlier chapters, I shall be brief. I do not think that having perceptual or mnemonic knowledge requires that one know that perception and memory are reliable. That is not required for what Sosa calls "animal knowledge." Suppose, on the other hand, reflective knowledge does require that one know that one's ways of forming beliefs are reliable. I have argued, following Sosa, that such knowledge need not be based on arguments free of epistemic circularity. If this is so, then the failure, even the long-term failure, of epistemologists to specify a justification in detail for our common sense beliefs, where this is understood as giving a non-circular argument for the reliability of our ways of forming common sense beliefs, implies nothing about the possibility of having reflective knowledge. Reflective knowledge simply does not require the sort of argument BonJour claims it does. The particularist's claims to knowledge, animal or reflective, are not defeated or defeasible by the sort of failure BonJour envisions. Consequently, the particularist may legitimately ignore the possibility of the sort of failure that concerns BonJour, and the particularist's claims to knowledge do not for that reason illegitimately rule out skepticism.

6.6 BUTCHVAROV'S OBJECTION

Chisholm writes, "We reject the sceptical view according to which there is no reason to believe that the premises of an inductive argument ever confer evidence upon the conclusion. If the sceptical view were true, then we would know next to nothing about the world around us."[28] Being a good particularist, Chisholm holds that since we do know such things, we know that this skeptical view is false. Panayot Butchvarov cites this passage

---

27 Laurence BonJour, *The Structure of Empirical Knowledge*, p. 13.
28 Roderick M. Chisholm, "On the Nature of Empirical Evidence," *Empirical Knowledge*, ed. by Roderick M. Chisholm and Robert J. Swartz (Englewood Cliffs, N.J.: Prentice-Hall, 1973), p. 232.

and warns, "We must guard against intemperate and dogmatic attitudes such as those expressed [by Chisholm]."[29] But why is Chisholm's attitude toward skepticism intemperate or dogmatic? Unfortunately, Butchvarov doesn't tell us. It is not as though Chisholm gives no reasons for rejecting skepticism. On the contrary, his reasons seem quite clear – skepticism implies that we know next to nothing about the world around us, but since that's false, it follows that skepticism is false. Perhaps Butchvarov thinks it is intemperate and dogmatic to claim that it is false that we know next to nothing about the world around us. But is such a claim really intemperate? That seems rather overstated. Indeed, perhaps itself a bit intemperate. Perhaps the claim is dogmatic? Dogmatic in the sense of an arrogant assertion? That seems rather harsh. Would it *really* be an arrogant assertion to claim one does know that there are other people? Perhaps it is dogmatic in the sense that Chisholm doesn't give any reasons in the passage cited for claiming that it is false that we know next to nothing about the world around us. But then wouldn't Butchvarov's charge that Chisholm's attitude is dogmatic be just as dogmatic, since he gives no reason for claiming that it is? And in any case, the mere fact that one asserts something without giving a reason for it does not imply that it is dogmatic. People non-dogmatically assert things everyday without actually giving reasons for them. Maybe the idea is that Chisholm asserts things without being able to give any reasons for his claims. But that's just false. Though they won't impress the skeptic, reasons can be given by Chisholm for thinking that he knows many things about the world around him, reasons having to do with his perceptual takings and what he seems to remember. It is hard to know why Butchvarov thinks Chisholm's attitude is dogmatic or intemperate.

I don't think that I have said anything in this chapter that will convince a committed methodist or skeptic that his position is wrong. I have considered both some reasons why methodism and DPJ might seem attractive and some criticisms of Chisholm's common sense particularism, but those reasons and criticisms do not seem to me to be very compelling. I wish I had something better or wiser to say in defense of common sense particularism, but I haven't. Like Chisholm, I do not pretend that I have avoided begging the question against the methodist or the skeptic, and anything further I could say would be question-begging in the same way

---

29 Panayot Butchvarov, *Skepticism about the External World* (Oxford: Oxford University Press, 1998), p. 8.

7

Common Sense and A Priori *Epistemology*

In this chapter, I consider some views about the nature of *a priori* knowledge and justification and their relationship to the common sense tradition. I do so for three reasons.

First, some philosophers have *both* adopted a common sense approach to the theory of knowledge and held that some epistemic principles are knowable *a priori*. Can one consistently do both? Whether one can consistently do both depends on the nature of *a priori* knowledge and justification. Some accounts of *a priori* justification, such as Chisholm's, treat basic *a priori* justification as certain and indefeasible. But this gives rise to what we may call "the problem of insulation." If epistemic principles are instances of basic *a priori* beliefs, and if basic *a priori* beliefs are indefeasible and thus cannot be reasonably rejected when they conflict with particular epistemic judgments, then how can particular epistemic beliefs be data for assessing those principles? The epistemic principles would be "insulated" from criticism from the standpoint of our particular epistemic beliefs, and that would be an unhappy result for the common sense particularist.

Second, it is worth thinking about the nature of *a priori* justification and knowledge because of the role that *a priori* justification, or claims to *a priori* justification, play in philosophical thought. Many philosophers have claimed that various metaphysical, epistemological, and moral claims are knowable *a priori*. Indeed, some might think that philosophy is primarily an *a priori* enterprise, that it is the *a priori* character of philosophical reflection that distinguishes it from other forms of inquiry such as scientific inquiry. If one thinks of philosophical inquiry as being exclusively or primarily an *a priori* enterprise, and if one thinks that basic *a priori* justification

135

cannot be defeated, then the appeal to various common sense propositions that are not known or justified *a priori* will seem illegitimate or unphilosophical. If our basic *a priori* beliefs are indefeasible, and insulated from defeat by our common sense beliefs, then, again, this may be seen as a reason to reject the common sense tradition.

Finally, some defenders of a Moorean response to skepticism go to the other extreme, rejecting most or all "philosophical" or "rational intuitions." William Lycan, for example, defends the Moorean response by casting doubt on the allegedly *a priori* intuitions that conflict with Moore's claims to knowledge about the external world. Lycan seems to suggest that skeptical arguments rest on allegedly *a priori* intuitions. He suggests that such *a priori* intuitions confer little or no epistemic justification, and so they are much less justified than the Moorean claim to knowledge with which they conflict. Thus, one is more justified in accepting the Moorean claims to knowledge than the premises of the skeptical argument. In his attempt to defend the Moorean response to skepticism, however, Lycan seems to be throwing out the *a priori* baby with the skeptical bath water, and that seems an awfully high price to pay in defending Moore. The truth seems to lie somewhere between these two extremes.

7.1 CHISHOLM ON EPISTEMIC PRINCIPLES AND *A PRIORI* KNOWLEDGE

Several philosophers have suggested that some substantive epistemic principles are knowable or justified *a priori*. For example, H. H. Price writes:

[T]he fact that a material thing is perceptually presented to the mind is *prima facie evidence* of the thing's existence and of its really having that sort of surface which it ostensibly has; . . . there is *some presumption in favour of* this, not merely in the sense that we do as a matter of fact presume it (which of course we do) but in the sense that we are entitled to do so.[1]

Price goes on to say, "Clearly, the principle is *a priori*; it is not the sort of thing we could learn by empirical generalization based upon observation

---

1   H. H. Price, *Perception* (New York: Robert McBride, 1933), p. 185.

of the material world."[2] Price is not alone in thinking that such general epistemic principles are *a priori*. More recently, Robert Audi writes,

[W]hen a visual belief arises in such a way that one believes something in virtue of *seeing that* it is so, normally the belief is justified. If I see that the tree is straight and, in virtue of seeing that it is, believe that it is, then (normally) I justifiably believe that it is. I say *normally* because one's justification can be overridden.[3]

Of this and similar principles, Audi writes, "I believe that it is more reasonable, though by no means obviously correct, to suppose that at least some principles about the conditions for justification are a priori. I would include various principles expressing the ways in which . . . justification is produced by basic sources."[4] Though Audi is clearly cautious about claiming that some epistemic principles are justified *a priori*, he suggests that it is reasonable to believe that indeed some are.

Chisholm's views about the epistemic status of epistemic principles are, at best, mixed. In *The Problem of the Criterion*, he defends his particularist approach to discovering general epistemic criteria. He writes, "The criteria that we formulate, if they are adequate, will be principles that are necessarily true."[5] Again, in his 1990 essay "The Status of Epistemic Principles," Chisholm presents the following epistemic principle:

(A) If (i) a person S thinks he perceives that there is an F, if (ii) it is epistemically in the clear for S that there is something that he perceives to be F, then it is beyond reasonable doubt for S that he is perceiving an F.[6]

Chisholm takes epistemic justification to be an evaluative notion. To say that a belief is "beyond reasonable doubt" is to make a favorable evaluation of that belief. Chisholm compares A with the following ethical principle that, for the sake of argument, we may pretend is true:

(B) If an act is such that (i) performing it would result in more pleasure and less pain than any other act that a person S could perform, and (ii) if the act is one of those that S is able to perform, then S ought to perform that act.

2 *Ibid.*, p. 186.
3 Robert Audi, *Belief, Justification, and Knowledge* (Belmont, CA: Wadsworth Publishing, 1988), p. 14.
4 *Ibid.*, p. 154.
5 Roderick M. Chisholm, *The Problem of the Criterion*, p. 37.
6 Roderick M. Chisholm, "The Status of Epistemic Principles," *Noûs* vol. 24, (April) 1990, p. 209.

Chisholm says that both A and B are *normative supervenience principles*. According to Chisholm, to say that A and B are normative supervenience principles is to imply that they are necessarily true. In every possible world, whoever satisfies the antecedent is in the evaluative or normative state described in the consequent. Chisholm adds:

A further feature of such principles is sometimes put by saying that they are "synthetic *a priori*". The expression "synthetic" is suggested by the fact that the principles cannot be said to be "true in virtue of their form". And since the principles are necessary, it is concluded that if we can *know* them to be true, then such knowledge is *a priori*.[7]

Chisholm suggests that insofar as normative supervenience principles such as A and B express something *necessarily* true, it seems that if they can be known, then such knowledge is *a priori*.

A year earlier, however, in the third edition of *Theory of Knowledge*, Chisholm again presents a variety of epistemic principles, including the following:

(C) If S *seems to remember* having been F, and if it is epistemically in the clear for him that he remembers having been F, then it is *beyond reasonable doubt* for S that he remembers having been F.[8]

(D) If S takes there to be an F and if it is beyond reasonable doubt for S that he is perceiving something to be F, then it is *evident* for S that he is perceiving something to be F.[9]

But here Chisholm claims that principles such as C and D are *not* known *a priori*: "It would not be plausible to say that they are *a priori* since many philosophers have understood them without thereby seeing that they are true."[10]

Chisholm seems clearly ambivalent about the *a priori* status of his epistemic principles. But we might note that Chisholm's ambivalence extends to other areas as well. For example, concerning our knowledge of what

---

7   *Ibid.*, p. 210.

8   Roderick M. Chisholm, *Theory of Knowledge*, 3rd edition (Englewood Cliffs, N.J.: Prentice-Hall, 1989), p. 68.

9   *Ibid.*, p. 72.

10 *Ibid.*, p. 72

is intrinsically good, he writes:

It has been held, not without some plausibility, that certain ethical sentences express what is synthetic *a priori* . . . consider the sentence, "All pleasures, as such, are intrinsically good, or good in themselves, whenever and wherever they may occur". If this sentence expresses something that is known to be true, then what it expresses must be synthetic *a priori*.[11]

Given these remarks one could take the axiological principle "If X is an instance of pleasure, then X is intrinsically good" to be a normative supervenience principle akin to epistemic principles such as C and D. We may say that it is necessarily true that whenever the antecedent obtains, so too does the normative or evaluative consequent. Yet here again we find that Chisholm has mixed views. First, recall Chisholm's claim that it is *implausible* that epistemic principles such as C and D are known *a priori* because many philosophers have understood them without seeing that they are true. Surely the same consideration would apply to the axiological claim. Many philosophers have understood the claim that "all pleasures, as such, are intrinsically good whenever and wherever they occur" without thereby seeing that the claim is true. Furthermore, we may note the stand Chisholm takes in the second edition of *Theory of Knowledge*. There he suggests that our knowledge of intrinsic value is not based on reason, that it is not a matter of *a priori* insight. Instead, Chisholm follows the Austrian tradition that locates knowledge of value in *das Wertgefuehl*, in our feeling for value and various emotional experiences. So, again, the ambivalence we find in Chisholm's writings concerning the *a priori* status of epistemic principles also extends to our knowledge of other normative and evaluative claims, such as claims about what is intrinsically good.

Let us turn to Chisholm's account of *a priori* knowledge in the third edition of *Theory of Knowledge*. His account, I suggest, is fairly traditional. He explicates it in terms of a series of definitions. The fundamental concept is that of an axiom:

(D1) h is an axiom = Df. h is necessarily such that (i) it is true, and (ii) for every S, if S accepts h, then h is certain for S.[12]

11 *Ibid.*, p. 36.
12 *Ibid.*, p. 28.

Given D1, the following propositions may be said to be axioms: *All men are men*; *if some Greeks are men, then some men are Greeks*; and *all round things have a shape*. Chisholm says that for those who really do consider these propositions, they may be said to be *axiomatic* in the following sense:

(D2) h is *axiomatic* for S = Df. (i) h is an axiom, and (ii) S accepts h.[13]

According to Chisholm, our *a priori* knowledge is not limited to what is axiomatic for us, for we know some things *a priori* because we can see that they follow from what is axiomatic for us. In this way, we can know the Pythagorean Theorem *a priori*, even though it is not axiomatic for us. To capture this broader notion of the *a priori* Chisholm suggests:

(D3) h is known *a priori* by S = Df. There is an e such that (i) e is axiomatic for S, (ii) the proposition e implies h is axiomatic for S, and (iii) S accepts h.[14]

Given this understanding of *a priori* knowledge, everything we know *a priori* is either axiomatic or we know that it follows from something we know with certainty and something that is axiomatic for us. *A priori* knowledge has a foundational structure. The foundation consists of what is axiomatic for us, and everything else we know *a priori* rests on what is axiomatic for us.

Chisholm's is a "strong" account of *a priori* knowledge. It is strong in its treatment of the foundation and in its account of the links between the foundation and the rest of what is known *a priori*. Let us consider the description of the foundation. Two features of the foundation make it very strong. First, what is for us foundational or basic *a priori* knowledge is *certain* for us, and certainty is the highest level of epistemic justification. If any proposition is less than certain for us, then our knowledge of that proposition is not foundational or basic *a priori* knowledge. Second, foundational or basic *a priori* knowledge is *indefeasible*. It is indefeasible in the sense that as long as one believes what is axiomatic, there is nothing that one could come to know, believe, or experience that would undercut one's justification for believing it. Recall that if a proposition *p* is an axiom, then *p* is necessarily such that if you accept *p*, then *p*

13   *Ibid.*, p. 28.
14   *Ibid.*, p. 29.

is certain for you. Thus, as long as you accept p, you are maximally justified in believing it, and nothing you can know, believe, or experience could be added to your evidence base and make you unjustified in believing p.

Chisholm's account of the *a priori* is also strong in its treatment of the supporting links between the foundations and the rest of our *a priori* knowledge. For you to have non-foundational *a priori* knowledge that p, there must be some proposition e such that e is axiomatic for you, and it must be axiomatic for you that e implies p. Thus, the non-foundational bits of *a priori* knowledge are connected by logical implication to the foundation, and this is a very tight connection. This view of the supporting links may be contrasted with certain foundational views of empirical knowledge that take various sensory states or ways of being appeared to as foundational. On these views, the fact that one is appeared to in a certain way provides evidence (or is a reason) for one's beliefs about external material objects even though one's being appeared to in that way does not imply that one's beliefs about material objects are true. For example, that you are appeared to in a whitish, roundish way provides some evidence for, though it does not imply, the proposition that there is a white, round object before you. Chisholm's account of the *a priori* forecloses the possibility of such purely non-deductive support for those bits of *a priori* knowledge outside the foundation.

Let us consider how well Chisholm's strong account of the *a priori* fits with his common sense particularism and the view that epistemic principles such as C and D are known *a priori*. Given Chisholm's strong account of *a priori* knowledge and justification, the common sense particularist is in an awkward position. For, given Chisholm's strong account, it is hard to see how one could hold that particular epistemic propositions could be data for assessing epistemic principles such as C and D *if* such principles *are* known *a priori*. It is hard to see how one could adopt the stance of the common sense particularist of assessing such epistemic principles by how well they fit with our ordinary particular beliefs about what we know or are justified in believing. For suppose that those principles are basic or foundational bits of *a priori* knowledge. According to Chisholm's account, such principles would then be certain for us and indefeasible in the sense that we could not be unjustified in accepting them provided that we did accept them. Being items of basic *a priori* knowledge they would not depend for their justification on anything else that we know, and thus would not depend on our knowing particular epistemic propositions. But also, insofar as they are indefeasible, we would not be unjustified in accepting those epistemic principles as long as we did in fact accept them *even if* they conflicted with our particular epistemic beliefs. The fact that such principles conflicted with our particular epistemic beliefs would not make us unjustified in accepting them. Further, it is hard to see how one would be in a strong position to reject such principles if they were justified in a non-foundational way, for in that case they would be seen to be implied from what is certain for us. It is hard to see how it could be more reasonable to accept some particular epistemic propositions than the epistemic principle if indeed the epistemic principle is seen to be implied by what is certain for us. Thus, if epistemic principles such as C and D are known *a priori*, then it is hard to see how we could make sense of the common sense particularist's view that we may use our particular epistemic beliefs in assessing and rejecting various epistemic principles. Such principles would seem to be insulated from criticism or assessment from the standpoint of our particular epistemic judgments.

Of course, one way out of the difficulty is to deny that any substantive epistemic principles are known or justified *a priori*. Indeed, though Chisholm does sometimes seem to endorse the view that some substantive epistemic principles are known or justified *a priori*, it is hard to see how this can be so, given his strong account of the *a priori*. Given his strong account, it is very doubtful that C and D *are* known *a priori*. Indeed, given Chisholm's strong account of the *a priori*, it seems doubtful that *any* principles that are "normative supervenience principles" are known *a priori*.

Let us consider two arguments against our knowing epistemic principles such as C and D *a priori*. Consider the following argument:

Argument A
1. We know *p a priori* only if (i) *p* is axiomatic for us, or (ii) there is an *e* such that *e* is axiomatic for us and the proposition *e* implies *p* is axiomatic for us.
2. Epistemic principles such as C and D are not axiomatic for us.
3. There is no *e* such that *e* is axiomatic for us, and the proposition *e* implies C or *e* implies D is axiomatic for us.
4. Therefore, we do not know epistemic principles such as C and D *a priori*.

The first premise simply tells us what Chisholm's strong account requires for *a priori* knowledge. The second and third premises tell us that the sorts of epistemic principles Chisholm proposes cannot meet those requirements.

The second premise is true for the following reason. If epistemic principles such as C and D were axiomatic for us, then they would be certain for us. But since they are not certain for us, they are not axiomatic for us. It is doubtful that many proponents of those principles would claim that they are certain for us, and surely it is not as reasonable for us to accept those principles as it is for us to accept such things as $2 = 2$ or all men are men. Furthermore, even if we accept such principles, we typically do not think of them as indefeasible. Even when we accept them, we remain open to counter-examples or other forms of argument against them. We examine them and consider arguments against them. In practice, we do not assume that they are indefeasible. Thus, if our justification for believing them is less than certain or defeasible, then such principles are not axiomatic for us and not candidates for basic *a priori* knowledge.

Are these epistemic principles non-foundational items of *a priori* knowledge? This too is unlikely, for in order for them to be known in this way, it would have to be the case that there is some *e* that is axiomatic for us and such that it is axiomatic for us that *e* implies the principle in question. But since there appears to be no axiomatic implication between such principles and anything that is axiomatic for us, it appears that such principles are not instances of non-foundational *a priori* knowledge. If this is so, then premise 3 is true. Given the strong conception of *a priori* knowledge, it seems that principles such as C and D cannot be known by us *a priori*.

Let us turn to a second argument. As we have seen, Chisholm rejects the view that epistemic principles such as C and D are known *a priori* because "many philosophers have understood them without thereby seeing that they are true." Other philosophers have taken a similar stance toward other principles. For example, William Rowe rejects the view that the Principle of Sufficient Reason (PSR) is known "intuitively."[15] Like Chisholm, Rowe does not reject the view that we know some things intuitively. For example, Rowe suggests that we know intuitively the

---

15   William L. Rowe, "The Cosmological Argument," *Reason and Responsibility*, 8th edition, ed. Joel Feinberg (Belmont, CA: Wadsworth, 1993), p. 27. Rowe takes the Principle of Sufficient Reason to hold that there must be an explanation (1) of the existence of any being, and (2) of any positive fact whatever.

propositions expressed by the sentences, "Every triangle has three sides" and "No physical object can be in two different places at the same time." He says that we can apprehend the truth of these propositions "just by understanding and reflecting on them."[16] Still, Rowe says, "The difficulty with the claim that PSR is intuitively true, however, is that a number of very able philosophers fail to apprehend its truth, and some even claim that the principle is false. It is doubtful, therefore, that many of us, if any, know intuitively that PSR is true."[17]

I take Chisholm and Rowe to hold that no proposition is an instance of basic *a priori* knowledge if many philosophers have understood it without thereby seeing that it is true. This suggests the following argument.

Argument B
1. One has basic *a priori* knowledge that *p* only if it is false that there are many philosophers who understand *p* without thereby believing that it is true.
2. Many philosophers have understood C and D without thereby believing that they are true.
3. Therefore, it is false that one has basic *a priori* knowledge that C and D are true.

This argument would only show that there is no basic *a priori* knowledge of the principles in question. But, as noted earlier, it is also doubtful whether we have non-basic *a priori* knowledge of them.

We have focused here on arguments that C and D cannot be known *a priori*. But if we accept Chisholm's strong conception of *a priori* knowledge and justification, then it is very hard to see how *any* substantive epistemic principles can be known *a priori*. Chisholm's account of *a priori* knowledge sets the standard for *a priori* knowledge quite high. Indeed, it is hard to see how many substantive or interesting metaphysical or ethical principles could be known or justified *a priori* given such a high standard. To some this might be a welcome conclusion. But it would be hasty. I think Chisholm's account of *a priori* knowledge and justification is too strong. Let us now consider another view.

16 *Ibid.*, p. 27.
17 *Ibid.*, p. 27.

In this section, I will argue that we ought to adopt a more "modest" view about *a priori* knowledge and justification, one that does not require that basic *a priori* justification be certain and indefeasible. The chief weakness with arguments A and B is that they require too much for *a priori* knowledge. For this reason, neither argument provides a compelling reason for rejecting the view that we have *a priori* knowledge or justification for accepting some epistemic principles. Now, I do not intend to argue that we do, in fact, know C and D *a priori*. Rather I shall argue that we should not reject the view that they are known *a priori* because they do not meet Chisholm's high standard for *a priori* knowledge and justification.

One difficulty with both arguments A and B concerns the epistemic status of the first premises they employ. We may note that the first premises in each argument fail to satisfy the strong account's requirements for *a priori* knowledge. In neither argument does the first premise enjoy the certainty of "all men are men" or "all squares have a shape," and thus neither premise seems axiomatic for us. But neither does it seem that either premise is a bit of non-foundational *a priori* knowledge, something known by being seen to follow from what is axiomatic. Thus, one might ask the proponent of these arguments what justifies him in believing the first premises. Neither first premise would be, given the strong account, known *a priori*.

More importantly, the strong Chisholmian view of *a priori* knowledge that underlies argument A assumes that basic *a priori* justification must be certain and indefeasible. Why assume such things? The view that basic *a priori* justification comes in degrees, and need not be certain, has distinguished historical precedents. The view that intuitive justification comes in degrees was suggested by Bertrand Russell[18] and A. C. Ewing, who held that basic *a priori* judgments need be neither certain nor

---

18 For example, Russell writes, "It should be observed that, in all cases of general principles, particular instances dealing with familiar things, are more evident than the general principle. For example, the law of contradiction states that nothing can both have a certain property and not have it. This is evident as soon as it is understood, but it is not so evident as that a particular rose which we see cannot be both red and not red." If the general principle is less evident than the particular instance, then the general principle is not maximally warranted. Bertrand Russell, *The Problems of Philosophy* (Oxford: Oxford University Press, 1912), pp. 112–13.

indefeasible.[19] More recently, Alvin Plantinga has taken a similar view,[20] and Laurence BonJour claims that *a priori* justification need not be certain.[21] Others have taken a similar stand.[22] But among the clearest opponents of the view that basic *a priori* knowledge must be certain and indefeasible is Thomas Reid. Reid asks us to consider the case of a mathematician having completed a demonstration.

> He commits his demonstration to the examination of a mathematical friend, whom he esteems a competent judge, and waits with impatience the issue of his judgment. Here I would ask again, Whether the verdict of his friend, according as it has been favorable or unfavorable, will not greatly increase or diminish confidence in his own judgment? Most certainly it will, and it ought.[23]

For Reid, the level of justification the man's belief enjoys can be affected by the testimony of his friend. Even though he might have *a priori* grounds for accepting the conclusion, the justification these grounds confer on his conclusion can be defeated or undercut by the testimony of others.

In the preceding example, Reid deals with the non-basic *a priori* justification one has for accepting the conclusion of an argument. Yet similar considerations apply to the level of justification of non-inferential *a priori* beliefs. Concerning "first principles," Reid asks, "Is it not possible, that

---

19   Ewing writes, "Many philosophers have preferred to limit the term 'intuition' to cases of certain knowledge, but there are many cases where something presents itself to one intuitively as deserving a certain degree of credence but falling short of certainty or where an intuition has some value but is confused and inextricably blended with erroneous assumptions and inferences." A. C. Ewing, *The Fundamental Questions of Philosophy* (London: Routledge and Kegan Paul, 1951), p. 41. He adds, pp. 50–51, "Arguments may well be available which without strictly proving either side to be wrong put a disputant into a position in which he can better see for himself whether he is right or wrong or at least cast doubt on the truth of his view."

20   Plantinga writes, "Intuitive warrant comes in degrees (and hence in less than maximal degrees); that makes it possible for the intuitive warrant for a given proposition to be defeated." Alvin Plantinga, *Warrant and Proper Function* (Oxford: Oxford University Press, 1993), p. 112.

21   Laurence BonJour, *The Structure of Empirical Knowledge*, p. 208.

22   Cf. Jerold Katz, "What Mathematical Knowledge Could Be," *Mind* vol. 104 (July) 1995, p. 511; Tyler Burge, "Content Preservation," *The Philosophical Review* vol. 102 (October) 1993, p. 461; Donna Summerfield, "Modest A Priori Knowledge," *Philosophy and Phenomenological Research* vol. 51 (March) 1991, pp. 49–50.

23   Thomas Reid, *Essays on the Intellectual Powers of Man*, Essay VI, Chapter 4, pp. 49–50.

men who really love truth, and are open to conviction, may differ about first principles?"[24] For Reid, honest disagreement about first principles is possible. "A man of candour and humility will, in such a case, very naturally suspect his own judgment, so far as to be desirous to enter into a serious examination, even of what he has long held as a first principle."[25] Reid appears to hold that in the face of such disagreement, it is natural and appropriate for us to be suspicious of our own judgment. I take him to hold that knowledge of such disagreement can lower the credence we ought to place in that judgment. For Reid, then, empirical knowledge or non-*a priori* considerations can lower or defeat the justification of those things we have some *a priori* ground for accepting. Plantinga agrees: "I am a philosophical tyro and you a distinguished practitioner of the art; you tell me that those who think about these things are unanimous in endorsing Meinong and rejecting my view that there aren't things that don't exist: then too, I should think, my view would no longer have warrant (or *much* warrant) for me."[26]

But it isn't only empirical or non-*a priori* considerations that can lower or defeat *a priori* justification. Plantinga calls our attention to the various assumptions that led to Russell's paradoxes, propositions such as "every property has a complement" and "there is a property of self-exemplification." Each of these propositions has a certain degree of plausibility or level of justification for us. Indeed, it is precisely because the initial assumptions seem so plausible, that each has "a ring of truth" to it, that their paradoxical implications seem so startling. Yet once we see what they imply, it is reasonable for us to reject one or more of these assumptions. Our justification for believing some of these propositions is undercut or defeated by seeing what they imply. "No doubt Frege was rational in believing *a priori* that for every condition there is a set of just those things that satisfy that condition; but no doubt he was equally rational in rejecting that proposition later on, upon seeing where it led."[27] If the arguments advanced by Reid and Plantinga are sound, then we should reject the strong Chisholmian notion of *a priori* justification and knowledge that underlies argument A.

24 *Ibid.*, p. 603.
25 *Ibid.*, pp. 603–04.
26 Alvin Plantinga, *Warrant and Proper Function*, p. 112.
27 *Ibid.*, p. 110. I use a similar example in *Intrinsic Value* (Cambridge: Cambridge University Press, 1994), p. 148.

Let us turn to argument B. The first premise tells us that one has basic *a priori* knowledge that *p* only if it is false that there are many philosophers who understand *p* without thereby believing it. Why should one think this premise is true? I suggest that there are at least two different reasons. First, one might think that there is a basic *a priori* ground for believing that *p* only if *p* is "doxastically compelling." In other words, one might accept the following preposition:

(E) One has a basic *a priori* reason to accept *p* only if anyone who grasps and considers *p* will believe it.

If E is true, someone's not believing *p* upon the comprehending consideration of it would imply that there is no *a priori* ground for believing it. There are at least three points to make about such a view.

First, E does not fit well with the view defended earlier that basic *a priori* justification is defeasible, for on that view one could have *both* an *a priori* ground for believing *p* and a defeater for that ground (such as the testimony of an expert or seeing that *p* implies something absurd). If E were true, then since *p* is doxastically compelling, one would be unable to give up belief in *p* in the face of defeating reasons. One would be in the epistemically awkward position of being compelled to hold a belief one knew one was not justified in believing. Second, we should distinguish E from F:

(F) One has a basic *a priori* ground for believing *p* only if anyone who grasps and considers *p* has a ground for believing it.

F, at least initially, seems a plausible thesis, but unlike E, it does not raise problems about defeated *a priori* justification. Further, F does not imply E, since one can have a ground for believing something and yet fail to believe it. So, one might opt for the weaker, more modest F without committing onself to E. Finally, why should we think that E is true? Why should someone's failure to believe *p* upon grasping and considering it imply that no one has an *a priori* ground for believing it? Suppose that Smith has some disorder that allows him to grasp and consider *p*, but prevents him from believing it. Or suppose that Smith has decided to embrace skepticism, and refuses to believe anything other than his skeptical principles. It hardly seems to follow that others would have no *a priori* ground for believing *p*. Finally, we should be open to the possibility that some might simply have greater powers of rational insight, so that what might enjoy basic *a priori* justification for some might not for others. So, for example, it seems possible that there be beings for whom the Pythagorean Theorem, or some other proposition for which the normal human mind requires proof, could be known in the basic *a priori* way in which we humans know that all bodies are extended. If this is so, then we should reject *both* E and F.

Let us consider a second possible reason for accepting the first premise of argument B, for the view that one has basic *a priori* knowledge that *p* only if it is false that many philosophers understand *p* without accepting it. This second reason might be gleaned from the remarks of Reid and Plantinga – namely, that the empirical knowledge of certain kinds of disagreement might weaken or defeat whatever *a priori* ground one has for accepting a proposition. On this view, knowing that competent philosophers have considered epistemic principles such as C and D without believing them would weaken the level of justification those principles have for me, or defeat whatever ground I have for believing them. On this view, knowledge of such disagreement would preclude my knowing such principles *a priori*.

There are several points worth making about this way of supporting argument B. First, we should note that the mere fact of disagreement does not necessarily lower the level of justification one might have for believing a proposition. Suppose, for example, someone denied that all men are men or that if some men are Greeks, then some Greeks are men. Knowledge of such disagreement would not make us any less justified in believing these propositions. It would simply make us doubt either the sincerity of the one denying the propositions or his intellectual competence. Second, suppose we know that competent philosophers have understood *p*, but do not believe it. Even if we assume that this weakens our level of justification for believing *p*, why should we assume that it weakens it below the level of justification required for knowledge? As Reid says, such disagreement may be a reason to suspect our own judgment, but it does not follow that we are no longer sufficiently justified in believing *p* to know it. Third, suppose, for example, that one finds that the disagreement is based on a mistaken notion of what *a priori* knowledge requires, or that those who reject the proposition do so because they mistakenly think that they have counter-examples to the principles in question. In this case, it is not clear that one could not be sufficiently justified in believing *p* to know it. Even if such disagreement were a defeater for believing *p*, this defeater could itself be defeated, and the mere fact of disagreement would not imply that one lacked knowledge.

We should emphasize that according to our more "modest" approach to *a priori* knowledge and justification, disagreement over principles need not be unreasonable or mere blind stubbornness to see what is obvious. If basic *a priori* justification is defeasible, then two philosophers could both understand an epistemic principle and reasonably disagree about its truth. This could happen if one has (or merely thinks he has) reasons that defeat his justification in believing it. One philosopher might have (or merely think he has) counter-examples to or arguments against the principle in question. But the existence of disagreement does not show that the epistemic principle can have no *a priori* status. It does not show that one cannot have a defeasible *a priori* ground for believing it or that one cannot be sufficiently justified in believing the principle to know it.

Again, my aim in this section has not been to defend the view that we do know Chisholm's epistemic principles C and D *a priori*. My aim has been rather to reject the view that *a priori* justification must be certain and indefeasible. In this respect, I would say that *a priori* justification resembles perceptual and mnemonic justification, each of which seems to come in varying degrees and each of which is susceptible to defeat.

7.3 LYCAN'S DEFENSE OF THE MOOREAN RESPONSE TO SKEPTICISM

As we saw in Chapter 1, Moore holds that it is more reasonable for us to believe various common sense and ordinary propositions such as "I know this is a finger" than one or more of the premises of skeptical arguments for the conclusion that we do not know such things. William Lycan agrees with Moore's claim. But Lycan thinks that the reason that Moore's claim is true is that skeptical arguments rest on some *philosophical* premise that is based on "intuition." Lycan takes a dim view of such intuitions as sources of epistemic justification.

Lycan asks us to consider the Moorean proposition (a), "I had my breakfast before lunch," and the metaphysical proposition (b), "Temporal modes such as pastness and futurity are monadic properties of events." Some metaphysicians such as McTaggart have argued against the reality of time, and held that propositions such as (a) are false because they conflict with (b). But Lycan claims that it is far more reasonable for us to accept (a) rather than (b). Moore has, says Lycan, excellent grounds for believing (a). For one thing, he remembers that he had his breakfast before his lunch. But there are no equally good reasons in favor of (b). Lycan writes:

We may wonder where metaphysical premises (often called "intuitions") come from. Are they deliverances of the *lumen naturale*? Does the Third Eye of the metaphysician's mind get a rare look at a Platonic Form? Perhaps they just articulate features of our ordinary way of conceiving things. Whatever; their epistemic credentials are obscure, and more importantly, they are shoddy. A metaphysician who claims to "just know" that such an abstract premise is true ("This is a deep intuition") cannot be taken very seriously. But Moore has excellent grounds for the competing proposition (a): He always has breakfast before he has lunch, and he specifically remembers doing so today in particular. A forced choice between (a) and (b) has got to go in favor of (a).[28]

Lycan adds, "Moreover, as is notorious, a priori metaphysical views historically have little staying power; one philosophical era's fundamental principles are often rejected in the next era as ludicrous superstition. No *purely philosophical* premise can ever (legitimately) have as strong a claim to our allegiance as can a humble common-sense proposition such as Moore's autobiographical ones. Science can correct common sense; metaphysics and philosophical 'intuition' can only throw spitballs."[29] Lycan clearly takes a dim view of allegedly *a priori* intuitions.

Of course, it is not only metaphysical "intuitions" that conflict with Moore's humble common sense claims. Lycan thinks that skeptical arguments also rely on purely philosophical premises, albeit epistemological premises, that conflict with such Moorean claims as "I know this is a hand." We might illustrate Lycan's view by considering the following familiar skeptical argument:

1. If one is to know that *p*, then one must exclude (rule out) every possibility that one knows to be incompatible with one's knowing that *p* (where "excluding" means "knowing not to be the case").

---

28 William Lycan, "Moore Against the New Skeptics," *Philosophical Studies* vol. 103 (March) 2001, p. 40.
29 *Ibid.*, p. 41.

2. One knows that "this is a hand" is incompatible with "I am a handless brain in a vat being deceived into thinking I have hands."
3. One does not know that it is not the case that "I am a handless brain in a vat being deceived into thinking I have hands."
4. Therefore, one does not know "this is a hand."

The first premise is our familiar Principle of Exclusion (PE). PE and similar principles are often used in skeptical arguments. But PE is a purely philosophical proposition. It is an allegedly *a priori* intuition of the sort whose credentials are, according to Lycan, "shoddy." So Lycan would, I think, conclude that it is more reasonable for us to reject PE than to reject the Moorean proposition, "I know this is a hand."

It is worth noting that the strong conception of *a priori* knowledge endorsed by Chisholm would lead us to reject the view that one knows PE *a priori*. One might do so for reasons analogous to those for rejecting the view that substantive epistemic principles such as C and D are known *a priori*. One might hold that PE is not axiomatic for us insofar as it is neither certain nor indefeasible. PE does not seem to be certain for us. It is not as reasonable to believe as "2 = 2" or "all men are men." So, given the strong account of *a priori* knowledge, PE would not seem to be a bit of basic or foundational *a priori* knowledge. Could PE be a bit of non-foundational *a priori* knowledge? That too seems doubtful. For it is not clear that there is any *e* such that *e* is axiomatic for us, and the proposition *e* implies PE is axiomatic for us. So the strong Chisholmian account of *a priori* knowledge and justification would apparently imply that we do not know, and are not justified in believing PE.

To many, however, including Moore himself, Lycan's defense of the Moorean response to skepticism simply goes too far. Moore himself seems to have accepted something very close to PE. Concerning a similar sort of skeptical argument, Moore writes, "I agree, therefore, with that part of this argument which asserts that if I don't know now that I'm not dreaming, it follows that I don't *know* that I am standing up, even if I both actually am and think that I am."[30] Moore does not seem to think that the problem lies in the philosophical premise that is some variant of PE. Unlike Lycan, Moore does not base his response to the skeptical argument on the claim that the epistemic credentials of philosophical intuitions in

---

30   G. E. Moore, "Certainty," *Philosophical Papers*, p. 247.

general are shoddy or that they cannot sometimes be reasonable to believe or provide us with instances of knowledge. Moreover, even if we think, with Moore, that it is more reasonable for us to believe "I know this is a hand" than the premises of the skeptical argument, it is not clear that it is PE that should be rejected. Could it not be premise 3 that ought to be rejected? Perhaps we might find that 3 rests on dubious considerations such as the sensitivity requirement on knowledge. In short, we might reject this skeptical argument without condemning all purely philosophical premises based on alleged *a priori* intuitions. Indeed, why should we condemn as shoddy all purely philosophical premises, and reject all intuitions? As Earl Conee notes in his response to Lycan, some of them seem as respectable as any Moorean common sense proposition.[31] The proposition that if one knows that p, then p is true, seems to be a purely philosophical proposition known *a priori*. Yet it is as respectable as any proposition in the Moorean camp. Conee suggests, plausibly, that the degree of epistemic justification that attaches to one's intuitions might vary in degree from the certain to the worthless. There is no good reason to reject them all. But if we take this view, then we ought to reject the strong conception of *a priori* knowledge and justification as well, and opt for the more modest view.

7.4 MODEST *A PRIORI* KNOWLEDGE AND COMMON SENSE PARTICULARISM

Whether or not one thinks *a priori* intuition can provide some epistemic ground for accepting an epistemic principle, we should not overlook the importance of *other* sources of justification for such principles. One such source is explanatory coherence. One might hold that it is reasonable for us to accept some substantive epistemic principles in virtue of their cohering with and explaining particular epistemic facts that we know or are justified in believing. On this view, we would have some justification for accepting various epistemic principles in virtue of their being the best explanatory account available to us for particular epistemic facts. Thus, we might accept an epistemic principle such as C in virtue of its role in explaining why various beliefs about the past are justified. C might, for example, strike one as the best explanation for the fact that one is justified

---

31 Earl Conee, "Comments on Bill Lycan's 'Moore Against the New Skeptics'," *Philosophical Studies* vol. 103 (March) 2001, p. 56.

in believing that one had eggs for breakfast, along with a great many other facts about what one is justified in believing. Similarly, one might hold that it is reasonable to accept D in virtue of the fact that it is the best explanation one has for the fact that one is justified in believing that one is perceiving, say, a dog. Of course, to treat such explanatory coherence as a source of justification is not incompatible with holding that we also have some independent *a priori* ground for accepting such principles. One could, after all, certainly have *both* sorts of justifications. But even without claiming that we have some *a priori* insight into the truth of a principle, we might have some justification for accepting it in virtue of its explanatory coherence.

Of course, sources of justification can sometimes conflict. If explanatory coherence is a source of justification, it might be reasonable for us to abandon some epistemic principles that seem plausible *a priori* in favor of different principles that provide a better overall explanatory account of our particular epistemic data. Even if we have some *a priori* intuition that a given principle is true, it might be more reasonable for us to reject it in favor of another principle that provides greater explanatory coherence. This would be, in principle, no different than rejecting various beliefs we might be inclined to accept on the basis of perception and memory when they fail to cohere with our other beliefs (as when I reject my memory belief that my doctor's telephone number is so-and-so after repeatedly dialing, only to reach a local bank). Beliefs that issue from perception, memory, and rational intuition *can* fail to be justified when they conflict with other things that cohere better with our other beliefs. But, again, just as this does not imply that we can have no perceptual or mnemonic grounds for belief, it does not imply that we can have no *a priori* ground for accepting some epistemic principles rooted in rational intuition.

The modest view of *a priori* knowledge and justification allows that whatever justification our *a priori* intuition might confer on an epistemic principle could be defeated by the fact that such principles conflict with particular, contingent epistemic propositions that we find, on balance, to be more reasonable. Thus, even if we find that some epistemic principle has an intuitive "pull," we may find that it is more reasonable, on reflection, to abandon that principle because it conflicts with what we take to be particular instances of knowledge and justified belief. The mere fact that those epistemic principles have something to be said in their favor would not thus imply that they "trump" our particular epistemic judgments. The principles would thus not be insulated from criticism. Given this fact, we can say that the possibility that we have some *a priori* basis for some epistemic principles is compatible with common sense particularism.

Similarly, we might find, for example, that there is an intuitive pull toward some of the epistemic principles employed in skeptical arguments. It might be that we have some *a priori* ground for accepting such principles. We need not think that such principles are epistemically shoddy or that there is nothing in their favor epistemically. Still, we may hold, along with Moore and Lycan, that it is more reasonable for us to accept our particular epistemic beliefs than it is to accept those principles.

But do we have some *a priori* ground for believing any epistemic principles? I think so. And I think the principle that if one knows that *p*, then *p* is true is such a principle. Furthermore, I assume that the principle of exclusion, PE, is an example of such a principle. Of course, as we saw in Chapter 5, there are philosophers attracted to relevant alternative accounts of knowledge and justification that would tell us that PE is false, and opt for a related yet different principle. If, however, the arguments of this chapter are sound, then we should not hold that neither of us enjoys *a priori* justification for our belief in our principles simply because the principles that we accept lack certainty or because there are others who deny them.

Yet what about epistemic principles such as C and D? And what of those "normative supervenience principles" that Chisholm endorses? The modest view leaves *open* the possibility that we could have some *a priori* grounds for accepting epistemic principles such as C and D. Indeed, one might hold that the level of justification is, in some cases, sufficient for *a priori* knowledge. It is, again, more plausible to think that we have *a priori* grounds for accepting such principles if we accept the modest view rather than Chisholm's strong account. Still, whether C and D are known *a priori* will depend on a variety of considerations. Suppose, for example, that one held that a source of belief X is a source of epistemic justification only if X is generally *reliable*. Given this view, it is not plausible to hold that principles C and D could be known *a priori*, since it is not a necessary truth that memory or perception are generally reliable. Now, whether such general reliability is necessary for a source of belief to be a source of justification is, of course, controversial, and so the claim that principles such as C and D are knowable *a priori* will also be controversial. Still, if the

8

Particularism, Ethical Skepticism, and Moral Philosophy

The previous chapters have focused on the common sense tradition and epistemology. We have been concerned primarily with the epistemological views of Reid, Moore, and Chisholm, and the main objections considered have dealt primarily with the epistemological status of the sorts of beliefs that common sense philosophers take as data. In this final chapter, I will take up certain issues in moral philosophy and consider these issues in light of what we have said about the common sense tradition.

There are, of course, certain similarities in the epistemological views of Reid, Moore, and Chisholm. They all reject skepticism about the external world and other minds. They all endorse some form of foundationalism, holding that there are some propositions that are known *immediately* or *basically*. But there are also areas of important disagreement. There are differences about the nature of perception and sensing. Furthermore, I think we may take them to hold different views about the nature of epistemic justification. Though all three hold some version of foundationalism, Reid may be taken as holding some form of externalist foundationalism, and Chisholm rejects such a view. With respect to the question, "What makes justified beliefs justified?" there is reason to think they would offer different answers.

When we turn to their moral philosophy, the situation is similar. There are certain similarities in the ethical or meta-ethical views of all three. For example, Reid, Moore, and Chisholm hold that we do *know* some ethical propositions, including some propositions about what is intrinsically good or bad. They are all, in this respect, ethical cognitivists. Moreover, each of them would hold that we have *immediate* or *basic* knowledge of some ethical or evaluative propositions. They do not agree, however, on *which* ethical propositions we know immediately. Moore, for example, held that

157

a certain form of the utilitarian principle was self-evidently true, and Reid takes various moral propositions that Moore would have rejected to be self-evidently true. Moreover, when we consider the question, "What makes right acts right?" we do not find any common answer. On this central question of ethical theory, they simply do not agree. Moore, as noted, was a utilitarian, who thought that the rightness of particular actions was a function of their consequences. But there is no reason to attribute such a view to Reid or Chisholm.

On certain important questions in both epistemology and ethics, then, we do not find agreement among the main figures of the common sense tradition. If we think of an epistemological theory as offering us a detailed answer to the question, "What makes justified beliefs justified?" then there simply is no common sense epistemological theory, at least not in the sense that there is such a theory accepted by the main figures in the common sense tradition. Similarly, if we think of a moral theory as providing an answer to the question, "What makes right actions right?" there is, in the same sense, no common sense moral theory. Still, in the epistemological sphere, Reid, Moore, and Chisholm are united in the view that we can pick out particular instances of knowledge and justified belief and use these beliefs in assessing criteria of knowledge and justification, as data for assessing and developing epistemological theories. This sort of epistemological particularism is common to all three. But we may ask whether an analogous sort of particularism can or should be employed in the moral sphere. May we assume that we can pick out particular instances of right action, and use these for assessing criteria of right action? Is the approach that they adopt in epistemology, and that I have tried to defend, one that we should employ in ethical theory?

If we follow the particularist approach in ethics, then we assume that we can pick out particular instances of right and wrong action. We will assume that in some cases, we know or we are justified in believing that some particular actions are right or wrong. I assume that in some cases, the degree of epistemic justification we have for believing some actions right or wrong is rather high. I assume, for example, that I am highly justified in believing that it would now be wrong for me to rape and kill my secretary and that it would be wrong for me now to torture my father to death. I think there are, in fact, many cases in which we have such highly justified moral judgments about particular cases. Consider, for example the following particularly grisly example from the local paper about a man in a nearby town who had a dispute with his sister over some money she owed him. He went to his sister's apartment, only to find that she was not home. However, his fourteen-year-old niece and two-year-old nephew were home. He slit the throat of his niece, took both children and drove them to a local bridge, and threw them in the creek below. His nephew drowned, but his niece survived. She wandered out to a local highway, where a couple driving by found her and rushed her to the local hospital. The uncle's slitting the throat of his niece and drowning his nephew were morally wrong. Moreover, I would say that I know this or that I am at least highly justified in believing this. It is, I think, beyond reasonable doubt that his actions were wrong. Moreover, I would say that it is beyond reasonable doubt that it was right for the passing couple to stop and help the injured niece. I am sure that I have many harebrained moral beliefs, and that my views on tax policy and health care in the United States are highly questionable. But I am quite confident in my judgments about certain of the actions of the uncle and of the passing couple, and I take them to be highly justified epistemically. As a particularist, I would assume that I could take these beliefs as data for developing and assessing criteria of right action.

Now, the view that one can know or that one can be epistemically justified in believing *any* moral or ethical propositions is, of course, controversial. Let us take *ethical skepticism* to be the view that no moral or ethical proposition can be known or epistemically justified. There are many reasons why ethical skepticism might seem plausible. A full treatment of the grounds for ethical skepticism would take us too far afield.[1] For the moment, however, I shall make the following points.

Many philosophers have offered analyses of moral language that imply that ethical skepticism is true. Non-cognitivist analyses of moral language hold that morally evaluative sentences have no truth value, that strictly speaking they are neither true nor false. If moral sentences have no truth value, then strictly speaking they cannot be objects of knowledge. If one can be epistemically justified in believing that p only if p has a truth value, then no one can be epistemically justified in accepting a moral sentence. There are two main versions of non-cognitivism in ethics, *emotivism* and *prescriptivism*. Emotivism holds, in its simplest form, that our moral utterances are mere expressions of our attitudes, and thus are not true or false. Thus, when one says "Murder is wrong," one means something like "Murder! Boo!" Similarly, when one says, "Gratitude is good," one means something like "Gratitude! Hurray!" Such emotional ejaculations express

---

1 I discuss some of these arguments in "Epistemology and Ethics," *The Oxford Handbook of Epistemology*, ed. Paul K. Moser (Oxford: Oxford University Press, 2002), pp. 479–512.

the speaker's attitude but lack truth value. Prescriptivism emphasizes the action-guiding role of moral language. According to prescriptivism, when one says "Murder is wrong," one is attempting to guide people's conduct. Moral language, on this view, is best understood in terms of imperatives. Thus, when one says "Murder is wrong," one means something like "Do not murder!" and when one says "Gratitude is good," one means something like "Show gratitude!" Many sophisticated non-cognitivist analyses of moral language were developed in the twentieth century by philosophers such as A. J. Ayer, C. L. Stevenson, and R. M. Hare. Many of these analyses are far more sophisticated than the simple versions noted earlier. Non-cognitivists need not deny that moral utterances can be reasonable or justified. Hare, for example, points out that the issuing of commands can be unreasonable. It can be unreasonable to issue conflicting commands such as "Shut the door!" and "Do not shut the door!" However, this sort of unreasonableness is not epistemic. For the non-cognitivists, there is no need to answer the question "How can one know what is right or wrong?" since, on their view, such knowledge and epistemic justification is not possible.

In spite of the popularity of non-cognitivist analyses, ethical cognitivism has remained stubbornly persistent. Let us take ethical cognitivism to be the view that some ethical propositions are true or false and that some people are epistemically justified in accepting them. (One could of course define "ethical cognitivism" as simply the view that some ethical propositions have a truth value. But this would be to leave cognition out of "cognitivism.") Again, a fully adequate defense of ethical cognitivism and critique of non-cognitivist analyses would be a daunting task, and one that would take us too far afield. I shall simply note here that there are a variety of considerations against non-cognitivist analyses of our ordinary use of moral language. First, we commonly take ourselves to be *asserting* something when we make a moral judgment, and the form of our judgment is typically declarative or assertive in form. In making a moral judgment, the ordinary user of moral language is not merely expressing his attitude the way one expresses disgust by uttering "Ugh!" or joy by exclaiming "Hurray!" Such attitudes might accompany most moral judgments, but the ordinary user of moral language takes himself to be describing or characterizing the object of his judgment. Second, we think that some forms of moral argument are deductively valid and others aren't. Consider, for example, the following argument: (1) If stealing is wrong, then it is wrong to encourage others to steal; (2) stealing is wrong; (3) therefore, it is wrong to encourage others to steal. This argument seems to be deductively valid. Ordinarily we take a valid deductive argument to be one in which the premises logically imply the conclusion. But if non-cognitivism is true, then the premises of this argument have no truth value, and if so it is hard to see in what way they could logically imply the conclusion. Third, moral sentences can meaningfully occur as the antecedent in conditional sentences, such as (1). But it is far from clear that mere prescriptions or imperatives or the expressions of attitudes can meaningfully take the place of such antecedents. What would it mean to say "If don't steal, then ... " or "If boo to stealing, then ... "? Fourth, our ordinary moral beliefs seems to reflect a commitment to ethical cognitivism. We believe that in some cases, a person ought to have known that what he did was wrong, that in some cases, a person should have known better than to act as he did. Similarly, we sometimes excuse a person from moral blame when we believe that he lacked the capacity to know what is right or wrong. That we accept this excuse without excusing everyone reflects the ordinary assumption that people have the capacity to know right from wrong.

In considering the plausibility of non-cognitivism in ethics, we may also consider its plausibility in epistemology. Many philosophers have suggested that epistemic concepts are *evaluative* concepts. They have suggested, for example, that when we take a belief to be an instance of knowledge, or to be justified, we are making a positive evaluation of it. Similarly, when we hold that a belief is unjustified or unreasonable we are making a negative evaluation of it. If epistemic concepts are evaluative, and if we can know that we know or that we are epistemically justified in believing various things, then it follows that we do have some evaluative knowledge. Non-cognitivist analyses of epistemic concepts such as "knowledge" and "epistemic justification" have not enjoyed the same popularity as non-cognitivist analyses of moral terms. A non-cognitivist analysis of epistemic terms would imply that sentences such as "He knows he has hands" and "She knows her name" are not true, and the sentences "He knows that the earth is flat" and "He knows that $2 = 3$" are not false. Claims to knowledge based on the most foolish superstitions would not be false, and claims to justification based on the best possible evidence would not be true. Given that knowing that p requires that p is true, one could never know that one knows anything. A non-cognitivist analysis of epistemic concepts would rule out epistemic knowledge. To many philosophers, such implications seem implausible. The implausibility of such claims is not limited to philosophers who think we *do* have epistemic knowledge, for many skeptical philosophers who deny that we

161

do know that we know do not hold that such epistemic claims lack a truth value. Many skeptics believe that claims to knowledge have a truth value, and some skeptics believe that knowledge claims are simply *false*. Given the evaluative nature of both epistemic and evaluative concepts, many philosophers would find that they are in the same boat, and that epistemic non-cognitivism is not very plausible. Why, then, should we think that ethical non-cognitivism is any more plausible? In any case, I will assume that ethical cognitivism is no worse off than epistemological cognitivism.

8.1 SOME CRITICISMS OF WIDE REFLECTIVE EQUILIBRIUM AND PARTICULARISM

In this section, I consider some objections to a particularist approach in moral philosophy. These objections do not presuppose or assume that ethical skepticism is true. They do not presuppose or assume that there can be no knowledge or epistemically justified belief in moral or ethical propositions. Still, they hold that there is something philosophically unsatisfactory in taking one's beliefs about particular instances of right or wrong action as data for developing and assessing criteria of right action. Many of these objections have been raised against the *method of wide reflective equilibrium*,[2] which also permits one to take one's beliefs about the rightness or wrongness of particular actions to be data. In the method of wide reflective equilibrium, one begins with one's (1) particular considered judgments, (2) beliefs about general principles, and (3) general background theories. One then seeks to achieve a coherent balance or "equilibrium" between these various elements. In some cases, this might require abandoning or revising some of one's particular judgments in favor of, say, a general principle that seems, on reflection, more reasonable. In other cases, one might give up or revise the general principle in favor of the particular judgment. The method of wide reflective equilibrium has been used in both epistemology and ethics. Just as the particularist epistemologist may take as data particular judgments about what he takes

---

2   In ethics, the method of wide reflective equilibrium figures prominently in John Rawls's *A Theory of Justice* (Cambridge, MA: Harvard University Press, 1971). See also Norman Daniels, "Wide Reflective Equilibrium and Theory Acceptance in Ethics," *The Journal of Philosophy* 76 1979; Michael DePaul, "Reflective Equilibrium and Foundationalism," *American Philosophical Quarterly* vol. 23 1986; Ernest Sosa, "Equilibrium in Coherence," *Knowledge in Perspective*.

himself to know or to be justified in believing, so too the particularist moral philosopher may take as data particular moral propositions. These might include such things as "It would be wrong for me to kill my secretary now," "I ought to give more to charity," or "It was wrong for that man to slit his niece's throat." He may also take as data various general moral principles such as "If an act is the breaking of a promise, then that act is *prima facie* wrong." Through the process of seeking overall coherence, the epistemologist or the moral philosopher seeks to improve his epistemic and moral beliefs, both particular and general, and to discover what makes acts right or beliefs justified.

Particularism in ethics and the method of wide reflective equilibrium have been criticized by several moral philosophers. Often these objections are analogous to those raised against the same approach in epistemology. We find, for example, objections based on concerns about (1) equally coherent yet incompatible systems, (2) vicious circularity, and (3) the epistemic status of our particular moral beliefs.

An objection based on the possibility of equally coherent alternative systems is raised, for example, in the following passage by Hare:

The appeal to moral intuitions will never do as a basis for a moral system. It is certainly possible, as some thinkers of our own time have done, to collect the moral opinions of which they and their contemporaries feel most sure, find some relatively simple method or apparatus which can be represented, with a bit of give and take, and making plausible assumptions about the circumstances of life, as generating these opinions; and then pronounce that this is the moral system which, having reflected, we must acknowledge to be the correct one. But they have absolutely no authority for this claim beyond the original convictions, for which no ground or argument was given. The 'equilibrum' that was reached is one between forces which might have been generated by prejudice, and no amount of reflection can make that a solid basis for morality. It would be possible for two mutually inconsistent systems to be defended in this way: all that this would show is that their advocates had grown up in different moral environments.[3]

Hare points out that mere coherence is not sufficient to guarantee justified or reasonable moral beliefs, for those beliefs and the resulting equilibrium might be rooted in mere prejudice. Someone deeply prejudiced, excessively self-interested, or brought up badly might be able to hold coherent

3   Richard M. Hare, *Moral Thinking* (Oxford: Oxford University Press, 1981), p. 12.

moral views. Surely we think it possible that some coherent bodies of moral beliefs can be unreasonable, even crazy.

I think Hare is right that it is possible for some coherent moral views to be unreasonable and deeply unsatisfactory. Still, Hare's complaint resembles Alston's worry about track-record arguments. As we have seen, Alston is worried that people with clearly objectionable ways of forming beliefs, such as gazing into crystal balls, might be able to produce track-record arguments for the reliability of gazing that are structurally similar to the track-record arguments that we might give for the reliability of perception and memory. The gazer could conceivably thus form a coherent body of beliefs about the reliability of gazing. Still, his beliefs about the reliability of gazing are unreasonable, even if coherent. But we may make the same response to Hare that we made to Alston – namely, that we need not treat all coherent bodies as being epistemically on a par. Even if we allow that coherence provides some boost to the epistemic status of beliefs, there are other factors relevant as well. As Sosa suggests, the aptness of a belief and the subject's intellectual virtue are also relevant. Even if Mr. Magoo can achieve a coherence in his beliefs comparable to our own, we need not hold that his beliefs are epistemically on a par with our own insofar as our beliefs are grounded in apt faculties of perception and his are not. So a defender of the method of wide reflective equilibrium and particularism in ethics need not hold that all coherent moral views are epistemically on a par. He need not hold that mere coherence is the only thing that matters for the reasonableness of one's moral beliefs.

Such a distinction has long been recognized in moral philosophy. Aristotle, for example, distinguishes between the beliefs of the practically wise and the merely clever. The merely clever man is very good at judging the means to his ends, yet lacking moral virtue he does not have the right ends. The beliefs of the merely clever man might enjoy a coherence equal to that of the practically wise man, but lacking as he is in moral virtue, his beliefs are not on a par with those of the practically wise. In other words, though their beliefs may be equally coherent, they are not epistemically as good. What raises the epistemic status of the beliefs of the practically wise man, what makes him "wise" and thus intellectually superior, is that his beliefs about what ultimately ought to be sought are rooted in virtue and those of the merely clever are not.

But how can we know which dispositions or ways of forming moral beliefs are virtuous? How can we tell which of them are reliable? To many, the use of our moral intuitions or moral judgments to defend the reliability of our ways of forming moral beliefs seems viciously circular. Consider the following passages by Hare and Brandt:

The intuitions that give rise to the conflict are the product of our upbringings and past experiences of decision-making. They are not self-justifying: we can always ask whether the upbringing was the best we could have, or whether the past decisions were the right ones, or even if so, whether the principles then formed should be applied to a new situation, or, if they cannot all be applied, *which* should be applied. To use intuition itself to answer such questions is a viciously circular procedure; if the dispositions formed by our upbringing are called into question, we cannot appeal to them to settle the question.[4]

Various facts about the genesis of our moral beliefs militate against the mere appeal to intuitions in ethics. Our normative beliefs are strongly affected by the particular cultural tradition which nurtured us, and would be different if we had been in a learning situation with different parents, teachers, or peers. Moreover, the moral convictions of some people derive, to use the words of Peter Singer, "from discarded religious systems, from warped views of sex and bodily functions, or from customs necessary for the survival of the group in social and economic circumstances that now lie in the distant past." What we should aim to do is step outside our own tradition somehow, see it from the outside, and evaluate it separating what is only a vestige of a possibly once useful moral tradition, from what is justifiable at present. The method of intuitions in principle prohibits our doing this. It is only an internal test of coherence, what may be no more than a reshuffling of moral prejudices.[5]

Brandt, like Hare, objects to the use of intuitions and the method of reflective equilibrium. Brandt rejects such a method since it "may be no more than a reshuffling of prejudices," and Hare complains that the equilibrium reached "is one between forces which might have been generated by prejudice." But, again, the defender of wide reflective equilibrium need not hold that all coherent bodies of belief are on a par. Still, how are we to tell which are the good or reliable ways of forming moral beliefs? Shall we appeal to our moral beliefs? Shall we use our ways of forming moral beliefs to determine which of our ways of forming moral beliefs are reliable? That, claims Hare, would be a "viciously circular procedure" and it would not "settle the question." For Brandt and Hare, the remedy or alternative is, as Brandt says, to "step outside" our own moral beliefs by appealing to

4 *Ibid.*, p. 40.
5 Richard Brandt, *A Theory of the Good and The Right* (Oxford: Oxford University Press, 1979), pp. 21–22.

non-moral beliefs to defend a moral criterion. In their view, we must seek an independent argument for a moral criterion, independent in the sense that it does not presuppose the truth of any of our moral beliefs. Thus, we find Brandt appeals to beliefs about "rational" action and desire, and Hare to beliefs about various logical principles, including principles about the logic of moral terms and various empirical, non-moral premises.

The demand that we step outside our moral intuitions and seek an independently established criterion of right action, one that will then allow us to determine which ways of forming moral beliefs are reliable, is similar to the demands we considered in Chapter 2. There we saw that BonJour holds that we need a non-circular meta-justification of our ways of forming empirical beliefs. And we saw that Fumerton argues that one cannot use a source or way of forming beliefs to support its own reliability.

Now, if Hare and Brandt's objection is rooted in the assumption that one cannot use a way of forming beliefs to support the reliability of that way of forming beliefs, then I think that the objection is unsound. Following Sosa, I argued in Chapter 2 that there is nothing illegitimate in such a procedure in principle. Indeed, if it were illegitimate, then Brandt and Hare would seem only to push the problem back a step. For one could surely raise the question about the reliability of those ways of forming beliefs that we might use to develop our moral criterion. Even if we get outside our ways of forming moral beliefs and defend a criterion by appealing to the logic of moral terms and various non-moral empirical premises, or by appealing to beliefs about what it is rational to do and desire, surely one could raise questions about the reliability of the ways in which *those* beliefs are formed. So, given the assumption that one cannot use a source to support the reliability of that source, we would seem only to have pushed the issue back. And how would we be ultimately any better off? Given the assumption in question, how could one support the reliability of those ways of forming beliefs?

So far we have considered objections to the method of wide reflective equilibrium based on concerns about equally coherent systems and vicious circularity. But one might object to the appeal to our moral judgments as data for criticizing and assessing moral criteria on the ground that they are pretty shaky epistemically. Recall Moser's complaint that appeals to our common sense beliefs about what we know are sometimes the result of special, even "biased" linguistic training, and that they are sometimes at odds with what science and perception tell us. So, too, one might hold that our moral beliefs, in general, are a rather shaky lot, and that from the standpoint of moral philosophy they are not to be trusted. This seems to be Brandt's point when he writes that "various facts about the genesis of our moral beliefs militate against the mere appeal to intuitions in ethics." He notes that our moral beliefs are strongly influenced by our particular cultural tradition, and would have been different with different teachers, parents, or peers. He cites with approval Singer's comment that the moral beliefs of some people derive from the vestiges of discarded religious systems, from warped views of sex and bodily functions, and from particular social and economic systems long past. Given these claims, it might seem that we ought to set aside our ordinary moral beliefs in seeking to discover criteria of right action, and appeal instead to beliefs that are more credible.

Even if we grant that there is much that is right in the remarks of Brandt and Singer, would it follow that we should eschew appeals to *all* moral beliefs as data? I don't think so. Even if we concede much in their comments, it does not follow that *none* of our moral beliefs is credible, justified, or instances of knowledge. My beliefs that I ought not torture my parents to death or kill my secretary are quite reasonable and justified. The same is true of a great many perfectly ordinary moral beliefs that I and others share. Many of these are such obvious truisms that we hardly ever bother to formulate them. These would include beliefs such as in general one ought not to swerve into the oncoming traffic, rob the local bank, kill one's children, and so on. Such beliefs are not merely the vestiges of discarded religious systems, from warped views about sex and bodily functions, and from particular social and economic systems long past. So even if some moral beliefs are dubious for the sorts of reasons Brandt and Singer give, some aren't.

Brandt and Hare point out that many of our moral beliefs, as well as our dispositions and habits of moral judgments, are deeply influenced by our upbringing and socialization. But does this fact support the view that they are somehow epistemically inferior to the sorts of beliefs to which they would appeal in the search for an independently established criterion? I don't see why it does. Much of what we know and are justified in believing is deeply influenced by culture and upbringing. Our beliefs about science, history, and geography are deeply influenced by our upbringing. Moreover, our upbringing and socialization influence many of our dispositions to form beliefs, including whether we form them critically, on the basis of evidence, and whether we reason more or less in accordance with the principles of logic. Indeed, even our beliefs about what it is rational to do and the logic of moral terms would seem to be influenced

167

by our upbringing and social milieu. That our beliefs in science, history, and geography were acquired through training and education within our particular cultural milieu does not imply that they are not instances of knowledge or that they are not epistemically justified. So there is no reason to think that anything follows about the epistemic status of our moral beliefs or dispositions from the fact that many of them are developed or influenced in the same way. Furthermore, the fact that other cultures have held different views about science, history, or geography does not imply that our views simply reflect the biased or prejudiced attitudes of our culture or that we lack knowledge in these areas. The mere fact that other cultures, or our own at different times, have held different moral beliefs does not imply that we lack moral knowledge or that all or most of our moral beliefs reflect biased and prejudiced attitudes.

Moreover, I would say that some of these moral beliefs are at least as justified for us, if not more justified, than the sorts of beliefs that Brandt and Hare would take as reasons or grounds for their particular moral criteria. For example, in arguing for a utilitarian criterion, Hare asks us to consider the following two propositions: (1) I now prefer with strength S that if I were in that situation, x should happen rather than not. (2) If I were in that situation, I would prefer with strength S that x should happen rather than not. Hare claims that it is a conceptual truth that to know (2), (1) must be true.[6] But is this conceptual truth *really* more evident than the proposition that it would be wrong to torture my parents now? Is that moral proposition *really* less evident than Brandtian propositions about what it would be rational for me to do? There are, I suggest, a great many moral propositions that are at least as justified for us as the sorts of claims that Brandt and Hare accept in defending their moral criteria. So, I think it is false that we have a good reason not to take such propositions as data on the ground that they are somehow epistemically inferior.

In sum, I do not think we should reject either particularism or the method of wide reflective equilibrium because of concerns about equally coherent systems or fears about vicious circularity, or because of the shaky epistemic status of our particular epistemic beliefs. Still, it is also important to note that if we accept the method of wide reflective equilibrium, we need not ignore the sorts of considerations that Brandt, Hare, and Singer point to as sources of error in forming moral beliefs. A proponent of wide reflective equilibrium can endorse the view that some moral beliefs

6   *Ibid.*, pp. 95–96.

depend on mistaken beliefs about non-moral facts, such as mistaken beliefs about the commands of God or the gods, the consequences of certain actions and policies, or the nature of a person. Disagreements and mistakes about non-moral facts can and do lead to mistaken moral beliefs. This proponent might also note that moral disagreements and errors can be the result of self-interest, partiality, and partisanship. There is no reason why the proponent of wide reflective equilibrium need ignore such causes of error in the course of moral reflection. The method is, after all, wide. Nothing that seems relevant need be excluded. Indeed, it seems that, given the relevance of such sources of error, the proponent of wide reflective equilibrium ought to take them into account.

What is more, the proponent of the method may concede that, about certain moral matters, many people are indeed unreliable. Still, someone quite unreliable about matters of state such as tax policy, distributive justice, and health care might be quite reliable about mundane moral matters such as not driving on the sidewalk or veering into oncoming traffic. Unreliability about some moral matters does not imply that one is unreliable about them all. The same, of course, is true about reliability with respect to non-moral matters. The sort of unreliability, noted by Brandt and Singer, that we find in some people about *some* non-moral matters concerning theological questions, sex and bodily functions, and economic and social conditions would not support the view that those people were unreliable about *other* non-moral matters. The pre-Socratic philosopher who is an unreliable judge of various biological, astronomical, and theological facts can be a highly reliable judge about other things, such as the existence of other people, their thoughts and feelings, and the size and shape of medium-sized objects in his environment. There is no reason, then, to assume that the proponent of wide reflective equilibrium or a moral particularist must treat all of his own moral judgments as being on a par. He may hold that the epistemic status of his moral beliefs comes in varying degrees, ranging from what is evident or obvious to what is merely more likely than not.

Finally, it should be clear that the proponent of the method of wide reflective equilibrium need not ignore the sorts of considerations and arguments presented by Brandt and Hare in attempting to establish a moral criterion. Nothing in the method requires that. The method does, however, maintain that such arguments and the proposed criteria should be assessed in light of those moral judgments that we find justified. Wouldn't we, after all, think that a criterion would be more reasonable for us to believe if it cohered with and explained those moral judgments that we took to be justified? That the proposed criterion could support and explain why it was wrong to veer into oncoming traffic or why it was wrong for me now to kill my secretary would be a mark in favor of the criterion. But this power of supporting a proposed criterion cuts both ways. If some proposed criterion implied that it was not wrong for me to do such things, or that we did not know such things, then would we not have good reasons for thinking that such a criterion was false?

8.2 JUSTIFIED BELIEF ABOUT PARTICULAR ACTIONS RECONSIDERED

I have assumed that we can know or be highly justified in believing that some particular actions are right or wrong. Such a view is characteristic of the particularist approach in ethics. But some philosophers who are not ethical skeptics suggest or hold that this view is mistaken. Some views about what is required for knowledge of the rightness or wrongness of particular actions imply that I do not know or that I am not highly justified in my moral beliefs about these particular actions. Some utilitarian writers, for example, hold that we can never know, or even form highly justified beliefs about, which particular actions are right or wrong. They hold, approximately, that it is right for a subject S to perform an act A if and only if the consequences of S's performing A are at least as intrinsically valuable as any alternative act that S could have performed. They claim that the rightness of particular actions depends on whether the total intrinsic value of the consequences of an act are at least as valuable as the total intrinsic value of the consequences of any alternative act the agent could have performed. But some utilitarian writers hold that we *cannot* know, or have highly justified belief about, the consequences of our actions, about the total intrinsic value of the consequences, or about the total intrinsic value of the consequences of our alternatives. Given that we cannot know with respect to any particular act that it maximizes utility, they conclude that we cannot know that any particular act is right or wrong.

We find this sort of skepticism about the rightness or wrongness of particular actions in Panayot Butchvarov, who endorses act utilitarianism.[7] Butchvarov takes seriously what he calls the position of the

---

7 Butchvarov says that "A right action is one that is (or was, or will be, or would be, or would have been), optimizing even if not optimific." Panayot Butchvarov, *Skepticism in Ethics* (Bloomington, IN: Indiana University Press, 1989), p. 19.

"empirical skeptic." The empirical skeptic "rests his case simply on what he thinks common sense would readily acknowledge: that we cannot know what actions are right because we cannot know what would naturally be described as their long-range consequences, although, like common sense, he finds no difficulty in understanding the idea that the totality of consequences of one action may be better than the totality of consequences of an alternative action."[8] Butchvarov ultimately concedes that the empirical skeptic is right. He concludes that we cannot know which particular acts are right or wrong. In his final chapter, he writes, "The skeptic concerning right and wrong seems to have won on the substantive issue before us in this chapter . . . We can and often do know good from evil, duty from offense, and virtue from vice, but it would seem, we cannot know right from wrong."[9]

Suppose we take the skeptical argument to be something like this:

Argument A
1. A particular act is right in virtue of its maximizing utility. Its being right supervenes on the fact that it maximizes utility.
2. Therefore, in order to know that a particular act is right, one must know that it maximizes utility.
3. But we cannot know what maximizes utility.
4. Therefore, we cannot know that a particular act is right.

If this is the argument, then one could reply by pointing out that 2 does not follow from 1. Even if the rightness of a particular act supervenes on the fact that it maximizes utility, it does not follow that knowledge of the rightness of a particular act depends on one's knowing that it has the property of maximizing utility. In Chapter 5, I considered the view that knowledge of a supervenient evaluative property depends on one's knowing a general principle about what the evaluative property supervenes upon. The view that it does depend on such knowledge is one reason for supporting methodism in epistemology. Yet I argued that such a view does not follow from the fact that evaluative properties are supervenient. I now also suggest that knowledge that a particular thing has a supervenient property does not necessarily require that one know that it has the underlying property on which the evaluative property supervenes. In other words, I suggest that if a thing X has a supervenient property F, and X has F in virtue of its having G, it does *not* follow that one's knowledge that X

8 *Ibid.*, p. 182.
9 *Ibid.*, 195.

has F epistemically depends on one's knowing that it has G. Consider our knowledge of mental states. Even if our mental states supervene on physical states of the brain, it does not follow that knowledge of mental states requires knowledge of the underlying brain states. One can know that one has various mental states without knowing anything about the underlying brain states, and even without knowing that one has a brain. Similarly, we can know that other people have various mental states without knowing anything about the state of their brains. I assume, then, that the fact that one sort of property supervenes on another sort of property does not imply that knowledge of the first sort of property depends on knowledge of the second. Consequently, I see no reason to agree with the claim that knowledge of an act's rightness depends on knowing that it maximizes utility even if an act's rightness does in fact supervene on its maximizing utility. Could it not be that just as we can know the mental states of others without knowing on what physical states those mental properties supervene, so too we might be able to know that some acts are right without knowing on what more basic properties their rightness supervenes?

Now, if knowledge of the rightness or wrongness of an act does not depend on one's knowing that it has the underlying property on which its rightness or wrongness supervenes, then on what does it depend? This seems to me to be a very difficult question, and one that I am not sure how to answer. But I will make the following tentative suggestion. Let us begin by considering the following remark by Reid:

When I grasp an ivory ball in my hand, I feel a certain sensation of touch. In the sensation there is nothing hard or external, nothing corporeal. The sensation is neither round nor hard; it is an act of feeling of the mind, from which I cannot by reasoning infer the existence of any body. But, by the constitution of my nature, the sensation carries along with it the conception and belief of a round hard body really existing in my hand. In like manner, when I see the features of an expressive face, I see only figure and colour variously modified. But by the constitution of my nature, the visible object brings along with it the conception and belief of a certain passion or sentiment in the mind of the person.

In the former case, a sensation of touch is the sign and the hardness and roundness of the body I grasp is signified by that sensation. In the latter case, the features of the person is the sign, and the passion or sentiment is signified by it.[10]

---

10   Thomas Reid, *Essays on the Intellectual Powers of Man*, Essay VI, Chapter 5, p. 638.

On Reid's view, certain features of the person are "signs" of their mental states. When we are presented with such signs, we tend to form certain beliefs about the mental states of others. Our dispositions to form such beliefs are, to use Sosa's term, "apt." We tend to form true beliefs about the mental states of others given the perception of these signs. The reliability of this way of forming beliefs is for us a source of knowledge of the mental states of others. The disposition to form true beliefs about the mental states of others can, of course, be developed and made more discriminating. With experience, one can become a more sophisticated and discriminating judge of others' mental states. Moreover, no reasonable adult forms beliefs about the mental states of others simply on the basis of perceiving the face, the tone of voice and so on. One must also be alert to defeaters such as whether the person is acting in a play or otherwise pretending. But in general it is the reliability of our dispositions to form beliefs about the mental states of others in the presence of certain signs that is the source of our knowledge of and justified belief about their states of mind. One need know nothing of the underlying physical states on which mental states supervene in order to have such knowledge. Now, I suggest that in some cases of moral belief, something similar takes place. When I consider, for example, the case of the local man who slit the throat of his niece in a rage over a dispute about an unpaid debt, I form the belief that his action was wrong. What confers a positive epistemic status on my belief about the wrongness of that act is that I am highly reliable about judging the wrongness of actions of that sort. That the act was a cruel life-threatening assault on the child done in a fit of rage over an unpaid debt is a sign or indicator of its wrongness. In close possible worlds, actions of that sort are almost always wrong. When I believe that actions of that sort are wrong, I am usually right in that belief. What the wrongness of the act supervenes on, whether it supervenes on the failure of the act to maximize utility or to treat another as an end in itself or to respect his right to be free from assault, I do not know. That is a hard and interesting question for moral theory. But I need not know what makes the act wrong in order to know that it is wrong any more than I need to know what brain states another has in order to know that he is sad. Just as one need not be a neurophysiologist in order to know what mental states others are in, or an epistemologist in order to know that one knows various facts about the external world, one need not be a moral philosopher in order to know that some acts are right or wrong.

The sort of view suggested here is close to that suggested by Bishop Butler. Butler held that "we are not competent judges [of] what is upon the whole for the good of the world."[11] In this respect, Butler agrees with Butchvarov about our inability to know in particular cases what maximizes utility. But Butler did not draw the skeptical conclusion. On Butler's view, if our knowledge of right and wrong in particular cases depended on knowledge of what maximizes utility, then we would have very little knowledge of the rightness or wrongness of particular actions. But he held that our knowledge of right and wrong does not so depend. He suggested that there are certain types of actions we are disposed to judge as right or wrong quite apart from a consideration of whether they maximize utility:

The fact then appears to be that we are constituted so as to condemn falsehood, unprovoked violence, injustice, and to approve benevolence to some preferably to others, abstracted from all consideration which conduct is likeliest to produce an overbalance of happiness over misery."[12]

On Butler's view we are, in fact, highly reliable judges of the rightness or wrongness of particular actions of certain types. Yet Butler also entertained the hypothesis that the disposition to judge actions of certain types as right or wrong and to act accordingly might also lead to the maximization of utility or "upon the whole for the good of the world." Butler also entertains the possibility that God has given us dispositions that tend toward the maximization of utility. He writes:

[W]ere the Author of Nature to propose nothing to himself as an end but the production of happiness, were his moral character merely that of benevolence, yet ours is not so. Upon that supposition, indeed the only reason of his giving us the above-mentioned approbation of benevolence to some persons rather than others, and disapprobation of falsehood, unprovoked violence, and injustice, must be that he foresaw this constitution of our nature would produce more happiness than forming us with a temper of more general benevolence."[13]

I am not endorsing Butler's hypothesis that God has so arranged our dispositions to judge in ways that tend to maximize utility. Still, it does seem that a utilitarian might agree with Butler that our knowledge of the rightness or wrongness of particular actions does not depend upon our knowing either (i) that a particular act does maximize utility, or (ii) that our disposition to judge particular actions leads us to maximize utility.

11 Bishop Butler, *Five Sermons*, ed. Stephen Darwall (Indianapolis: Hackett, 1983), p. 66.
12 *Ibid.*, p. 73.
13 *Ibid.*, p. 73–74.

In any case, I do not think that Argument A provides us with any compelling reason for accepting skepticism about the rightness or wrongness of particular actions. We may, I think, reasonably reject premise 2 (of Argument A). But let us consider another argument for skepticism about the rightness or wrongness of particular actions. Let us recall the Principle of Exclusion:

PE   If one is to know that p, then one must exclude (rule out) every possibility that one knows to be incompatible with one's knowing that p.

Now, consider again the case of the local man who slit his niece's throat. Let p = the local man's slitting his niece's throat was wrong. Let q = the local man's slitting his niece's throat maximized utility. According to act utilitarianism, q is incompatible with one's knowing p, since according to act utilitarianism, if q is true, then p is false. Now consider the following argument:

Argument B
1. If one is to know that p, then one must rule out every possibility that one knows is incompatible with one's knowing that p.
2. We know that q is incompatible with one's knowing p.
3. We cannot exclude q. We cannot know that not-q.
4. Therefore, we do not know that p.

If the premises of this argument are true, then we do not know that the local man's action was wrong. Clearly, the argument can be generalized to support the view that we can never know that *any* particular action is wrong. Such a view would be quite damaging to a particularist approach to ethics.

As we have seen, Butchvarov holds that we cannot know whether a particular act maximizes utility or not. Such a view has been shared by many others. It also seems, for example, to be Moore's view. Moore accepts a form of act utilitarianism. In *Principia Ethica*, for example, he writes that "Our 'duty,' therefore, can only be defined as that action, which will cause more good to exist in the Universe than any possible alternative. And what is 'right' or 'morally permissible' only differs from this, as what will *not* cause *less* good than any possible alternative."[14] He then goes on to write:

In order to shew that any action is a duty, it is necessary to know both what are the other conditions, which will, conjointly with it, determine its effects; to know

14   G. E. Moore, *Principia Ethica* (Cambridge: Cambridge University Press, 1903), p. 148.

175

exactly what will be the effects of these conditions; and to know all the events which will be in any way affected by our action throughout an infinite future. We must have all this causal knowledge, and further we must know accurately the degree of value both of the action itself and of all these effects; and must be able to determine how, in conjunction with the other things in the Universe, they will affect its value as an organic whole. And not only this: we must also possess all this knowledge with regard to the effects of every possible alternative; and then we must be able to see by comparison that the total value due to the existence of the action in question will be greater than that which would be produced by any of these alternatives. But it is obvious that our causal knowledge alone is far too incomplete for us ever to assure ourselves of this result. Accordingly it follows that we can never have any reason to suppose that an action is our duty: we can never be sure that any action will produce the greatest value possible.[15]

Again he writes:

It is difficult to see how we can establish even a probability that by doing one thing we shall obtain a better result than by doing another. I shall merely endeavour to point out how much is assumed, when we assume that there is such a probability, and on what lines it seems possible that this assumption may be justified. It will be apparent that it has never been justified – that no sufficient reason has ever yet been found for considering one action to be more right or more wrong than another.[16]

Neither Moore nor Butchvarov is an ethical skeptic. They both believe they know that some things are intrinsically good and that the act utilitarian criterion of right action is true. Yet each seems to hold that we cannot know that an action is right or wrong. As Moore says, "no sufficient reason has ever yet been found for considering one action to be more right or more wrong than another" because we cannot know all the consequences of an action and its alternatives, and what their intrinsic value is.

Moore and Butchvarov hold that we do not *know* whether a particular action will maximize utility. But can't we know that the *foreseeable* consequences of one action would be better than another? Can't we know, for example, that the foreseeable consequences of the local man's slitting his niece's throat are worse than the foreseeable consequences of some other action he could have performed? It does seem reasonable to believe that the foreseeable consequences of slitting his niece's throat are intrinsically worse than the foreseeable consequences of his refraining from doing so, and worse than the foreseeable consequences of some

15 *Ibid.*, p. 149.
16 *Ibid.*, p. 152.

alternative he might have undertaken, such as having a stiff drink and watching a good movie. Yet Butchvarov and Moore insist that what is relevant to the rightness or wrongness of an act is not the foreseeable consequences, but the *total* consequences of the act. And of the total consequences, we can have no knowledge. Moore says, "Our utter ignorance of the far future gives us no justification for saying that it is even probably right to choose the greater good within the region over which a probable forecast may extend."[17] Moore holds that even if we are justified in believing that the foreseeable consequences of an act are better than the foreseeable consequences of any alternative open to the agent, this does not justify us in believing that the act's total consequences are better than the total consequences of any alternative open to the agent.

If Moore and Butchvarov are right, then the third premise is true. But are they right? Other utilitarians are more optimistic about our ability to know or form highly justified beliefs about which particular actions maximize utility. It might be argued that we *do* know what kinds of actions *generally* lead to the best consequences. One might hold that *experience* has taught us over time what kinds of actions tend to maximize utility. This seems to be the position that Mill takes in *Utilitarianism*. Mill suggests that throughout human history, men have been discovering what sorts of actions tend to promote the maximization of utility. "During all that time mankind have been learning by experience the tendencies of actions; on which experience all the prudence as well as all the morality of life are dependent."[18] On this view, we come to know through experience, for example, that certain kinds of actions such as murder, theft, and the breaking of promises are usually such that they fail to maximize utility. Given this knowledge that certain sorts of actions generally fail to maximize utility, we may reasonably predict that particular instances of murder, theft, and the breaking of promises will also fail to maximize utility.

But do we, in fact, know on the basis of experience, as Mill suggests, that certain kinds of actions generally maximize utility and that others do not? Butchvarov and the empirical skeptics are unconvinced:

What past experience, he will ask, shows that even one act that has accorded with the rule will have had a totality of consequences better than that which would have resulted if the act had not been performed? After all, only a tiny fraction of these consequences have already occurred, and even a tinier one is known to us.

---

17   *Ibid.*, p. 153.
18   John Stuart Mill, *Utilitarianism*, p. 23.

One's keeping of promises in the past may *seem* to have led so far to nothing very bad and perhaps to some good. But only so far! . . . In any case, it is just false that one knows that most of one's actions of keeping a promise have had mostly good consequences in the past. One knows very little about what consequences most of them have had. One knows even less about the past consequences of other people's acts of keeping a promise. And, surely, one knows virtually nothing of the consequences that the alternative acts, whether one's own or that of others, would have had if those acts had been performed. The skeptic is certain to remind us that to know whether a certain contemplated action would be right, one must know not only what consequences it would have but also what consequences each of its alternatives would have. These are not epistemological, philosophical claims. They are claims that common sense readily acknowledges.[19]

Butchvarov rejects Mill's claim that experience has taught us that certain kinds of actions or dispositions are generally such as to maximize utility, and denies that we are empirically justified in believing that certain sorts of actions generally maximize utility. Others have also taken a skeptical stance toward our ability to know what actions will in fact maximize utility. Alan Donagan, a non–utilitarian, writes:

That the calculations which utilitarianism calls for cannot be made was pointed out, as we have seen, more than a century ago: by Adam Sedgwick for act utilitarianism, and by Whewell for rule utilitarianism. And perhaps the most puzzling thing about discussions of the subject at the present time is that what they pointed out is not commonplace . . . most have chosen to disregard what the practical incalculability of the utilities either of actions or rules may imply, and to occupy themselves with the logically interesting problems that arise in pure utilitarian theory on the assumption that ordinal utilities can be calculated."[20]

David Brink, a utilitarian, writes:

But even if some interpersonal comparisons of welfare can be made reliably or accurately, it would be disingenuous to claim that we are generally reliable at making interpersonal comparisons of welfare or at estimating the total, long–run consequences of alternative actions and policies with a high degree of accuracy. The causal mechanisms involved in many of these counterfactual situations are numerous and complex, our time is frequently limited, our information is also frequently limited, and calculations are often distorted because of prejudice, self–concern, and failure of imagination. For these reasons, there must be many cases

---

19   Panayot Butchvarov, *Skepticism in Ethics*, pp. 183–84.
20   Alan Donagan, *The Theory of Morality* (Chicago: The University of Chicago Press, 1977), p. 205.

in which estimates of what would maximize human welfare would be highly unreliable.[21]

In this passage, Brink is describing the difficulties that confront an individual agent trying to guide his action by determining what maximizes utility. But it seems clear that the same difficulties would confront anyone attempting to assess whether a particular action or policy does in fact maximize utility. Even in a supposedly "cool hour," would one not still be faced with limited time and information, counter-factual situations that are numerous and complex, and failure of imagination?

I think it is reasonable to believe that premise 3 is true. I am inclined to agree with Moore, Butchvarov, and Butler on this point. But must we then accept ethical skepticism about the rightness or wrongness of particular actions? No, for we may reject premise 2. It is, I think, more reasonable for us to hold that we know that it was wrong for the uncle to slit his niece's throat than that premise 2 is true. The claim that q is incompatible with our knowing that p rests on a highly controversial moral theory, one that faces many plausible objections. Even those sympathetic to some form of utilitarianism do not agree that *act* utilitarianism is true. It is far from clear that act utilitarianism is true, and far less clear that anyone *knows* that it is true. As we saw in the last chapter, Lycan pointed out the absurdity of rejecting the proposition that one had breakfast before lunch because it conflicted with some metaphysical theory about the nature of time. That is a typical Moorean move. It would be just as absurd to hold that one does not know that it was wrong for the uncle to slit his niece's throat because it conflicted with some controversial moral theory about the nature of right action.

Moore, in dealing with skeptical arguments about the existence of the external world, holds that is more reasonable for him to believe that he *does* have knowledge of the external world than it is for him to believe the premises of various skeptical arguments. And we should note that the sort of unreliability, noted by Brandt and Singer, that we find in some people about *some* non-moral matters concerning theological questions, sex and bodily functions, and economic and social conditions would not support the view that those people were unreliable about *other* non-moral matters. I suggest that we should make the same move here. It is, I believe, more reasonable for me to believe that I *do* know or am highly justified in believing that it was wrong for the local man to slit his niece's

21 David Brink, *Moral Realism and the Foundations of Ethics* (Cambridge: Cambridge University Press, 1989), pp. 255–56.

throat and that it would have been right for him to refrain from doing so than it is to believe *all* of the premises of this argument. I am inclined to think that the first premise is true. The first premise seems to me to be quite plausible. But with respect to the second and third premises, I do not think that either is as reasonable for me to believe as it is that I do know that it was wrong for the local man to slit his niece's throat.

Given Moore's approach to various skeptical arguments about the external world, it is striking that he would not also reject this sort of reasoning for skepticism about the rightness or wrongness of particular actions. Of course, there is no formal inconsistency in his taking himself to know various facts about the external world and in denying that he has any knowledge about the rightness or wrongness of particular actions. Still, I suggest that it is more reasonable for us to accept that we do know that some particular actions are right or wrong than it is to hold that *all* of the premises of Argument B are true, and that it is more reasonable for us to believe that we do know that it was wrong for the uncle to slit his niece's throat than it is to believe that premise 2 is true. Such a response might seem to some "dogmatic" or "intemperate," but I believe that it is neither. It is no less reasonable, I believe, than the approach that Moore himself takes in epistemology, an approach I have sought to defend at length throughout this book. If that approach is reasonable in epistemology in general, then I do not see why it is not also reasonable in moral epistemology or in moral philosophy.

Conclusion

I have defended the common sense tradition from a variety of philosophical objections. Among the most important of these objections are (1) that common sense philosophers fail to offer any non-circular proof for the reliability of their ways of forming beliefs, and (2) that they assume that they know various things without knowing a criterion of knowledge. We examined the first sort of objection chiefly in Chapters 2 and 3 and the second in Chapter 6. I have argued that neither of these objections provides a good reason for rejecting the basic approach of the common sense tradition to the philosophical questions that concern us.

I have not sought to prove that there is an external world or that there are other people who are conscious, or to prove a great many other things that may be considered matters of common sense. One does not need philosophy to know such things. One also does not need to be a philosopher to know that one knows things. You don't need to be a philosopher, for example, to know *that* you know there are other people. Instead, I have defended the view that we may assume that we do know much of what we ordinarily think we know and that we use such beliefs as data for philosophical reflection. When we think philosophically, we need not assume or pretend that we really don't know anything or that we don't know what we ordinarily think we know. We need not view what we ordinarily believe and take ourselves to know as mere matters of faith, as mere commitments, prejudices, unsupported yet firmly held beliefs, or hinge propositions with suspect epistemic credentials. We do not need to confine our data to the immediately evident testimony of reason and introspection. This is as true in ethics as epistemology. Though much of the focus of this book has been on epistemological matters and what we may take as data in epistemology, I showed in the last chapter that many of the arguments against the common sense tradition in epistemology have their analogues in ethics, and that they fare no better in ethics than in epistemology.

As I noted in the Preface, Reid holds that philosophy is rooted in the principles of common sense. But no one of good judgment confuses the roots with the branches, and Reid does not confuse philosophy with common sense. If we do not need philosophy to know many of the things we ordinarily think we know, it does not follow that we have no need of philosophy. The defense of the common sense tradition in philosophy that I have presented is itself a philosophical undertaking. It is a defense of one philosophical view against others. Moreover, the analysis of the concepts that interest us; the search for criteria of justification, knowledge, and right action; and the seeking of coherence between apparently plausible but incompatible views require us to go beyond what is evident to and widely believed by almost everyone. I am acutely aware that I have not offered any analysis of important philosophical concepts or defended any criterion of justification, knowledge, or right action. Of course, it has not been my intention to do so here. My goal was the more modest one of defending the common sense tradition against some philosophical objections, and to defend the view that it is not unphilosophical, dogmatic, intemperate, or question-begging, at least not in any intellectually vicious way.

Selected Bibliography

Alston, William. *Epistemic Justification*. Cornell University Press. 1989.

—— *The Reliability of Sense Perception*. Cornell University Press. 1993.

—— "Two Types of Foundationalism." *The Journal of Philosophy* 73 (1976): 165–85.

—— "Some Remarks on Chisholm's Epistemology." *Noûs* 14 (1980): 565–86.

—— "A 'Doxastic Practice' Approach to Epistemology" in *Empirical Knowledge*, 2nd edition, ed. Paul Moser. Rowman and Littlefield. 1996.

Amico, Robert P. *The Problem of the Criterion*. Rowman and Littlefield. 1993.

Audi, Robert. *Belief, Justification, and Knowledge*. Wadsworth. 1988.

—— *Epistemology: A Contemporary Introduction to the Theory of Knowledge*. Routledge. 1998.

Augustine, St. *The Essential Augustine*, ed. Vernon J. Bourke. Hackett. 1974.

BonJour, Laurence. *The Structure of Empirical Knowledge*. Harvard University Press. 1985.

—— *In Defense of Pure Reason*. Cambridge University Press. 1997.

—— *Epistemology*. Rowman and Littlefield. 2002.

Brandt, Richard. *A Theory of the Good and the Right*. Oxford University Press. 1979.

Brink, David. *Moral Realism and the Foundations of Ethics*. Cambridge University Press. 1989.

Burge, Tyler. "Content Preservation." *Philosophical Review* 102 (1993): 457–88.

Butchvarov, Panayot. *Skepticism about the External World*. Oxford University Press. 1998.

—— *Skepticism in Ethics*. Indiana University Press. 1989.

Butler, Bishop. *Five Sermons*, ed. Stephen Darwall. Hackett. 1983.

Chisholm, Roderick. *The Problem of the Criterion*. Marquette University Press. 1973.

—— *Theory of Knowledge*. Prentice-Hall. 1st edition 1966; 2nd edition 1977; 3rd edition 1982.

—— *The Foundations of Knowing*. The University of Minnesota Press. 1982.

—— "The Status of Epistemic Principles." *Noûs* 24 (1990): 209–15.

Chisholm, Roderick, and Robert J. Swartz, eds. *Empirical Knowledge*. Prentice-Hall. 1973.

Conee, Earl. "Comments on Bill Lycan's 'Moore Against the New Skeptics'." *Philosophical Studies* 103 (2001): 55–59.

DeRose, Keith, and Ted A. Warfield, eds. *Skepticism: A Contemporary Reader*. Oxford University Press. 1984.

Descartes, René. *The Philosophical Writings of Descartes*, ed. J. Cottingham, R. Stoothoff, and D. Murdoch. Cambridge University Press. 1991.

Donagan, Alan. *The Theory of Morality*. University of Chicago Press. 1977.

Elgin, Catherine. *Considered Judgment*. Princeton University Press. 1996.

Ewing, A. C. *The Fundamental Questions of Philosophy*. Routledge and Kegan Paul. 1951.

Fumerton, Richard. *Metaepistemology and Skepticism*. Rowman and Littlefield. 1995.

Hare, R. M. *The Language of Morals*. Oxford University Press. 1952.

____ *Moral Thinking*. Oxford University Press. 1981.

Hume, David. *A Treatise of Human Nature*, 2nd edition, ed. L. A. Selby-Bigge. Oxford University Press. 1978.

____ *An Enquiry Concerning Human Understanding*, ed. Eric Steinberg. Hackett. 1993.

Kant, Immanuel. *Prolegomena to Any Future Metaphysics*. Bobbs-Merrill. 1950.

Katz, Jerold. "What Mathematical Knowledge Could Be." *Mind* 104 (1995): 491–524.

Kvanvig, Jonathan, ed. *Warrant in Contemporary Epistemology*. Rowman and Littlefield. 1996.

Lehrer, Keith. *Thomas Reid*. Routledge. 1989.

Lemos, Noah. *Intrinsic Value*. Cambridge University Press. 1994.

____ "Epistemology and Ethics" in *The Oxford Handbook of Epistemology*, ed. by Paul K. Moser. Oxford University Press. 2002.

Lycan, William. "Moore Against the New Skeptics." *Philosophical Studies* 103 (2001): 35–53.

Mill, John Stuart. *Utilitarianism*. Hackett Publishing. 1979.

Moore, G. E. *Principia Ethica*. Cambridge University Press. 1903.

____ *Philosophical Studies*. Routledge. 1922.

____ *Some Main Problems of Philosophy*. Macmillan. 1953.

____ *Philosophical Papers*. George Allen and Unwin. 1959.

Moser, Paul, ed. *Empirical Knowledge*. Rowman and Littlefield. 1996.

____ "Epistemological Fission." *The Monist* 81 (1998): 353–70.

Moser, Paul, and Arnold vander Nat, eds. *Human Knowledge: Classical and Contemporary Approaches*, 2nd edition, Oxford University Press. 1995.

Murphy, Arthur E. "Moore's Defence of Common Sense" in *The Philosophy of G. E. Moore*, ed. Paul A. Schilpp. Open Court. 1968.

Plantinga, Alvin. *Warrant and Proper Function*. Oxford University Press. 1993.

Price, H. H. *Perception*. Oxford University Press. 1932.

Reid, Thomas. *Inquiry and Essays*, ed. Keith Lehrer and Ronald E. Beanblossom. Hackett Publishing. 1983.

____ *Essays on the Intellectual Powers of Man*. The M. I. T. Press. 1969.

Rowe, William. "The Cosmological Argument" in *Reason and Responsibility*, 8th edition, ed. Joel Feinberg. Wadsworth. 1989.

Russell, Bertrand. *The Problems of Philosophy*. Oxford University Press. 1912.

Schilpp, Paul, ed. *The Philosophy of G. E. Moore*. Open Court. 1968.

Sinnot-Armstrong, Walter. "Begging the Question." *Australasian Journal of Philosophy* 77 (1999): 174–91.

Sosa, Ernest. *Knowledge in Perspective*. Cambridge University Press. 1991.

____ "The Foundations of Foundationalism." *Nõus* 14 (1980): 547–65.

____ "How to Defeat Opposition to Moore." *Philosophical Perspectives* 13 (1999): 141–53.

____ "Reflective Knowledge in the Best Circles" in *Knowledge, Truth, and Duty*, ed. by Matthias Steup. Oxford University Press, 1983.

____ "Philosophical Scepticism and Epistemic Circularity" in *Empirical Knowledge*, 2nd edition, ed. Paul K. Moser. Rowman and Littlefield. 1996.

Steup, Matthias. *Contemporary Epistemology*. Prentice-Hall. 1966.

____ *Knowledge, Truth, and Duty*. Oxford University Press. 2001.

Strawson, Peter. "Skepticism, Naturalism, and Transcendental Arguments" in *Human Knowledge* 2nd edition, ed. Paul K. Moser and Arnold vander Nat. Oxford University Press. 1995.

Stroud, Barry. *The Significance of Philosophical Scepticism*. Oxford University Press. 1984.

Summerfield, Donna. "Modest a Priori Knowledge." *Philosophy and Phenomenological Research* 51 (1991): 39–66.

Van Cleve, James. "Reid on the First Principles of Contingent Truths." *Reid Studies*. 3 (1999): 3–30.

Vogel, Jonathan. "Reliabilism Leveled." *The Journal of Philosophy* (2000): 602–25.

____ "Tracking, Closure, and Inductive Knowledge" in *The Possibility of Knowledge*, Steven Luper-Foy, ed. Rowman and Littlefield. 1987.

Wittgenstein, Ludwig. *On Certainty*, ed. G. E. M. Anscombe and G. H. von Wright. Basil Blackwell. 1969.

Index

188